Voices from the Korean War

Voices *from the* Korean War

PERSONAL STORIES of AMERICAN, KOREAN, and CHINESE SOLDIERS

Richard Peters and Xiaobing Li

THE UNIVERSITY PRESS OF KENTUCKY

Publication of this volume was made possible in part
by a grant from the National Endowment for the Humanities.

Editorial and Sales Offices: The University Press of Kentucky
663 South Limestone Street, Lexington, Kentucky 40508-4008
www.kentuckypress.com

10   09   08   07   06   6   5   4   3   2

Library of Congress Cataloging-in-Publication Data
Peters, Richard A.
  Voices from the Korean war : personal stories of American, Korean,
and Chinese soldiers / Richard Peters and Xiaobing Li.
     p.   cm.
Includes bibliographical references and index.
     ISBN 0-8131-2293-7 (Hardcover : alk. paper)
  1. Korean War, 1950–1953—Personal narratives. I. Li, Xiaobing,
1954– II. Title.
  DS921.6.P37   2003
  951.904'28—dc21   2003014586
     ISBN 0-8131-9120-3 (pbk : alk. paper)
     ISBN 978-0-8131-9120-1

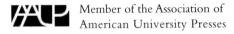

Contents

Maps

Photographs

Abbreviations

CCP	Chinese Communist Party
CCYL	Chinese Communist Youth League
CIA	Central Intelligence Agency
CINCFE COM	Commander-in-Chief, Far East Command (U.S.)
CINC UNC	Commander-in-Chief, United Nations Command
CO	Commanding Officer (UN)
CP	Command Post
CPVF	Chinese People's Volunteers Force
CUF	Communist United Front (POW Camps, UN)
DPRK	Democratic People's Republic of Korea (North Korea)
FDC	Fire Direction Center (UN)
FECOM	Far East Command (U.S.)
FO	Forward Observer
HQ	Headquarters
JCS	Joint Chiefs of Staff
KDP	Korean Democratic Party (South Korean)
KMAG	Korean Military Advisory Group (U.S.)
KMT	Kuomintang (Taiwan)
KNP	Korean National Police (South Korea)
KWP	Korean Workers' Party (North Korea)
MASH	Mobile Army Surgical Hospital

MLR	Main Line of Resistance
NCO	Non-Commissioned Officer
NKPA	North Korean People's Army
PG	Prisoner Guard (POW Camps, UN)
PLA	People's Liberation Army (China)
POW	Prisoner of War
PRC	People's Republic of China
R&R	Rest and Recuperation
RCT	Regimental Combat Team
ROC	Republic of China (Taiwan)
ROK	Republic of Korea (South Korea)
ROKA	Republic of Korea Army
UN	United Nations
UNC	United Nations Command
UNF	United Nations forces
UNTCOK	United Nations Temporary Commission of Korea
U.S.	United States
USAF	United States Air Force
USO	United Services Organization (U.S.)
WWII	World War II

Note on Transliteration

THE KOREAN NAMES of persons, places, and terms are translated by the co-authors, who follow the traditional East Asian practice that the surname is usually written first, as in Kim Il Sung. Exceptions are made for a few figures whose names are widely known in reverse order, such as Syngman Rhee. If a place has different spellings in Korean and English literature, parentheses are used at its first appearance—for example, Hahwaokri (Hagaru-ri).

The *pinyin* romanization system is applied to Chinese names of persons, places, and terms. The transliteration is also used for the titles of Chinese publications. A person's name is written in the Chinese way, the surname first, such as Mao Zedong. Some popular names have traditional Wade-Giles spellings appearing in parentheses after the first use of the *pinyin,* such as Jiang Jieshi (Chiang Kai-shek), as do popular names of places like Beijing (Peking).

Preface

EXPLAINING THE METHODS employed to collect these soldiers' stories poses something of a problem, in part because three different nationalities are involved—American, Korean, and Chinese. Since the co-authors worked independently, we proceeded quite differently. Consequently, as co-authors we decided to describe the process in the same way, independently, and to break it down by nationality. We will begin with the recollections of the American veterans.

Stories by American Soldiers (Dr. Richard Peters)

Obtaining stories of American veterans of the Korean War was undoubtedly much simpler than collecting stories on the Chinese and Korean veterans, but it was not without some problems. One might assume that since I served in Korea during the war, I needed only to contact some of the men in my unit, the Fifth Regimental Combat Team. But like many veterans, I had not kept in touch with a single person. Nor did I belong to any of the established veterans' organizations where one could expect to meet Korean War veterans.

Fortunately, an active chapter of the Korean War Veterans Association existed in Oklahoma City. I joined the chapter and began attending their monthly meetings. I was pleased to learn that the veterans in the chapter represented a large number of the units that had served in Korea during the war. After becoming acquainted with some of the members, I encouraged them to write (or tape) their stories about the war with the hope they would someday be published. I encouraged them to write about their noncombat experiences as well as their time in combat, because hard work, boredom, and even humor are also part of war. Eventually, some of the veterans began to write down their wartime experiences. These stories varied greatly in length and style. Sometimes I made extensive changes and sometimes only minor editing and grammatical changes. In all cases, I returned my copy of the story to the veteran, who then had the opportunity to make any corrections and perhaps add a bit of new material that he had failed to recall earlier. Eventually, often after lengthy telephone conversations, the story was finished.

Some veterans who did not write their own stories still helped the project along by providing the names of others they had served with in Korea who might be willing to tell their stories. This usually led to a telephone call and sometimes to another story on the war.

Stories by Chinese Soldiers (Dr. Xiaobing Li)

The Chinese and North Korean war stories were both difficult to obtain and complicated by the tedious job of translating them into English. As a native of China, I assumed the responsibility for collecting and translating the stories of the Chinese soldiers, a project that has consumed several years. The reader will notice that, unlike the Americans in this book, the stories from Chinese soldiers were nearly all from officers. Since the Chinese army at the time was essentially a peasant army, most of whom were illiterate, this is understandable. I gathered these unique reminiscences from several different sources, all the result of my research in China. Some of the stories are the result of personal interviews with CPVF soldiers. While in Beijing in 1997, I received valuable assistance from the China Society of Strategy and Management Research (CSSM), and was permitted to interview some of the retired officers and veterans who had served in the Korean War. Between 1998 and 2000, while in Harbin, Heilongjiang Province, Northeast China, I was permitted to meet several dozen Korean War veterans for individual and group interviews with the help of the regional military command and the Center for Archives and Information, Provincial Academy of Social Sciences, Harbin.

It is important to point out that only in recent years have these Chinese officers and soldiers felt comfortable talking about their Korean War experiences. Fortunately, many of them had kept personal papers, diaries, letters, and photographs that served as important checks on their memories. This direct testimony by Chinese soldiers has only recently been made available in China, and only now to an English-language audience.

*Stories by Korean Soldiers (The co-authors
on behalf of Dr. Walter Byung Jung)*

Obtaining and translating the Korean sources, while fewer in number, posed essentially the same problems as the Chinese sources. Here, the co-authors are deeply indebted to our colleague at the University of Central Oklahoma, Walter Jung, who has made an enormous contribution to this book. A native of South Korea and the author of *Nation Building: A Geopolitical History of Korea,* he is quite familiar with the Korean War and its historical significance. For this project he obtained written permission from the Institute of Defense Military History, a Korean government research institute, to use the contents of articles that earned recognition in the institute's nationwide search for the best stories by Korean War veterans. From this collection he selected those veterans whose wartime conduct was most exemplary. Before translating these stories into English he interviewed the original authors to ascertain each story's accuracy. In addition to this invaluable contribution, he has served as a consultant and a source of information for the co-authors on "all things Korean" throughout the writing of this book.

Comments on the Scope of the Book

The co-authors would like to remind the reader that while it is true the bulk of the fighting in Korea was carried out by American, Korean, and Chinese nationals, there were many other countries involved in the war. Altogether, sixteen nations sent ground forces to Korea to serve under the United Nations Command. Some nations sent hardened battle units, made up of professional soldiers, while others sent only small medical detachments. Collectively, however, the many countries that participated under the UN Command played an important part in the war. The authors regret that time and space has not allowed us to include the stories of these veterans, many of whom performed their duties heroically.

Also, our apologies to the men and women who served in the air forces and navies of all nations in the UN Command. This book is limited to the land battles of Korea, but anyone with even the most elementary knowledge of the Korean War is immediately made aware of the enormous contributions of the air and naval forces. The landing at Inchon would not have been seriously considered without UN control of the air and the seas. Nor is it likely the marines and GIs would have escaped from the Chosin Reservoir trap. Indeed, without air and naval control the outcome of the war could have been quite different.

One final point. The stories of all of the soldiers included in this book are based on their memories. Memory, of course, is not infallible, especially after so many years have passed. But if these veterans have occasionally erred, it is most likely an error of detail, usually relating to time and place. All of this pales in comparison with the advantages of reading the stories as told by the veterans themselves in their own direct, raw testimony. No secondary source on the war, no matter how scholarly, can convey to the reader their thoughts, feelings, and frustrations in the same way. This is best done by those who fought in the war—the Korean War veterans.

Acknowledgments

MANY INDIVIDUALS HAVE contributed to this book and deserve recognition. First, we would like to thank Provost Don Betz, Dean of Liberal Arts T.H. Baughman, and Chair of History and Geography Kenny Brown at the University of Central Oklahoma (UCO). They have been very supportive of the project over the past several years. Joaneta Randell and Zhou Mei have provided secretarial assistance. The Faculty Merit-Credit Program, sponsored by the Office of Academic Affairs at UCO provided funding for our travels and student assistants.

We also wish to thank our Chinese colleagues and collaborators at the China Society of Strategy and Management Research, Beijing, and the Center for Archives and Information (CAI) in the Heilongjiang Provincial Academy of Social Sciences, Harbin. We especially appreciate the hard work of Zhang Tiejiang, CAI Director, who in 1998–2000 made the many arrangements necessary for interviewing the Chinese veterans.

A special thanks to the members of the Korean War Veterans Association of Oklahoma and its president of many years, Harold Mulhausen. Several members of the association contributed personal stories to the book, and Harold as president strongly supported the project from the beginning. Thanks also to Mike Gonzales, curator of the Forty-fifth Infantry Division Museum in Oklahoma City, who made available some of the photographs that appear in the book.

Our thanks to John Osburn, who has reproduced nine photos used in the book. Helen Peters not only made an important contribution to editing the manuscript, but her computer skills have done much to compensate for the meager computer skills of her husband. Others have contributed to the book, sometimes by reading parts of the manuscript and sometimes by just sharing their knowledge. These invaluable colleagues are Charles Neimeyer, Donald Duffy, Jeff Plaks, Stanley Adamiak, and Herman Fullgraf, all current, former, or retired UCO professors. Finally, thanks to Robert Sevier, a retired army officer.

Part One

The Korean War

A Short History

Chapter 1

Background and Origins of the War

IT IS ONE of the more unfortunate and ironic events in history that Korea, a nation that prior to 1945 included the most homogeneous and united of all peoples, should become a nation divided. Whatever differences may have existed in regard to caste or class, the Korean people speak the same language throughout the peninsula and, with minor variations between north and south, are of the same culture. This cruel fate is made even more tragic by the fact that the Korean people were divided by other powers—clearly the victims of Cold War politics.[1]

The tragedy of Korea, however, began long before the Korean War. Thanks to victories over China in 1894 and Russia in 1905, between 1905 and 1945 Japan governed Korea as a colony, with the blessings of Great Britain and the United States. The Japanese ruled harshly and backed up their policies with brutal police and army forces as they strived to destroy all vestiges of Korean culture. While Korea did make economic progress under Japanese rule, the political climate remained repressive. In the words of one historian, "Japanese imperialism stuck a knife in old Korea and twisted it, and that wound has gnawed at the Korean national identity ever since."[2]

The Japanese occupation was made even more difficult for Koreans to accept by their close cultural ties to China and their view of the Japanese as products of inferior culture. Partially for these reasons, in the end the Japanese were unable to extinguish Korean culture and nationalism. When World War II ended in 1945, Korean nationalists, bonded by their common hatred of the Japanese, competed for leadership in the attempt to establish a free and independent Korea.[3] The two strongest Korean nationalists to emerge as postwar leaders were Syngman Rhee and Kim Il Sung. Despite the divergent paths their lives took, both resisted Japanese rule during the occupation and both shared a strong belief in Korean unity and independence.

Born in 1875, Rhee participated in anti-Japanese activities and worked on behalf of Korean independence as a youth. Not surprisingly, this brought him spells of imprisonment and torture. Immigrating to the United States after a failed revolt in 1919, Rhee headed a self-styled Korean government-in-exile, married a gifted Austrian woman, earned a Ph.D. from Princeton University, and pursued a successful academic career. His goal, however, remained the same—to return to his native country and establish a free and independent government.[4]

Much of the early life of Kim Il Sung (1912–1994), the future leader of North Korea, is surrounded in myth and remains obscure. He apparently established himself as a young guerrilla fighter against the Japanese, and at times commanded several hundred guerrillas. It is also believed Kim joined the Chinese Communist Party in the 1930s and fought against the Japanese along the Korea-Manchuria border. Sometime in 1939 or 1940, he made contact with the Soviets and became an officer in the Soviet army. Stationed in the Khabarovsk district near the Manchurian border, Kim became the commander of a Korean battalion with the rank of captain in a multiracial brigade. Specifically, his job was to train cadre for the Korean People's Army (KPA). When the Soviets swept through Japanese-occupied Manchuria and northern Korea in 1945, Kim returned to his native land. On October 10, Kim and sixty-six other officers, who became the core of the North Korean high command, were carried to the port of Wonsan in a Russian cargo ship. Carefully groomed by the Soviets, in February 1946 he was appointed chairman of the Interim People's Committee, the principal instrument of civil government in North Korea.[5]

Meanwhile, in the midst of World War II, the Allied powers discussed Korea at several of their wartime conferences. At the Cairo Conference in late November 1943, Generalissimo Jiang Jieshi (Chiang Kai-shek), who feared postwar Soviet designs on Korea, persuaded President Franklin D. Roosevelt and Prime Minister Winston Churchill to join him in supporting Korean independence. The joint communique, issued just after the conference, stated that "The aforesaid three great powers, mindful of the enslavement of the people of Korea, are determined that in due course Korea shall become free and independent."[6] The Yalta and Potsdam conferences later reaffirmed the principle of an independent Korea. The Soviet Union, by signing the Potsdam Declaration of July 26, 1945, thus accepted the Cairo declaration on Korea, at least according the U.S. interpretation.[7]

What Roosevelt had in mind for postwar Korea was a multipower trusteeship that would include the United States, Great Britain, China, and the Soviet Union. He believed it would be many years before Korea was ready for independence—hence the phrase "in due course" at Cairo. Only Roosevelt, however, supported the trusteeship enthusiastically. The British and the French were primarily concerned with their own empires, while Stalin had little to say on Korea during wartime conferences.[8]

Korean nationalists, such as Syngman Rhee, were naturally offended by the "in due course" phrase, which seemed to postpone any chance of an immediate "free and independent" Korea. On August 8, 1945, the Soviet Union entered the Pacific war, and within a few days the Soviet army had occupied the northern provinces as far south as Pyongyang. The Americans, who had no large number of troops closer to Korea than Okinawa, realized that it was essential for the two powers to reach an agreement on the respective occupation zones before disarming the large Japanese garrisons in Korea. About midnight on August 10–11, two young colonels, Charles H. Bonesteel and Dean Rusk (the future American secretary of state), were directed to draw a military demarcation line across Korea that would divide the peninsula into American and Russian occupation zones. Without consulting the Korean leaders, they chose the 38th Parallel, in part because it would place the capital city of Seoul in the American zone. Surprisingly, the Soviets made no objections and General Douglas MacArthur made the decision public on August 15, the official date of the Japanese surrender and the liberation of Korea.[9]

On September 8, 1945, American troops arrived in Korea under the command of Lieutenant General John R. Hodge, who began the task of setting up the military government. Often referred to as the "Patton of the Pacific," Hodge was a hero of the Okinawa campaign and a competent soldier, but he lacked the political, intellectual, and diplomatic skills needed for the difficult and often thankless task of an occupation commander. He failed to sense the deep loathing the Koreans had for the Japanese and the strong patriotic feelings they felt for their newly liberated country. Hodge callously included Japanese officials and well-known Korean collaborators among his advisors, and subjected the Korean people to the same repressive laws they had endured under Japanese rule.[10] The Korean people, through no fault of their own, were under the authority of another "occupation" force and faced the strong possibility their nation would be divided.[11]

The Soviets, in contrast, arrived in North Korea with a highly trained political staff, complete with public relations and propaganda personnel. The Soviets presented themselves as liberators who entered Korea to disarm the hated Japanese army and to facilitate a "democratic revolution." While initially popular, the Soviets were still foreigners, and tension soon developed between the Soviet soldiers and the Korean people, who wanted real independence. Unlike the Americans, who governed South Korea with direct military control, the Soviets maintained indirect control by delegating governing power to the North Koreans. After a few months, however, it became clear that only those Koreans who held the correct political views could expect to play a role in the new government.[12]

President Truman attempted to follow the basic outlines of Roosevelt's policy for Korea and to prepare Korea for the time it would become free and independent. American policy still envisioned placing a united Korea under a four-power trusteeship consisting of the United States, Great Britain, China, and the Soviet Union. In December 1945, at a meeting in Moscow, the United States did win Soviet acquiescence to a modified version of the trusteeship that provided for the election of a provisional government for a unified Korea. To prepare Korea for the elections, a joint Soviet-American commission was established, but the all-Korean elections were never held.[13]

Unfortunately, while the Moscow agreement shortened the period of the trusteeship to no more than five years (Roosevelt had thought it would last forty years or more), Koreans of all political persuasions in both the North and South greeted the agreement with demonstrations and work stoppages. They wanted immediate independence; five years was too long to wait. Also, signs of the "two" Koreas were already beginning to emerge. In the North, the Soviets had clearly placed their trust in Kim Il Sung as the Korean leader most capable of establishing a socialist state. The Soviets also supported the people's committees that sprang up throughout Korea after the war for the purpose of securing Korea's independence, but were soon under the effective control of the political left. In the South, the Americans opposed the committees and backed Syngman Rhee, who had returned to Korea in October. Finally, the emergence of the Cold War saw a hardening of relations between the two super powers and found an echo in U.S.-Soviet relations in Korea. Truman, accepting Soviet expert George Kennan's view that Soviet expansionism must be contained, increasingly adopted a get-tough policy toward the Soviet Union, a nation that fully understood such a policy.[14]

Thus, the high hopes many Koreans had for independence following World War II were soon dashed in both the North and the South. In the North, Kim Il Sung, backed by the Soviets, proceeded to eliminate all those who stood in the way of his establishing a Communist Korea. An opportunist, Kim quickly saw the advantages of developing a close relationship with Stalin. Publicly, however, he presented North Korea to the world as the very model of independence. South Korea he pictured as nothing more than the puppet of Washington and Wall Street.[15]

In the South, very little about the occupation went smoothly for the Americans. In the early months the pressure came from the political leftists, especially the Communists, who sought a fundamental change in the political and social structure of Korea. As in the North, Communist-led "people's committees" emerged, which the American military government under Hodge suppressed. This suppression, however, when combined with the efforts of the conservative landowners to block plans to redistribute land to the peasant tenants, spawned widespread dissatisfaction, resulting in further disorder and even guerrilla activities.[16]

To counter the threat from the left, the Americans allied themselves with the Korean landowners and businessmen on the right, many of whom had enjoyed a privileged status under Japanese rule. They also embraced Syngman Rhee, who was both fervently anti-Japanese and anti-Communist. Supported by General MacArthur and other prominent Americans, on October 16, 1945, Rhee had arrived in Korea (in MacArthur's personal plane) and gathered around him the parties on the right to form the Korean Democratic Party (KDP). He soon emerged as the most powerful political leader in South Korea.[17]

Syngman Rhee's demand for the immediate unification of Korea and the formation of a national government, however, proved to be a serious problem for the Americans, who wished to focus first on bringing order and stability to the peninsula. The Americans quickly discovered this would not be an easy assignment, made more difficult by the lack of a democratic or liberal party in Korea. There was no "middle" in Korean political life, only very poor peasants and a small elite of wealthy landowners and businessmen. Thus, the Americans faced the unhappy dilemma of supporting people who on one hand were essentially anti-democratic, but on the other hand strongly anti-Communist—the single most important criteria in determining U.S. policy in the Cold War era.[18]

As the trusteeship unraveled, the United States began to abandon its goal of a united Korea in favor of an independent South Korea. To accomplish this, the U.S. turned to the United Nations. In October 1947, the American delegation requested that the UN sponsor an election for a Korean government to be supervised by a United Nations Temporary Commission, or UNTCOK (the "Temporary" was later dropped). As expected, the Soviets refused to allow UNTCOK to enter its zone. In February 1948, the UN adopted a resolution giving UNTCOK the authority to supervise the election where feasible, that is, in the South. The election, resulting in the selection of a National Assembly for South Korea, was held on May 10, 1948.[19]

The South Korean Communists, represented by the South Korean Workers' Party, opposed the UN-sponsored election. Believing the election would divide Korea permanently, they attempted to prevent it by carrying out acts of sabotage, guerrilla activities, and rioting. The Korean National Police (KNP), who were firmly in the hands of Rhee's KDP, responded by employing the most brutal methods to repress the Communists and left-wing sympathizers. Such methods made it appear that the chances for true democracy were no better in the South than in the North. Nevertheless, determined to prevent the Communists from taking over the South Korean government, the United States backed the autocratic Rhee.[20]

Since the Communists and left-wingers boycotted the elections on May 10, the newly elected National Assembly naturally represented Rhee's conservatives and right-wingers. In a symbolic gesture on behalf of the Korean people's desire for a united Korea, one hundred seats, representing North Korea, were left vacant. A constitution was drawn up and signed on July 17, after which the Assembly promptly elected Rhee the first president of the Republic of Korea (ROK). The Republic was officially proclaimed on August 15, 1948, the third anniversary of the liberation, with MacArthur on the podium. Despite evidence the police had corrupted the voting process, the UN followed by recognizing the Republic as the only legitimate government in Korea.[21]

At this same time the birth of the ROK Army (ROKA) took place. The Korean Military Advisory Group (KMAG), made up of five hundred American officers and men, replaced the military government, and the Truman administration moved toward building and equipping a South Korean army strong enough to defend itself from attack. The members of the KMAG both retained operational control of the ROK Army and served as its advisors as long as U.S. combat troops remained in Korea.

The Americans still had serious concerns over whether President Rhee would use the ROK Army responsibly, but they realized South Korea needed a military force to defend itself against a hostile North Korea. While Hodge both disliked and distrusted Rhee, he knew he had to work with him because there was no other suitable alternative.[22]

When South Korea formed its government in 1948, Kim Il Sung still had the option of joining the new government, although representatives from the South in the National Assembly would have outnumbered those from the North by about two to one. Allied to the leftist parties in the South, however, North Korea would have still wielded considerable influence in a united Korea. Kim, of course, chose—or was forced to choose—another path. On September 9, 1948, he proclaimed the formation of the Democratic People's Republic of Korea (DPRK) in Pyongyang.[23] While Soviet pressure on Kim was undoubtedly very real, recent scholarship suggests that Moscow's influence on Kim and North Korea's puppet state status has been exaggerated.[24]

Whatever degree of influence Moscow may have exerted on Premier Kim, it is clear he soon constructed a totalitarian state that resembled its sponsor in many ways. Freedom of the press ceased to exist, efforts were made to insure conformity of thought, and police surveillance was everywhere. A constitution, drafted in 1947 and implemented in September 1948, offered no protection for individual rights. The North Korean army expanded rapidly, soon augmented by the return of thousands of Korean soldiers whom Kim had dispatched earlier to fight for Mao Zedong (Mao Tse-tung) in the Chinese Civil War. Beginning in 1948, thousands of these battle-hardened soldiers filtered back home. They would play a huge role in the Korean War.[25]

Meanwhile, by 1948 the Rhee regime had begun to face serious problems from organized guerrilla activities. Supported by North Korea, the rebels were a mixture of Communists, leftists, and sometimes bandits, held together by their common hostility to the Rhee government. Most commonly they attacked local police stations, both because of their hatred for the national police and because the police stations kept the records on political dissidents. Operating in small units, the guerrillas would take over a town, grab the needed food and supplies, and then retreat into the woods and hills. Their brushes with the police were marked with extreme brutality on both sides; torture and murder were routine. Not until the spring of 1950, after an aggressive counterguerrilla campaign that may have claimed as many as one hundred thousand lives, did the Rhee regime manage to put down the rebellions. The brutal reprisals, however, further alienated many Koreans from the Rhee government. At the same time, the guerrilla operations were a disappointment for Kim Il Sung. They failed to overthrow Rhee and to win widespread support for Communism among the South Korean populace.[26]

Satisfied the North Korean government was in good hands, at the end of 1948, the Soviets suddenly withdrew their troops from North Korea. Indirectly, this had the effect of increasing the pressure on the Americans to pull out their troops, especially since American policy had always been to withdraw from Korea as soon as possible. No American politician wanted to maintain large numbers of American troops in places like Korea when they believed the main threat to peace was in Europe, not the Far East. In 1947, the Joint Chiefs of Staff backed up this view by reporting to the president that Korea remained outside U.S. strategic interests.[27] Recent events in Europe strengthened the Truman administration's view that Europe should be America's first line of defense. In 1948, the Communists took over the Czech government, and when the Berlin crisis followed only a few months later, tension between the Soviet bloc and the Western powers increased to dangerous levels. The fear of a huge Soviet army marching westward into western Europe was very real.[28]

Political pressure on the Truman administration to withdraw American troops from South Korea also came from Congress, which was determined to cut back on military spending.[29] Since only a limited number of troops was available in the Far East, the military believed the pressure of other commitments made it unwise to keep large numbers of American troops in Korea, where the terrain was unfavorable to the use of armor. The growing strength of the ROK Army, which reached about one hundred thousand by the end of 1949, also seemed to justify the departure of American troops. Ignoring the bitter complaints of Rhee, in June 1949 the last of the American troops pulled out, leaving only those who remained as a part of the KMAG Command.[30]

Once the Soviet and American troops had left Korea, border clashes took place with increasing regularity, especially on the Ongjin peninsula. Brigadier General William Roberts, head of the KMAG, reported to Washington in August 1949 that while both sides were at fault, the South actually initiated more battles than the North. Neither Kim Il Sung nor Syngman Rhee, it appears, made any serious effort to prevent their armies from attacks across the 38th Parallel. General Roberts, who had the unenviable job of attempting to train and equip the ROK Army while at the same time trying to restrain its aggressiveness, at one point threatened to remove the KMAG from Korea if the attacks continued. These attacks, when combined with the general distrust of Rhee, were among the reasons the Americans refused to arm the ROK Army with the tanks and heavy artillery it would need later to stop the invading North Korean army.[31]

On January 12, 1950, Secretary of State Dean Acheson spoke to the National Press Club in Washington on the subject of U.S. policy toward China. The American defensive perimeter in Asia, he said, ran from the Aleutian Islands to Japan to the Ryukyu Islands (Okinawa) and down to the Philippines. If an attack should occur anywhere in this area, it must be met first "by the people attacked," and second by the "commitments of the entire civilized world under the Charter of the United Nations."[32] Since it appeared Acheson had left Korea out of the defensive perimeter, his political opponents later vilified him for inviting an attack from North Korea, even though the "defensive perimeter" referred to by Acheson had been backed up by both the Joint Chiefs of Staff and MacArthur.[33] How Pyongyang reacted to Acheson's speech is surrounded in controversy, but there is evidence that Kim used the speech in his effort to persuade Stalin to support the invasion.[34]

In view of the frequent border clashes and even some intelligence reports indicating the North Koreans were preparing to invade South Korea, it is reasonable to expect that a state of military readiness existed on the part of both the ROK Army and their American allies. But this was not the case, and when the attack came on June 25, 1950, it came as a surprise to nearly everyone.[35] At the time, most Americans assumed the attack was provoked by Stalin, with the support of Mao Zedong. Clearly, the Soviet Union and China were involved; Kim Il Sung would never have attacked without their acquiescence. But the story of their involvement is a complicated one, unraveled, at least in part, by the opening of Soviet archives in recent years. Here, the story can only be briefly traced.

Inspired by the Communist victory in China, Kim Il Sung had sought Stalin's approval for the unification of Korea by military force even before 1950, but without success. Determined, in late March and early April 1950 he secretly visited Moscow, where, it appears, Stalin reluctantly approved Kim's plan to invade South Korea, but only after consultations with Mao.[36] Stalin did not wish to risk war with the United States, but since the American

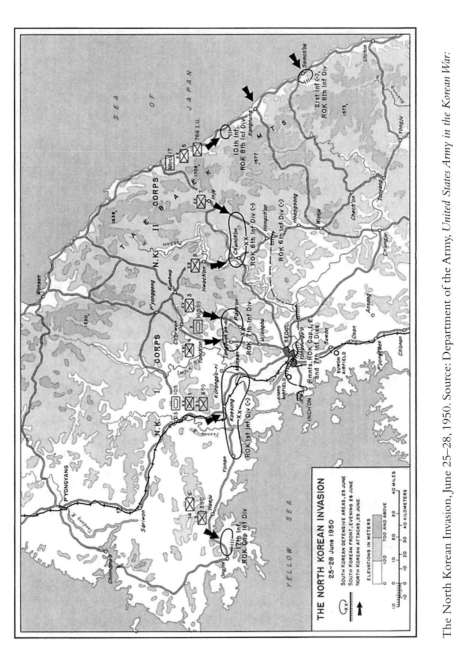

The North Korean Invasion, June 25–28, 1950. Source: Department of the Army, *United States Army in the Korean War: South to the Naktong, North to the Yalu* (Washington, D.C.: U.S. Government Printing Office, 1961), Map III.

army had pulled out of Korea, there seemed to be nothing to prevent the North Korean army from rolling over the ROK Army in a matter of days—which Kim had promised to do. In this event, Stalin would find it embarrassing if he had withheld support for a Communist ally. On the other hand, he did not wish to shoulder the responsibility for anything that went wrong, such as the entry of the United States into the war. The responsibility for this, he thought, belonged to the Chinese. Therefore, Stalin demanded that Kim seek approval from Mao before he would give his final approval for the attack.[37] "If you should get kicked in the teeth," Stalin reportedly said to Kim in Moscow, "I shall not lift a finger. You have to ask Mao for all the help."[38]

This way, Stalin had nothing to lose; the onus of the attack would fall on Mao and Kim, regardless of its success or U.S. reaction. If Kim moved quickly and decisively, North Korea would overrun South Korea and present the world with a *fait accompli*. Even if the U.S. did intervene, it would take many months to move masses of men and materiel into Korea. American intervention would lead to an increase in hostilities between Washington and Beijing, but to the cynical Stalin this was not all bad because it would increase Mao's dependence on the Soviet Union. At the very least, a war in Korea would test American resolve and draw U.S. power away from Europe.[39]

The relationship between Kim Il Sung and Mao Zedong prior to the outbreak of the war is even more difficult to establish. It does appear, however, that Kim made a secret visit to Beijing in May 1950 to secure Mao's blessing for the attack on South Korea. After explaining how Stalin had approved the plan—which Mao had verified—Kim asked Mao only for his approval, not military assistance. At the time, Mao feared a North Korean invasion might interfere with other and higher priorities, such as economic recovery and his plans for reclaiming Taiwan (Formosa) from Jiang Jieshi's Nationalists (hopefully, with help from Moscow). He could not, however, express his fear of American intervention in Korea without admitting to Stalin the likelihood of the same American intervention in Taiwan, which would jeopardize expected Soviet support. And how could he fail to support a plan so recently approved by Stalin, who was generally recognized as the leader of the Communist movement worldwide and of the nation with which Mao had just concluded a mutual assistance agreement?[40] Reluctantly, Mao agreed that Korea must be unified, even before the liberation of Taiwan. He did express concern, however, that the Japanese or Americans might enter the war, which would prolong the conflict.[41]

Stalin's and Mao's approval of the attack, even if given reluctantly, proved to be the green light for the outbreak of the Korean War. In the weeks immediately before the war, massive quantities of Soviet weapons began arriving at the North Korean port of Chongjin.[42] On June 25, 1950, the North Korean forces under Kim attacked, beginning on the Ongjin peninsula in the west, then spreading to other parts of the front. The frequent border clashes along the 38th Parallel made it an easy matter to elevate the civil conflict into a general war, and Kim did not hesitate to accuse the South of invading the North. While Rhee must bear his share of the responsibility for the civil conflict, the responsibility for the general war clearly rests on the shoulders of Kim. Stalin and Mao Zedong may have given their approval, but they did not initiate the war, despite the fact many Americans thought so at the time.[43]

Chapter 2

The Opening Phase
South toward Pusan, North to the Yalu

WHEN THE NORTH Korean army invaded South Korea on June 25, 1950, it is hard to conceive of a nation more ill-prepared for war than the United States, psychologically as well as militarily. World War II had ended only five years earlier, a war in which Americans had fully committed themselves to the defeat of the Axis powers. Young men and women had volunteered for military service by the thousands; others had turned to defense work. Children had collected rubber, paper, and scrap iron, and everyone with a whit of soil had planted a victory garden. Every family with a son or daughter in the service had proudly displayed its blue star in the window, or sadly, a gold star in the event one of them had been killed in the war.

When the war finally ended in 1945, the GIs were welcomed home as heroes who had triumphed over the evil genius of Hitler, Mussolini, and Tojo. While there were problems, such as finding jobs and housing for the vets, the majority of Americans were optimistic about the future. Most had high hopes for the United Nations as a means of preserving the hard-earned peace and keeping the Communists in check. Since the United States alone possessed the atomic bomb, there could be no serious threat to American security. The bomb would also serve to deter the expansionist tendencies of the Soviet Union. A sizable navy and air force might be necessary, but a large and expensive army was clearly an anachronism and unessential in the atomic age.

Accordingly, the United States proceeded to downsize all of its armed forces with all deliberate speed. During World War II the American armed forces had peaked at near 12 million men; by 1950 this figure had dropped to about 1.6 million. The army had suffered the most severe cuts, and when the Korean War broke out in 1950, it had been reduced to only 596,000 men. While the United States had four divisions in Japan (Seventh, Twenty-fourth, Twenty-fifth, and First Cavalry), their regiments were short an entire battalion. Neither did they have the best equipment. Instead of the 3.5-inch rocket launcher, they had only the 2.36-inch, an inferior weapon that had already proved its inability to stop enemy tanks during World War II. Nor could the United States realistically count on the forces of Syngman Rhee and his ROK Army to stop an invasion by Kim Il Sung's North Korean army. When the American troops pulled out of South Korea in 1949, they left the ROK Army with no tanks, no fighter aircraft, and no heavy artillery, despite frequent border clashes and the well-known hostility between the leaders of the two Koreas.[1]

The American divisions in Japan were not only understrength in numbers, they were also inadequately trained. The occupation troops lived in a laid-back peacetime atmosphere that did little to prepare them for the realities of combat, either physically or psychologically. They had plenty of leisure time, with excellent clubs for both officers and noncoms, access to a free railway system, and for one-twentieth of a second lieutenant's pay they could have a Japanese maid or "boy-san" to do the laundry and cleaning. Simply put, they were not combat ready, and some GIs paid dearly for this in the early days of the war.[2]

When Americans first learned of the war in Korea, most thought this was the work of the Soviet Union, the godfather for all the Communist states. If North Korea invaded South Korea, this could only have been the result of Stalin's devilish work. Neither North Korea nor Communist China, most Americans believed, would act alone,[3] and they were not eager to send their sons and husbands to faraway Korea, where they could be killed fighting against the "second" team.

President Truman, of course, was fully aware of the strong aversion to war on the part of the American public. However, he also knew that the Communists had taken over Czechoslovakia in 1948, had attempted to take over West Berlin the same year, and had defeated Jiang Jieshi's Chinese Nationalists in 1949. Communist success in Korea, he feared, would place Japan within easy striking distance of Red troops. Clearly, the expansion of Soviet Communism must be contained. On June 27, Truman authorized MacArthur to use the U.S. air and naval forces at his disposal to support the ROK Army south of the 38th Parallel. On the same day the United Nations Security Council, thanks to the absence of the Soviet delegate, adopted the U.S. resolution requesting that all members of the UN give assistance to South Korea. Three days later, on June 30, Truman boldly authorized MacArthur to make full use of the U.S. ground troops he had under his command in the Far East for the purpose of repelling the Communist aggressor.[4]

On July 1, 1950, 403 disoriented GIs from the Twenty-fourth Infantry Division, under the command of Lieutenant Colonel Charles Smith, arrived in Pusan from Japan. Although U.S. air and naval forces had already moved into the combat zone, these soldiers in Task Force Smith were the first American troops to engage the North Korean army on the ground. This engagement took place on July 5, in fighting south of Seoul, near Osan. Outnumbered and inexperienced, the fighting went very badly for these men and for the additional troops that poured into Korea during the early weeks of the war. Armed with the inferior 2.36-inch rocket launcher, the GIs in Task Force Smith were unable to stop the heavy Russian-built T-34 tanks. Both the American and the ROK armies were pushed southward, toward Pusan.[5]

During the summer of 1950, the UN forces continued to retreat. While some units fought bravely, others withdrew in disorder. There were occasions when units in both the American and ROK armies abandoned weapons and equipment in their haste to escape the fast-moving North Koreans. As the summer passed, however, more American divisions arrived, with tanks and heavy artillery. All the units, including the ROK Army and the newly arrived units from other UN countries, were placed under the authority of Lieutenant General Walton H. Walker, commander of the Eighth Army. While driven back to a defensive perimeter around Pusan, the Eighth Army finally halted the advance of the North Koreans along the Naktong River. The UN forces were aided by the inadequate supply system of the North Korean army, which could not keep up with the advance of their frontline troops.

Clearly, the Pusan perimeter fighting represented a very critical stage in the war for both sides. The possibility that the North Korean forces might push the UN forces off the Korean peninsula was very real and would likely have occurred had it not been for the mastery of the air and seas by the U.S. Air Force and Navy.[6] Immediately following the outbreak of war, the modest U.S. Navy in the Far East began transporting troops and equipment to the peninsula, an action that was absolutely essential to prevent a Korean "Dunkirk." Quickly enlarged, the U.S. and UN naval forces continued to play an important role in the war by cruising along Korea's coastline, repeatedly shelling North Korean troop concentrations, supply lines, and other strong points, sometimes with the big sixteen-inch guns of battleships. As the war continued, the UN navies imposed a blockade on the entire peninsula so tight that the Communist forces could not even use their own ports in North Korea, such as Wonsan and Hungnam, to supply their troops. Throughout the war, loaded troopships made their way from Japan to Pusan unmolested by the enemy.[7] After the war, Sergei G. Gorshkov, Admiral of the Fleet of the Soviet Union, stated that "Without the extensive active employment of the Navy, the interventionists would hardly have been able to avoid a military defeat in Korea."[8]

Ironically, despite the attention military strategists gave to the future role of the U.S. Air Force following World War II, it was still ill-prepared for the type of air war required in Korea. During the early Cold War years the strategists believed the primary mission of the air force should be directed toward the Soviet Union, which required an ultra-heavy nuclear bomber, like the new B-36 (which was never deployed in Korea). Fighter aircraft, such as the new swept-wing F-86 (which was deployed in late 1950), were designed to intercept Soviet bombers. The Korean War, however, called for close air-ground operations, especially in the early months of the war. Armed with F-80 jet Starfighters and the World War II propeller driven planes then available in the Far East Air Force (F-51 Mustangs, F-4U Corsairs, B-26 Invaders, C-47 Skytrains), they went to work. The North Korean air force, equipped with Soviet-built WWII aircraft, offered no serious challenge, so the fighter pilots devoted themselves largely to strafing, bombing, and dropping napalm on the invading Communist troops. The heavy bombing role was carried out by the four-engine World War II B-29, primarily against industrial targets in North Korea.[9]

The near disaster in the Pusan perimeter fighting was followed almost immediately by the great success story of the Korean War—the amphibious landings at Inchon, just west of Seoul. MacArthur began planning the operation almost from the beginning of the war. It was a daring plan, and on July 13, at a meeting in Tokyo, a special deputation of the Joint Chiefs of Staff made it clear they considered it too risky. Their concerns included the dangerous approaches to the port and the notoriously high tides. MacArthur, however, strongly defended his plan. By the end of August, MacArthur's will had prevailed over the Joint Chiefs of Staff. They were not prepared to challenge this legendary hero of World War II, who with five stars outranked them all by at least one star. Besides, at a time when it was uncertain the UN forces could even hold out in Korea, who had any better ideas?[10]

The landings, carried out on September 15, 1950, succeeded beyond all expectations. The First Marine Division and the Seventh Division, now a part of the newly formed X Corps under the command of MacArthur's

chief of staff, Major General Edward M. Almond, overcame the tide problems and drove inward. By the end of the month, they had liberated Seoul.
At the same time, Eighth Army forces under Walker began driving north
from the Pusan perimeter. After initially putting up strong resistance, the
North Korean army collapsed. Some units dropped their weapons and retreated into the hills on a scale equal to or greater than the ROK Army's
retreat during the first week of the war. As the UN forces advanced to the
north, they also became painfully aware of the many atrocities committed by
North Korean troops earlier in the summer.[11]

Unfortunately, Almond's X Corps failed to drive across the neck of
Korea to the east coast. As a result, most of the North Korean army managed
to slip into North Korea to fight another day. Walker, unhappy when X
Corps carried out the Inchon invasion under a separate command, placed
the blame squarely on General MacArthur. In his view, MacArthur should
have ordered Almond's "public relations brigade" to strike directly across the
neck, instead of opting for the symbolic capture of Seoul.[12]

Despite this failure, nobody could deny that Inchon represented a brilliant and much needed victory for the UN forces. But it did come at a price,
which would become clear in the next several weeks. Since MacArthur
almost alone had fought for Inchon, and over the objections of the Joint
Chiefs of Staff, the success of the operation enhanced his reputation as a
military genius to such God-like dimensions he was virtually unchallenged
in making forthcoming decisions.

Surprisingly, no decision had been made about what the UN forces
were to do when they reached the 38th Parallel, and this quickly became the
next great debate. MacArthur, supported by President Rhee, wanted to cross
the 38th, drive into North Korea, and inflict a total defeat on the Communist aggressors. The UN resolution, however, had provided authorization
only to repel the North Korean army, not to invade North Korea. The British especially questioned the wisdom of crossing the 38th Parallel.[13] The big
problem: would the Chinese enter the war if UN troops approached the
Yalu River? MacArthur and his staff insisted they would not and vigorously
relayed this view to Washington. While MacArthur has been widely criticized for his blindness on this issue, Washington must share the blame. The
Truman administration, following the Inchon triumph, saw an opportunity
to win a total victory over the Communist aggressors. According to General
Bradley, chairman of the Joint Chiefs of Staff, the view persisted, supported
by the CIA, that neither the Soviets nor the Chinese Communists were

prepared to risk global war over Korea, and "China was not militarily capable of unilateral intervention"; consequently, "there would be no Soviet or Chinese communist intervention in Korea."[14] In the end, Washington supported MacArthur. On September 27, the Joint Chiefs of Staff sent MacArthur a directive that authorized him to destroy the North Korean armed forces. MacArthur quickly concluded this provided him with all the authority he needed to pursue the enemy above the 38th Parallel. On October 7, the UN General Assembly followed with a vaguely worded resolution approving UN troops north of the 38th Parallel for the purpose of establishing an elected, unified government.[15] "My mission," MacArthur stated at the Senate hearings in 1951, "was to clear out all North Korea, to unify it and to liberalize it."[16] Clearly, a wider war now became a real possibility.

On October 9, the UN forces crossed the 38th Parallel (the ROK forces had crossed on October 1), and the drive to the Yalu began. Since the North Korean army had been largely destroyed, no major problems were expected. MacArthur assigned the eastern part of North Korea to X Corps under Almond, and the central and western part to the Eighth Army under Walker. The two commands were separated by the Taebaek Mountains.

Meeting no strong opposition on the ground, and with total control of the air, Eighth Army forces moved northward rapidly. On October 19, the First Cavalry entered Pyongyang, the capital of North Korea. On October 26, elements of the First ROK Division reached the Yalu, and on November 1, elements of the U.S. Twenty-fourth Division reached Chonggo-dong, only eighteen miles from the Yalu. Optimism swept the UN Command; the end of the war seemed imminent. But it was not to be.

Chapter 3

China Enters the War

WASHINGTON, OBVIOUSLY, HAD concluded that neither China nor the Soviet Union would intervene if the UN forces advanced north of the 38th Parallel. By late September, however, Washington had already received a disturbing report indicating Mao had called for a major build-up of the Chinese army. Even more ominous, in an October 1 speech at Beijing, Premier Zhou Enlai (Chou En-lai) warned that the Chinese people "will not tolerate foreign aggression and will not stand aside should the imperialists wantonly invade the territory of their neighbor."[1] The premier followed up the next day by informing the Indian ambassador to China, K.M. Panikkar, that China would intervene if the UN forces crossed the 38th Parallel.[2] Clearly, neither the Truman administration nor MacArthur in Tokyo heeded these warnings.

As the UN forces advanced north toward the Yalu, Beijing prepared for war. Mao still found the decision to go to war a difficult one, however, despite the pressure to intervene. Following the Inchon landings, Kim Il Sung had dispatched two of his top aides to Beijing and asked Mao for emergency help, but the Chinese were not ready to make any firm commitment. Stalin, following the landings, also pleaded with the Chinese to go to the aid of the North Koreans. According to Chinese sources, the Soviet leader promised to provide air cover for the Chinese troops and to send Russian troops in the event the Chinese army faltered. Still, Mao hesitated. Most disturbing to Mao, if the Chinese armies intervened and were pushed back, would Stalin really send troops as promised in order to save China? Also of concern, if China became involved in a war with the United States, China's dependence on Stalin would inevitably grow, an unsavory thought to Mao. Finally, all hope of conquering Taiwan would vanish indefinitely.[3]

Despite his hesitance, step-by-step Mao moved closer to intervention. On October 1, Stalin telegraphed Mao and encouraged him to send "volunteer" Chinese soldiers into North Korea for the purpose of defending the area north of the 38th Parallel.[4] On October 2, Mao directed the Chinese Politburo to pass a resolution to send these Chinese troops into North Korea, beginning on October 15. The same day, Mao cabled Stalin of China's decision to send volunteers into Korea to "fight the United States and its lackey Syngman Rhee."[5]

Although Chinese preparations for war accelerated, Mao refused to give the green light, perhaps held back by the reservations expressed by some of the other members of the Politburo.[6] As Mao pondered his options, however, he concluded the reasons for entering the war outweighed the reasons for remaining neutral. Profoundly distrustful of the United States, Mao believed that after a victorious war in Korea the Americans would attempt to make China their next victim. Already U.S. naval action had effectively blocked the conquest of Taiwan, which for Mao was itself a sufficient cause for war.[7] The Soviet presence and the Sino-Soviet alliance, Mao believed, would keep the war limited and non-nuclear, and the U.S. involvement in Europe would prevent the Americans from making a total commitment to a war in Korea. If the war dragged on indefinitely, the U.S. would be under pressure from its European allies to conclude a peace agreement. In the meantime, China must fight to prevent the presence of a large and hostile army on the Manchurian border. This not only threatened China's industrial base, but the United States would also use North Korea as a springboard for operations inside China. The U.S., Mao believed, would never accept the permanent loss of China to the Communists. Since a war between the United States and China, at some future date, was inevitable, the Chinese might as well select the time and place. Better to fight in Korea than China, Mao reasoned, because an invasion of China obligated the Soviets to send troops in accordance with the Sino-Soviet treaty. Thus, either American or Russian troops would occupy Chinese soil. Mao, of course, found both alternatives unacceptable.[8]

Although some members of the Chinese Politburo still expressed views in opposition to the war in meetings held after October 4,[9] on October 8 Mao issued an official order for the Chinese People's Volunteers Force (CPVF), under the command of General Peng Dehuai, to enter the war. On October 19, Peng's armies crossed the Yalu and moved into North Korea. Mao gave specific instructions that the operation should be kept "absolutely secret" and that the crossing of the Yalu must take place only between dusk and 4:00

A.M. After taking cover in the mountains of North Korea, the Chinese troops would watch the American and UN armies push northward toward the Yalu and wait for orders to attack.[10]

In this way, quietly and unconventionally, the Chinese entered the Korean War. In many respects the Chinese army was unconventional, because it reflected the ideas of its creator, Mao Zedong. Chinese tactics and strategy in conducting the war need to be understood in this context.

Mao had long studied the military strategists, especially the fourth century B.C. Chinese writer Sun Tzu and the nineteenth-century Prussian army officer Karl von Clausewitz. A committed Communist, Mao accepted the basic Marxist-Leninist idea that the origin of modern wars was rooted in class conflict, which made war inevitable.[11] "Political power," Mao wrote in an often quoted maxim, "grows out of the barrel of a gun."[12] If an army expects to win, it must "become one with the people so that they see it as their own army"; political training should be of "equal importance" to military training.[13]

Chinese soldiers, Mao believed, must possess both fighting spirit and high morale for success on the battlefield. "Weapons are an important factor in war, but not the decisive factor; it is people, not things, that are decisive."[14] If the soldiers grasped the issues at stake, they were more likely to make sacrifices, endure hardships, and fight bravely. Good relationships between the officers and the soldiers, built on the basis of "brotherhood and comradeship," would also contribute to high morale.[15]

Conditions for high troop morale, Mao believed, favored the Chinese over the Americans. American soldiers, he thought, were incapable of enduring hardships, were afraid to die, and were politically unmotivated, because they had invaded a country belonging to others and were fighting an unjust war. In contrast, Chinese soldiers had developed a "stronger political consciousness and higher combat spirit," were "brave and willing to sacrifice life and blood and capable of bearing hardships and heavy burdens," attributes that would compensate for their inferior firepower.[16]

Mao's military tactics were based on years of guerrilla warfare fighting, usually against superior forces with greater firepower. The most basic principle in war was "to preserve one's own strength and destroy that of the enemy."[17] To accomplish this, Mao wrote that commanders should concentrate a superior force against the enemy, completely encircle the enemy forces, and—when the right moment arrived—wipe them out. "In this way, although inferior as a whole (in terms of numbers), we shall be absolutely superior in every part and every specific campaign." In addition, special efforts should be made to attack when the enemy is on the move, and to avoid a battle of attrition.[18] Commanders must adhere to the principle of mobile warfare, and while they should fight to win, they should retreat when victory is impossible. Mao firmly believed that by following these principles, a weak army could defeat a stronger army.[19]

While the Chinese army, which moved into North Korea, certainly embodied many of the strengths favored by Chairman Mao, it nevertheless had a number of problems. It moved almost entirely on foot and possessed little in the way of motor transport, armor, artillery, and air support. The troops were supplied with a wide range of equipment, most of it Soviet, Japanese, or American, that required different calibers for the small arms and created huge supply problems. Their communications were primitive, and the famous whistles, bugle calls, and cymbals that accompanied their attacks were used as a substitute for radios more than for the psychological effect. The troops wore cotton-quilt uniforms, which were quite warm but almost impossible to dry when wet. For shoes, they wore a low-cut canvas shoe, which provided inadequate protection from the cold and contributed to frostbite. They ate rice, parched wheat, soybean, and corn flour; when they were on the move, all of this was cooked into concentrated cakes and packed into a sock. Since they were not issued name tags, some left their names on scraps of paper inside their clothing for identification. Political commissars, responsible for maintaining orthodoxy of thought, always accompanied the Chinese armies.[20]

Once in North Korea, the Chinese troops took to the mountains as they had been instructed. They moved mostly at night, avoided the main roads, and hid away during the day in camouflaged tents or in the villages. American reconnaissance aircraft found them difficult to detect; even the brown uniforms of the Chinese soldiers matched the brown hills and villages of the winter landscape in Korea. Unimpeded by heavy weapons, such as artillery, they would rely upon their mobility, concealment, and nighttime surprise attacks, all of which would prove to be very effective in the early months of the war.[21]

Chapter 4

The Chosin Reservoir Retreat and Advance to the North

ON OCTOBER 25, 1950, the ROK First Division captured the first Chinese soldier, a clear indication Chinese troops were entering North Korea. The prisoner reported thousands of Chinese soldiers had already crossed the Yalu and were holing up in the mountains while the UN forces advanced north. In late October and early November, after waiting patiently for the right opportunity, the Chinese troops sprang the trap. They set fires to the forests north and northeast of Unsan to obscure UN aerial observation, then emerged from the hills, sometimes behind the UN lines. They attacked the ROKs first and then the Americans. The Eighth Regiment of the U.S. First Cavalry Division was mauled trying to escape a Chinese roadblock near Unsan.[1] Amazingly, despite the seriousness of the attacks, both Eighth Army headquarters and Far East Command refused to believe the main body of the Chinese army had entered the war, and no orders for a general withdrawal were given. MacArthur's intelligence chief, Major General Charles A. Willoughby, thought the "most auspicious time" for the Chinese to intervene had passed, and he cavalierly dismissed captured Chinese prisoners as stragglers or volunteers of no real significance. Urged on by MacArthur, the UN forces even continued the advance whenever possible. Then, on November 6, for reasons which are still not clear, the Communist forces broke off their attacks and withdrew back into the hills as suddenly as they had appeared. Optimism returned—on to the Yalu.[2]

Meanwhile, in the X Corps area east of the Eighth Army, Almond's First Marine Division and Seventh Division had landed at Wonsan and Iwon Harbors, respectively, in preparation for their drive to the Yalu. The landing of the marines at Wonsan, however, did not go exactly by the book. Forced to remain on the crowded transports for over a week while the navy cleared

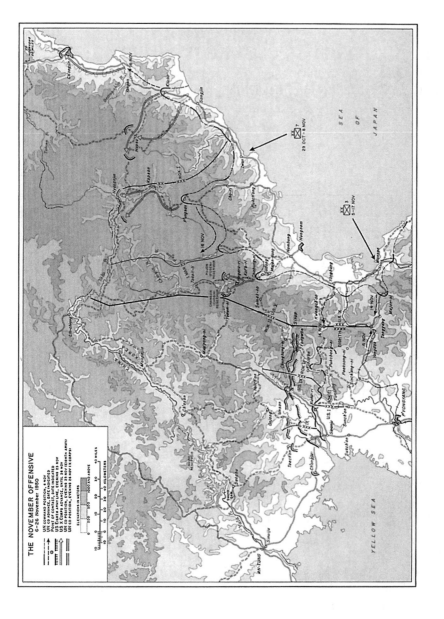

The UNF November Offensive, November 6–26, 1950. Source: Department of the Army, *United States Army in the Korean War: Policy and Direction: The First Year* (Washington, D.C.: U.S. Government Printing Office, 1972), Map VI.

mines from the harbor, they finally disembarked on October 26 only to discover the ROKs had already arrived by land. More embarrassing, Bob Hope and his USO show had also arrived before the marines, and this made the A.P. wire.[3] Despite the delays, the First Marine Division moved north into the Chosin Reservoir area. They advanced more slowly, however, than either the U.S. Seventh Division or the ROKs, which annoyed Almond. Major General Oliver P. Smith, the division commander, feared the dispersal of his marines placed them at risk, and he so informed Almond.[4] Nevertheless, they advanced, through Koto-ri, Hagaru-ri, and Yudam-ri, all destined to become part of the hallowed marine tradition.

On the east side of the reservoir, where there were no Chinese forces, the Seventh Division advanced easily against weak North Korean opposition. On November 21, elements of the Seventh Division's Seventeenth Regiment actually occupied the town of Hyesanjin and the surrounding area all the way to the Yalu River. MacArthur immediately sent his "Heartiest congratulations" to Almond.[5] Clearly, the ground war was going well.

The U.S. Air Force (USAF), however, faced its first serious challenge about the same time the UN ground forces were achieving their maximum penetration of North Korea. On November 8, 1950, MiG-15s, the latest Soviet jet fighter, appeared suddenly over the Yalu and jumped a formation of B-29s and its escort of F-80 jet fighters. It took only a few encounters for American pilots to realize their straightwing F-80s were no match for the new sweptwing MiG-15s.

Recognizing that the UN mastery of the air over Korea was in jeopardy, in December the USAF rushed to Korea a wing of the new, sweptwing F-86 Sabre jets, the only fighter in the U.S. arsenal capable of dueling with the MiG-15s.[6] They also dispatched the straightwing F-84, but like the F-80, it could not compete with the MiGs and was soon relegated to ground support. After some initial losses, especially among the B-29 bombers, American pilots met the challenge and resumed their control of the skies over Korea. Fighting largely in "MiG Alley" near the Yalu, the air war between the Sabre jets and the MiGs provided the little glamour that existed for an otherwise most unglamourous war. Americans waited anxiously for news of the latest air battles involving their local heroes, such as Major James Jabara of Wichita, Kansas, who became the first jet ace in the war.[7]

Although suspected at the time, the Soviet archives have now confirmed that Soviet pilots were flying the MiGs, using bases in North Korea and Manchuria.[8] Soviet authorities, however, required the pilots to do everything possible to conceal their true nationality. They wore Chinese uniforms, were restricted from flying over UN-controlled territory, and were forbidden (in theory) from speaking Russian in radio transmissions. If captured, they were expected to identify themselves as Chinese of Russian extraction. One Soviet pilot shot down behind UN lines ejected safely and then shot himself.[9] American pilots were also restricted, and they fumed when they got MiGs in their gun sights but could not pursue them north of the Yalu (many did anyway). When MacArthur complained about enemy reinforcements pouring over the Yalu bridges, the Joint Chiefs of Staff gave permission to attack the bridges, but only the Korean side of the spans; Manchurian air space must not be violated. MacArthur's predictable reaction to the JCS orders: "The most indefensible and ill-conceived decision ever forced on a field commander in our nation's history."[10]

November 23 was Thanksgiving Day in Korea. On or near that day, American troops were served a turkey dinner with all the trimmings. No effort was spared to reach all the troops, even if this meant airdrops.[11] Morale remained generally high; after all, it appeared the UN armies were within striking distance of a total victory. MacArthur even suggested, perhaps partly in jest, that if the troops advanced fast enough, "maybe some of them could be home by Christmas."[12] It was not to be.

After about a three-week lull, on the night of November 25–26 the Chinese attacked in force. The first blow fell on the ROK Eighth Division, followed by strong attacks on the American Second Division. A day later, November 27, they hit the First Marine Division and Seventh Division in the X Corps area. Chinese tactics, in all cases, were virtually the same. While the UN forces advanced to the north on the roads, the Chinese penetrated the surrounding mountains and remained under cover. When they emerged, they hammered the UN forces with mortars and small arms fire and threw up roadblocks behind them to prevent their escape. It was a formula they repeated over and over in Korea.

Again the UN armies were forced back, toward the 38th Parallel. The hard-hit Second Division managed to cut through the Chinese roadblocks but suffered such heavy losses it was combat ineffective and had to be pulled out of action to rebuild. Some of the most bitter fighting took place in the Chosin Reservoir area, where both the Seventh Division and the First Marine Division were forced to fight their way through Chinese roadblocks while being pounded by Chinese shellfire from the surrounding hills. Those engaged in this retreat, "The Chosin Few," as they now call themselves with pride, endured unbelievable hardships. The fighting was not only intense, the men also had to fight in temperatures that often dipped to more than twenty degrees below zero. Automatic weapons, if not fired regularly, froze up. Frostbite forced the evacuation of hundreds of men. Fortunately, this was possible because of a short runway hacked out by engineers at Hagaru-ri, where C-47 pilots battling terrible weather conditions brought in supplies and took out the casualties. When the Chinese blew a bridge at the Funchilin pass just south of Koto-ri, C-119 transports dropped the necessary bridge spans by parachute. Within hours engineers had repaired the bridge that provided the only escape possible. The retreat required the maximum effort from everyone; cooks and clerks became riflemen. Smith's well-known explanation of the retreat, in response to a reporter's question—"Retreat, hell— we're attacking in another direction"—made headlines in the United States and has been forever associated with the marines at the Chosin Reservoir.[13] Finally, with much support from UN fighter-bombers, most of the men made it to the port of Hungnam. On December 24, 1950, the U.S. Navy evacuated the men to Pusan to regroup and fight another day. Then the navy bombarded the abandoned port into a heap of wreckage.[14]

Meanwhile, in Washington the Chinese entry into the war effaced the recent optimism brought about by the UN offensive and revived the old fear that UN forces might yet be pushed off the Korean peninsula. It also revived the fear that atomic weapons might be necessary to stop the charging Communist forces in Korea. President Truman did not help matters at a press conference on November 30. In response to a question about the possible use of atomic bombs, he stated that in order to meet the military situation the United States would include "every weapon that we have."[15] A hastily prepared press release later the same day did little to clarify the issue. World reaction against the use of atomic weapons in Korea was strong, no doubt strengthened by the Soviet explosion of its own bomb in 1949. In Britain, the uproar in the House of Commons over the bomb prompted Prime Minister Attlee to pay a personal visit to Washington in early December for reassurances on this issue. He urged Washington to accept a negotiated cease-fire in Korea, even if this meant UN withdrawal.[16]

In late November, following the fighting that took place during the first entry of the Chinese into the war, the Chinese Sixty-sixth Army Headquarters issued a report on its perceptions of the performance of the American forces as well as its own army. They commented favorably on the American "coordinated action of mortars and tanks," the "great hazard" of American "aircraft strafing and bombing," and the "very active" American artillery. Their estimate of the American infantry, however, was less complimentary. The report described the Americans as "weak, afraid to die," unfamiliar with "night fighting or hand-to-hand combat," and "afraid when the rear is cut off." In future operations, the report concluded, as its "main objective" the Chinese forces "must fight its way rapidly around the enemy and cut off their rear," while avoiding "highways and flat terrain" so American tanks and artillery could not hinder their attack operations.[17]

While the retreat had revived speculation about the UN pulling out of Korea, that speculation was soon countered by General J. Lawton Collins, Army Chief of Staff. On December 8, he returned from a fact-finding tour of Korea. He reported that while the situation was serious and that it might be necessary to retreat to a line south of Seoul, the UN forces could hold in Korea, even without major reinforcements.[18]

During December, the Communist forces continued to push the UN forces southward along the entire front in what proved to be the largest retreat in U.S. military history. They paid a heavy price for their success in casualties, however, and by late December their supply lines, repeatedly hammered from the air, had been stretched to the breaking point. Exhausted, the Chinese offensive temporarily came to a halt.

On December 23, a freakish jeep accident claimed the life of Lieutenant General Walker. That night, General MacArthur called General Collins in Washington and requested Lieutenant General Matthew B. Ridgway as Walker's replacement to command the Eighth Army. Ridgway was an offensive-minded officer and a true WWII hero, and MacArthur had high respect for his strong leadership ability. Although stationed in Washington at the time, Ridgway's duties as the deputy chief of staff for operations and administration had kept him well informed on operations in Korea. Ridgway left Washington immediately for Tokyo, where he stopped briefly on December 26 for a meeting with MacArthur. When he asked MacArthur if he had permission to attack, providing conditions were favorable, the general replied: "The Eighth Army is yours, Matt. Do what you think best."[19]

Pleased, Ridgway flew to Korea the same day and immediately met with his top commanders. He found the leadership in "many instances sadly lacking," and he criticized them openly for their "timidity about getting off the scanty roads" and their "lack of imagination" in dealing with an enemy they "outmatched in firepower and dominated in the air and on the surroundings seas." The main problem, Ridgway believed, was how to restore the "lost confidence and lack of spirit" among the troops. Ridgway also saw Syngman Rhee, in order to impress him with "our determination not to be driven from the peninsula, and to go on the offensive again as soon as we could marshal our forces."[20]

Ridgway was eager to attack, but knew he first had to deal with a pending Chinese offensive, which intelligence expected imminently. It came on New Year's Eve, preceded by an extensive artillery barrage. Reluctantly, Ridgway ordered his troops to fall back to the south bank of the Han River, and on January 3, to evacuate Seoul. At one point, frustrated by truckloads of ROK soldiers scurrying south without either orders or their equipment, Ridgway personally stood in the middle of the road waving his arms frantically to stop the retreat. To restore order, he set up straggler posts in the rear manned by American military policemen.[21]

While the Communist offensive in January 1951 succeeded in pushing the UN forces south about fifty or sixty miles across the peninsula, it also cost the Communist armies an estimated thirty-eight thousand casualties. More than half of these casualties were the result of air attacks by American pilots, who bombed and strafed the Communist forces unmercifully during their advance.[22]

Fortunately, most of the UN armies retreated in good order with their equipment intact. Once the Communists armies had exhausted their offensive capacity, Ridgway ordered a new defensive line established in the vicinity of the 37th parallel. Known as the "D Line," it ran from Pyontaek in the west to Samchok on the east coast. This line proved to be as far south as the Eighth Army would go for the remainder of the war.

Reinforcements and additional equipment were pouring into Korea, and Ridgway was ready to take the offensive. He now had under his command not only I Corps and IX Corps, but also X Corps, which had been rebuilding in the Pusan area following the Chosin Reservoir fighting. Beginning in late January, the spring of 1951 is notable for a series of UN "limited" offensive operations, all intended to push the Communist forces back to the 38th Parallel or beyond. They were also designed to take full advantage of superior UN firepower and to inflict maximum casualties on the enemy while keeping UN casualties at a minimum. Eighth Army Headquarters gave each operation a name (Thunderball, Roundup, Killer), and each pushed the line further to the north toward a new defensive line, also named (Topeka, Kansas, Utah).[23]

Cautiously, in the spring of 1951, the UN forces worked their way north—toward the 38th Parallel. Unlike the uneven advance of the UN forces in the fall campaign, they moved forward as a solid front, and units remained in contact. This did much to prevent the Communist armies from flanking the road-bound columns of UN troops and setting up roadblocks behind them, a common tactic in earlier campaigns. The fighting was often intense, and the Communist forces were still capable of carrying out their own offensive operations for limited periods of time. They paid dearly for any success, however, because any large-scale attack forced the Chinese troops into the open, where UN air power and artillery inflicted horrendous casualties on them.

Chipyong-ni, just northwest of Wonju, was the scene of an intense battle in mid-February. A Communist offensive, launched on February 11, had succeeded in surrounding the U.S. Second Division's Twenty-third Regiment and its attached French battalion. Supplied from the air, the U.S. and French troops managed to hold on until finally relieved by a task force from the First Cavalry Division. This gutsy defense, which cost the Communist forces an estimated five thousand casualties, allowed the UN forces to retain the initiative and resume the advance to the north a few days later. Ridgway thought the battle a turning point that symbolized the confidence the Eighth Army had lost during the December withdrawals. Both the Twenty-third Regiment and the French battalion received the American Distinguished Unit citation for their heroic defense against far superior forces at Chipyong-ni.[24]

On March 15, UN forces captured the battered capital of Seoul for the second time, and a few days later they moved into Chunchon. When the advance brought the UN troops close to the 38th Parallel, Washington decided to make the crossing a tactical decision rather than a political one. Since in Ridgway's opinion this mystic line was "neither defensible nor strategically important," he decided, with MacArthur's approval, to "continue the advance."[25] By early April, UN troops had reached the Kansas line, a few miles north of the 38th Parallel.

The UN armies were now fighting with professionalism and spirit, and Ridgway had reason to be pleased. Attention, however, now shifted from the battlefield to politics—the Truman-MacArthur controversy. Essentially, MacArthur wished to carry the war to the Chinese in a way that contradicted Washington policy. He had proposed, sometimes publicly, a blockade of the Chinese coast, the use of Chinese Nationalist troops on Taiwan, and bombing targets on the Chinese mainland. All of these proposals were well known in Washington, and all had been rejected to prevent a wider war.

As the Eighth Army approached the 38th Parallel, Truman thought the timing right for a negotiated settlement. On March 20, in a statement cleared with Secretary of State Dean Acheson, Defense Secretary George Marshall, and President Truman, the Joint Chiefs of Staff informed MacArthur that the United Nations was now prepared to discuss the "conditions of settlement in Korea," and that "further diplomatic effort" should be made "before any advance with major forces north of the 38th Parallel."[26] MacArthur, however, considered a negotiated settlement that failed to punish the Communist aggressors unacceptable. On March 24, without notifying anyone in Washington, he issued his own "routine communique," which essentially torpedoed Truman's plans for a negotiated peace. MacArthur belittled China's military weaknesses and its failure to accomplish the conquest of Korea by force "even under inhibitions which now restrict the activity of the United Nations forces. . . ." The general went on to say that an "expansion of our military operations to his coastal areas and interior bases, would doom Red China to the risk of imminent military collapse."[27]

President Truman was furious. The statement was "in open defiance of my orders as President and as Commander in Chief" and "a challenge to the authority of the President under the Constitution," Truman wrote in his memoirs. MacArthur "left me no choice—I could no longer tolerate his insubordination."[28] A few days later, the general gave the president yet another reason to act. On April 5, Congressman Joseph W. Martin, the House minority leader, read a letter from MacArthur on the House floor. In the letter, MacArthur asserted that "if we lose the war to Communism in Asia the fall of Europe is inevitable. . . ." He ended the letter with his often quoted statement, "There is no substitute for victory."[29]

Truman was determined MacArthur must go, and he received full support from the Joint Chiefs of Staff. On April 11, 1951, in an unpopular move, Truman relieved MacArthur from his command. The general returned to the United States to deliver his celebrated "old soldier's" speech before a joint session of Congress and received a ticker tape parade in New York City. He returned a hero to many (but not all) Americans, but especially to the "limited war" and Truman critics. Ridgway replaced MacArthur in Tokyo, and Lieutenant General James A. Van Fleet, at the time in the States, took over the Eighth Army.[30]

Meanwhile, the war went on. On April 22, a quarter million Chinese troops attacked along a forty-mile front, complete with a massive artillery barrage, bugles, drums, flares, and whistles. They managed to break through two ROK divisions, and one of the breaches opened the way for another drive on Seoul. The UN forces withdrew about twenty-five miles to a line just north of Seoul, which Van Fleet did not name (the "No-Name Line") but expected the Eighth Army to hold. Once again the Chinese forces could not sustain the attack. Hit repeatedly from the air, by the end of April the offensive had run its course, and the Chinese fell back for resupply and replacements with very heavy losses.[31]

The exhaustion of the Communist armies presented the Eighth Army with the opportunity to seize the initiative and retake ground lost during the recent Communist offensive. Although Van Fleet had only been in Korea about a week, he was eager to attack, and on May 20, the UN armies again headed north on a broad front. By early June they had driven beyond the Kansas line to the Iron Triangle, the Hwachon Reservoir, and the Punchbowl area. During the advance Eighth Army troops also captured an unusually large number of prisoners. Many of them were clad in rags and in poor physical condition, suffering from malnutrition and low morale. UN commanders also reported the Communists had abandoned unprecedented amounts of equipment during their retreat, indicating disorganization.[32]

Once the Chinese and North Korean troops had retreated to their defensive positions, they began to dig in, as if they were planning to stay for a while. They dug tunnels and built bunkers strong enough to withstand all but direct hits from the American 155mm guns. They would not easily be dislodged from these positions. Perhaps the time to talk peace in Korea had finally arrived.[33]

Chapter 5

Truce Talks and Prison Riots

CLEARLY, THE BATTERED Communist forces lacked the firepower to break through the UN lines on a wide front. Realistically, they could no longer expect to recapture Seoul and drive into South Korea. They could achieve temporary success in limited sectors, but even this success came at the cost of huge casualty figures. On the UN side, even if the firepower and troops to drive the Chinese back to the Yalu were available, the will to do so was lacking, especially in Washington and among the other UN participants. Although Ridgway believed the Eighth Army, if ordered to do so, "could have pushed right on to the Yalu in the spring of 1951," he also believed the "price for such a drive would have been far too high...."[1] In June, Van Fleet did order limited operations to consolidate the UN positions, but nothing more. Unless one side or the other was willing to pay the cost in casualties and equipment required to carry out a major offensive, which would have been enormous, the war was effectively stalemated.[2]

The Truman administration was more than ready for peace talks. Secretary of State Acheson, at the MacArthur hearings in early June, had implied a willingness of the U.S. to accept an armistice based on the 38th Parallel provided certain conditions were met. On June 23, the Soviet ambassador to the UN, Jacob Malik, after talks with the American government's Soviet Union expert, George Kennan, suddenly called for discussions leading to a cease-fire and an armistice that provided for the mutual withdrawal of forces from the 38th Parallel. When the Beijing *People's Daily* followed by endorsing the Soviet proposal, it appeared the key players in all the warring powers except South Korea were ready to talk. Syngman Rhee, of course, adamantly opposed any settlement that left Korea divided.[3]

Given the green light by Washington, Ridgway followed up with some timely peace-feelers. In a radio message on June 30, Ridgway indicated his willingness to name a representative to begin discussions for a cease-fire and armistice. He suggested the meeting take place on a Danish hospital ship in Wonsan Harbor. The Communist reply, signed by Kim Il Sung for North Korea and Peng Dehuai for the Chinese People's Volunteer Forces, came two days later. They suggested talks begin on July 10 at Kaesong, a neutral site between the lines. Ridgway agreed to the changes.[4]

When the UN delegation under Vice Admiral Turner C. Joy met for the first time at Kaesong on July 10, hopes were high for an early end to the fighting. They quickly discovered, however, that the Communists were more interested in using the talks for propaganda purposes and making the UN look like losers than real peace. They began by surrounding and bringing under Communist control the "neutral" city of Kaesong. When the UN delegation arrived under a white flag, as previously agreed, the Communists presented this to the world as a token of surrender. When the delegates took their seats, the Communists sat in high chairs, while the UN delegation sat in low chairs. At some meetings the two delegations sat for hours in silence and just glared at each other across the table. It was an ominous beginning for the peace talks, which were to drag on for more than two years.[5]

During the early weeks of the talks, the major disagreement on the agenda occurred over the demarcation line. The Communists insisted the cease-fire line should be along the 38th Parallel, which the Truman administration had seemed to endorse when first suggesting the peace talks. During the ensuing fighting, however, the UN forces had moved into areas north of the 38th Parallel, areas that provided a more natural defense, and Ridgway insisted the line must be in keeping with the military realities. He did not object to surrendering some areas south of the parallel that could not be easily defended, but he wished to retain a buffer zone established along the general line of battle, much of which was north of the 38th.[6]

Finally, after the talks were suspended in August and after UN forces took Heartbreak Ridge and Bloody Ridge in bitter fighting, the talks resumed on October 25. This time, at Ridgway's insistence, they took place at the village of Panmunjom, about midway between the two lines. Ridgway favored a tough, hard-line position in dealing with the Communists, and opposed a cease-fire until agreement on the demarcation line had been reached. This often put him at odds with Washington, which backed a softer stand to create more favorable conditions for peace. On November 14, after rejecting Ridgway's appeals, the Joint Chiefs of Staff ordered Ridgway to "press for an early settlement" of the fighting. Accordingly, Ridgway ordered Van Fleet to cease all major offensive operations and seize only the terrain needed for defense, such as outposts. In this way, the UN negotiators hoped that the existing main line of resistance (MLR) could be frozen into the final demarcation line on the effective date of the armistice. To implement this proposal, the UN negotiators insisted that a cease-fire must take place within thirty days. On November 27, the Communists accepted the proposal, but when the thirty days passed, no agreement on a cease-fire had been reached. The Communists instead used the time to strengthen their defensive positions, well aware of the growing war weariness among the Western powers and confident that time was on their side. When the war finally ended nineteen months later, the final demarcation line differed only slightly from the MLR as it existed at the end of 1951.[7]

While the negotiators agreed on the demarcation line, they could not agree on the details for implementing an armistice, especially the methods of supervision. During the spring of 1952, the negotiators went back and forth on these issues, sometimes making progress and sometimes meeting for only five or ten minutes before stalking out of their truce tents.[8]

It was the POW issue, however, that deadlocked the negotiations and, in effect, extended the war. Despite all the emotion and appropriation of the issue for propaganda purposes by both sides, the matter was quite simple. The United States insisted that the repatriation of POWs should be strictly voluntary, and the Communists insisted that all of their prisoners should be returned home. The issue was made more contentious by the exchange of POW lists, which the Communists had reluctantly agreed to on December 18, 1951. During the early months of the war, the Communists had reported through radio broadcasts and news releases the capture of over 65,000 prisoners. When the UN Command received the lists, however, they were shocked to learn the Communists held only 7,142 ROK soldiers and 4,417 UN personnel, for a total of 11,559 prisoners.[9] What happened to the others?

On the POW issue, President Truman took a personal interest, undoubtedly haunted by the memory of thousands of desperate Russian prisoners the Western Allies forced to return in 1945 to an uncertain fate in Stalin's Russia. He insisted that the UN position of "voluntary" repatriation must not be compromised. On May 7, 1952, in a public statement, Truman stated bluntly that there would be no "forced repatriation of prisoners of war," despite the insistence of the Communists. "We will not buy an armistice by turning over human beings for slaughter or slavery," the president continued.[10] He could not have made his position more clear.

Unfortunately, the Communists were equally adamant on this issue. If a massive number of Communist prisoners declined repatriation and the glories of their system in favor of freedom, this would constitute a major propaganda setback. This is precisely what happened. In April, after screening, the UN Command reported that only 70,000 of the 132,000 prisoners held in UN custody were willing to go home. The Communists, of course, found these figures humiliating and totally unacceptable. Even the UN negotiators were disturbed by these events. They were much more interested in ending the war than scoring propaganda victories and knew this would interrupt the progress of the truce talks.[11]

The POW issue not only deadlocked the peace negotiations, it also had other tragic consequences. It played a major role in sparking riots in a number of the UN prison camps. One of the worst—and the best known—took place at Koje-do.

During the early months of the war, the North Korean captives were in the care of the ROK Army. When the number of captives swelled, however, as a result of the swift UN advance into North Korea, the U.S. Army assumed the responsibility for captured Communist prisoners. Many of them were detained in hastily constructed prison compounds built on islands surrounding the peninsula, such as Koje-do, a small island off the coast of South Korea. The 150,000 Communist prisoners were guarded by a mix of American and ROK soldiers, nearly all without experience in prison camp duty.[12] The administration of the camps can only be described as chaotic, in part because no effort had been made to separate the Communists and the anti-Communists. As a result, hard-core militants on both sides battled it out in the camps while the American and ROK guards watched but did nothing. There is even evidence Communist military leaders ordered some of their more promising and dedicated cadre to intentionally fall into enemy hands on the battlefields and enter the UN prison camps, where they could organize the prisoners.[13]

Once prisoners inside the camps understood the UN Command insisted on voluntary repatriation, the hard-core Communists went to work on the non-Communist prisoners, that is, all of those who refused to return to China or North Korea. While beatings were most common, on occasions the Communist prisoners convened kangaroo courts inside the compounds and sentenced the recalcitrant prisoners to death, sometimes by torture. Where non-Communists were in control of the compound, they meted out justice in much the same way. The result was total pandemonium, and it created a huge public relations problem for the UN Command, which Communists worldwide exploited in the propaganda war. General Ridgway and Admiral Joy actually favored an increase in the number of Communist prisoners volunteering to return, because they knew a larger and more acceptable figure to the Chinese would facilitate the signing of an armistice. They could not, however, tolerate the brutal methods employed by the Communist zealots in the camps. They had to be stopped. But first, the UN had to regain control of the camps. The attempts to do this sparked the riots at Koje-do in May 1952.[14]

The problems at Koje-do go back as far as the summer of 1951, when several prisoners were killed inside the compounds. In February 1952, the UN began the process of screening the prisoners one by one to determine who wished to be repatriated to China and North Korea and who did not. This had the effect of increasing the disorder, however, and the riots and murders inside the compounds continued. On February 13, to enforce the screening, U.S. troops moved into one of the compounds and fought a pitched battle with Communist resistance groups, resulting in casualties on both sides. Nevertheless, the screening of prisoners continued, except in compounds controlled by Communist hard-liners, which General Ridgway decided were all eligible for repatriation. Then a foolish act by the American commandant of the island, Brigadier General Francis T. Dodd, changed everything. Despite warnings from UN intelligence sources of a Communist plot to make him a prisoner, on May 7, 1952, Dodd met with representatives of Compound 76, who managed to drag him into the camp. Brigadier General Charles F. Colson took command and, after negotiating with the Communist prisoners, managed to secure the release of Dodd on May 10, but only after signing a humiliating confession. The entire affair received intense media coverage and amounted to a major propaganda victory for the Communists. Soon afterward, Generals Dodd and Colson found themselves colonels and retired from the army. Order gradually returned to the camps, in part because many of the American and ROK guards were replaced with other UN troops. Nevertheless, the prisoner riots were more than embarrassing to the UN Command; they also undercut the high moral ground the UN had assumed when it endorsed the principle of voluntary repatriation.[15]

Chapter 6

Trench Warfare and Peace

IN THE MEANTIME, the war went on. Since the end of 1951, when the two sides agreed on the demarcation line, the nature of the war had changed. It was no longer a war to "win," and every UN soldier soon knew it. Instead, it had now become a stalemated war of the trenches, the most forgotten part of the forgotten war. Yet, about 45 percent of all U.S. casualties tragically occurred after the beginning of the truce talks.[1] Much bloody fighting lay ahead, but the front lines remained essentially unchanged. Both sides just dug in and prepared to stay.

Back in the States, without movement and big battles, news of the war gradually dropped off the front pages. Once it became a war of the trenches, casualty figures generally declined and thus became less of an issue. A new rotation plan meant that no GI would be doomed to Korea indefinitely. Most Americans, unless they had a family member involved, went about their business without paying much attention to the war. They did find the war frustrating and wanted it over. At the same time, the majority of Americans seemed determined to "stay the course" in Korea and even supported Truman's position on the POWs, which deadlocked the negotiations. Besides, the wrath of Senator McCarthy's "Red-hunters" could come down hard on anyone who suggested a pullout in Korea and peace at any price. So, most Americans patiently waited it out and, unlike during Vietnam, never became actively involved in opposition to the war. When young men received their draft notices, they went silently into the service without protest, not eagerly, but they went.[2]

On the front lines, however, all UN soldiers still found the war to be very real. Even without major Communist attacks, which were rare except in the final weeks of the war, there were still patrols, guard duty, work details, wiring parties—all part of the routine. For excitement, there were frequent incoming mortar and artillery rounds, and on occasions, firefights with the enemy. Frequently, small units of Chinese and North Korean soldiers infiltrated the UN trenches, killed as many UN soldiers as possible with grenades and small arms fire, then slipped away only to repeat the process a few nights later. The attacks always took place at night, so soldiers on guard duty hoped for a cloudless night with a bright moon.

Sometimes UN Command sent down orders that a particular hill must be taken, perhaps to consolidate the line, or perhaps it gave the enemy too much of an advantage. Such an order virtually guaranteed hard combat and high casualties for those involved, and it was not always easy for frontline soldiers to see the purpose in such attacks. To most soldiers, the hills in Korea looked amazingly similar, including those selected for an attack.

Some of the most hazardous duty in Korea for UN soldiers, and the scenes of some of the bloodiest fighting, took place on the outposts. Located well in front of the MLR, and usually on hill crests, outposts were built to provide an early warning against surprise attacks. They consisted of well-constructed bunkers housing command posts and artillery observation posts, all connected by telephone to the MLR. Down the hill, but linked by trenches to the command post, were still more trenches, manned by UN soldiers well equipped with grenades and small arms. Since they would most likely spot the enemy first, they were expected to warn the others. Barbed wire entanglements and minefields ringed the entire outpost to prevent rapid infiltration by the enemy. Outposts were usually defended by platoons or companies, which were relieved every four or five days.[3]

In contrast, the Communists built their defenses around tunnels rather than trenches, a decision no doubt prompted by the UN control of the air space over the front. Using their huge manpower resources, they cut tunnels into the mountains to connect the front and reverse slopes, then added miles of intercommunication tunnels with unlimited storage facilities. Chinese artillerymen could wheel a 76mm field gun to the entrance of the tunnel, fire a round, and quickly withdraw the gun to safety within the tunnel. General Maxwell Taylor, the last commander of the Eighth Army in Korea, rated the Chinese defenses superior to the German defenses during WWII.[4]

For the most part, UN Command fought the Korean War with WWII weaponry. There was one notable exception—the helicopter. Despite some limitations, such as its vulnerability to enemy ground fire and adverse weather conditions, it played a major role in the war. Helicopters were used for battle-

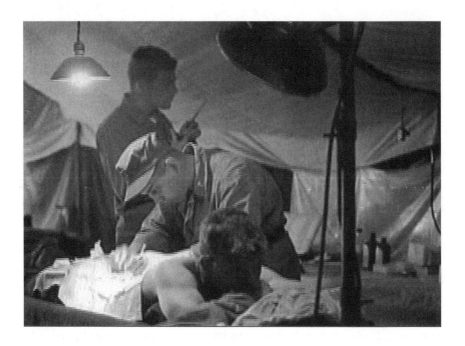

Tending to a wounded soldier in a MASH unit. (Courtesy of Forty-fifth Infantry Division Museum)

field observation, air–sea rescue, transport of men and supplies, and for the evacuation of the wounded.[5]

Because of the film and television series *M*A*S*H,* there is no more enduring image of the Korean War for most Americans than a helicopter landing at a MASH unit with wounded soldiers. Like the helicopter, MASH (Mobile Army Surgical Hospital) units were relatively new. Designed late in World War II, they were essentially field hospitals intended to provide emergency surgery to stabilize and prepare the severely wounded for evacuation, often to Japan. Located near the front lines, MASH units were prepared to move as often as necessary to keep pace with combat operations. When helicopters brought in the wounded, they arrived at MASH units in a fraction of the time required by litter jeeps and ambulances. The combination of MASH units and helicopters, plus other medical advances at the time, clearly improved the survival rates for wounded American and UN soldiers in Korea.[6]

In sharp contrast, the Chinese and North Korean medical services, which were inadequate by any standard, nearly collapsed by early 1951 when UN armies went on the offensive. Much of the problem rested with their inability to evacuate their wounded in a timely manner. Since UN air forces controlled the airspace, the Communists could not safely evacuate their wounded soldiers until nightfall, and even then over the most primitive roads. Wounded soldiers evacuated by train also had to wait it out during the day; the trains ran only at night. Since this flawed evacuation system was combined with serious problems pertaining to medical equipment, medicines, sanitation, and nutrition, survival chances for wounded Chinese or North Korean soldiers were much lower than for UN soldiers.[7]

As the war continued, UN Command began to realize that for the sake of morale the men needed a break in the routine of combat and training. While serving on the front line, soldiers had no opportunities to go to bars or clubs, and passes were unknown. When in reserve, they might occasionally see a movie or a USO show, but that was about it. Otherwise, soldiers in Korea experienced little but snow and bitter cold in the winter, rain and mud in the spring, humid heat in the summer, and monotonous mountain ridges all year. To boost morale, during the early part of 1951 the Eighth Army initiated a new program that provided each soldier with the opportunity to spend five days in Japan for "rest and recuperation" (R&R). For most soldiers, this meant club life and women, but for everyone it meant the opportunity to take a real bath, get dry and warm, sleep in a bed, and eat something other than army chow. Just getting out of Korea provided a big morale boost for everyone, even if only for a few days.[8]

During March 1951, the Eighth Army adopted another new program—a rotation system for all UN personnel, based upon points. As modified in March 1952, soldiers received four points a month for frontline duty, three points for service in an intermediate combat zone (divisional reserve), and two points for service elsewhere in Korea. The magic number was thirty-six points, and any soldier who collected four points each month could rotate in nine months. While individual soldiers appreciated knowing there were limits to their service in Korea, critics have often pointed out that the system damaged combat effectiveness by lessening comradery and adhesion to the unit. Also, by the time the new men had become proficient soldiers they had accumulated so many points that some were more focused on going home than on their jobs. Soldiers could measure their rotation date with some accuracy, and many did not hesitate to remind others they were a "short-timer" when they neared the end of their service in Korea.[9]

Toward the end of the war, when it appeared the negotiators were near

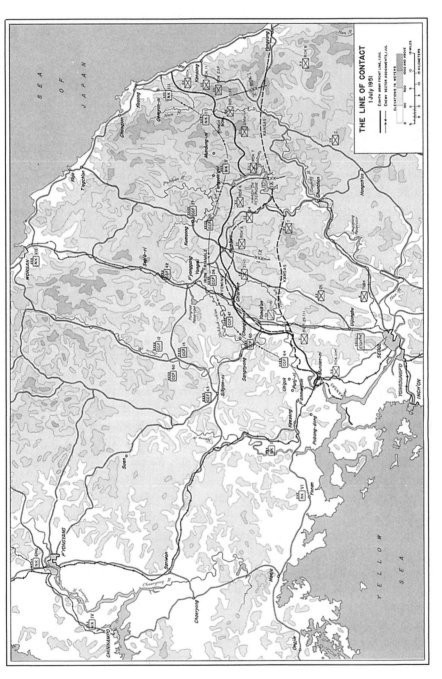

The Line of Contact, July 1, 1951. Source: Department of the Army, *United States Army in the Korean War: Truce Tent and Fighting Front* (Washington, D.C.: U.S. Government Printing Office, 1988), Map I.

A battery of 105mm howitzers, the standard artillery piece used by the American army in Korea. (Courtesy of Forty-fifth Infantry Division Museum)

an agreement, the intensity of the fighting actually picked up. In part, this was because the Communists were trying to strengthen their military position for the purpose of strengthening their negotiating position. Also, they wished to prove they had more staying power and were more willing to make sacrifices than the UN forces. Consequently, the Communists ordered frequent attacks, usually against one of the outposts scattered across the peninsula in front of the MLR. The names of some of these outposts became well-known, such as Old Baldy, Bunker Hill, and Pork Chop Hill. While the size of the Communist forces assaulting these outposts varied greatly, the fighting was consistently savage for those involved. Some of these outposts changed sides several times during the war. In April 1953, the fighting was especially intense on Pork Chop, and the heroic defense of the outpost prompted Hollywood to turn the story into a movie starring Gregory Peck.[10] Between June 10 and 18, 1953, the Chinese made a serious attempt to take Outpost Harry in the central sector, attacking in regimental strength. Each night one company from either the Third Division, the Fifth Regimental Combat Team, or the Greek Expeditionary Force defended the outpost, but only for one night. After one night, each company suffered so many casualties it was pulled off the line and replaced by another company before the next round of attacks came on the following night. An estimated 4,118 U.S. and Greek soldiers participated in the fighting on Harry, and 2,422 soldiers, or 59 percent, were killed or wounded. Artillery rounds fired, on both sides, reached record proportions. Ironically, it was during June, just weeks before the end of the war, that the UN Command fired more artillery rounds than any other month of the war (2.7 million rounds).[11]

Despite this increase in the fighting, by the spring of 1953 there were some positive signs in favor of an armistice. General Dwight D. Eisenhower, now president, publicly stated his determination to do everything possible to bring the war to an end. Accordingly, the Eisenhower administration dropped hints that if the deadlock in the peace negotiations were not broken soon, the Chinese Nationalists could be unleashed to invade the mainland and the U.S. might employ atomic bombs in Asia. After this, Eisenhower wrote later in his memoirs, the "prospects for armistice negotiations seemed to improve."[12] Stalin's death on March 5, however, probably had more to do with improving the prospects for peace than Eisenhower's threats. Only ten days after the death of Stalin, the new Soviet leader, Georgi M. Malenkov, seemed to extend an olive branch when he declared there was no existing dispute between Moscow and Washington that could not be solved peacefully. Eisenhower, replying in a cautiously worded speech, challenged Malenkov to match his words with deeds, including "an honorable peace" in Korea.[13]

It is difficult to assess how these hints of new directions coming from Moscow and Washington affected the thinking in Beijing. At the very least, it must have created uncertainty among the Chinese leaders. It is even possible Moscow may have applied pressure on China and North Korea to end the war.[14] It is also possible the Chinese were war weary and more than ready to quit. They badly needed their resources to rebuild their nation after years of civil war. Since they had pushed the UN forces back from the Yalu, they could claim a victory. Kim Il Sung may not have been so eager for a truce, but he could hardly continue the war alone.[15]

Whatever the reasons, events began to move in the direction of an armistice. The big break came on March 28, when Chinese and North Korean negotiators suddenly agreed to a previous International Red Cross proposal for an exchange of the sick and wounded POWs. Two days later, the Chinese foreign minister, Zhou Enlai, issued a statement that promised a breakthrough on the POW issue, suggesting that all POWs who did not wish to be repatriated should be turned over to a neutral state.[16]

On April 20, Operation Little Switch began. The UN Command delivered 6,670 sick and wounded North Korean and Chinese prisoners, while receiving a total of 684 UN prisoners. This was clearly a sign the Chinese were ready for peace.[17]

The negotiators at Panmunjom were now able to carry on discussions with the serious intent of breaking the deadlock on the POWs. There were still many problems, however, such as the problem of determining which of the neutral nations would assume the responsibility for those POWs who did not wish to return home. Finally, on June 7, the negotiators came together on this difficult issue. Based on a proposal made earlier by India, prisoners who did not wish to be repatriated would be turned over to a five-member Neutral Nations Repatriation Commission. The commission would assume responsibility for these prisoners for a maximum of 120 days and, if necessary, attempt to relocate them. The road was now clear for an armistice.[18]

Not surprisingly, as the two sides drew closer together trying to work out the last details, Syngman Rhee became a major obstacle to a settlement. Rhee was opposed to any armistice that did not provide for a united Korea with himself in control. In April, he had even threatened to withdraw the ROK forces from UN Command and continue the war alone. He made radio broadcasts, staged mass rallies, and issued press releases—all aimed at undermining the talks. Most serious, on June 18 he directed the ROK prison guards to release about twenty-five thousand North Korean prisoners who had refused repatriation. Not surprisingly, the prisoners quickly melted into the hills of South Korea, While infuriated, the Communist negotiators did not allow Rhee's action to sabotage the peace negotiations. A few days later Rhee promised that while he would not sign the armistice, neither would he obstruct it.[19]

On July 23, staff officers reached agreement on the final demarcation line, and the stage was set for the signing. At 9:57 A.M., on a windy July 27, the delegates entered the building at Panmunjom from opposite sides and took their place behind the tables in an atmosphere that has been described as "marked by cold courtesy on both sides." Generals William K. Harrison for the UN and Nam Il for North Korea sat down without a word of greeting and began to sign the first of nine copies of the armistice agreement. By 10:12 the signing was completed, and the two men departed through their exits as silently as they had entered. In the distance the sound of artillery could still be heard; both sides continued heavy shelling until 10:00 that night, when the armistice went into effect. At that moment the sky suddenly lit up with dozens of multicolored flares, signifying the end of the war. It was exactly two years and seventeen days since the talks had begun.[20]

On August 5, in accordance with agreements reached during the negotiations, the prisoner exchange began at Panmunjom. Known as Operation

Big Switch, the Communists returned 3,597 Americans by the time the exchange ended on September 6.[21] Twenty-one Americans refused repatriation, although nearly all of them eventually left China. Many of the UN prisoners arrived emaciated and in a pitiable physical condition, the result of years of mistreatment in POW camps. All would have their own horror stories to tell about the camps. Unfortunately, not many Americans wanted to hear them. Subjected to hours of interrogation, even on their voyage home, American POWs returned only to discover their country was torn by the Red Scare, led by Senator Joe McCarthy. They were asked not about their sufferings and hardships, but about brainwashing and collaboration. It is little wonder that for most of them it was years before they would talk openly about their experiences, and some have remained silent to this day.[22]

The Communist prisoners, in their eagerness to show their countrymen they were uncontaminated by capitalist handouts, often threw away their cigarettes and stripped off their clothes and boots before arriving at the exchange point. But at last it was mercifully over, three years, one month, and two days after the invasion of South Korea.[23]

The price in American lives for containing Communist aggression was not cheap. A total of 36,914 Americans lost their lives on the battlefields of Korea from war related causes. In addition, 3,960 non-Americans in the service of the United Nations Command died in Korea. Estimates of Korean casualties vary widely, however, largely because of incomplete records and the intermingling of the populations of North and South Korea. When deaths caused by disease, exposure, and starvation are added to the violent deaths, UN officials believe as many as 900,000 lives may have been lost in South Korea alone. The North Korean government has never provided official casualty statistics on the war, but the South Korean government claims the NKPA lost nearly 300,000 in deaths alone. Casualty figures for the Peoples Republic of China are equally vague. After the war, the U.S. armed forces estimated Chinese military casualties at more than one million, with deaths exceeding 500,000.[24]

When the GIs arrived back in the States, most were treated neither as heroes, as were many WWII veterans, nor with hostility, as were many Vietnam veterans. The majority were simply received in silence, and sometimes with the question, "Where have you been anyway?" Most Korean veterans accepted this reality, quickly put the war behind them, and got on with their lives. Nobody was more eager to forget America's forgotten war than the men who had fought it—the Korean War veterans.

Part Two

Many Faces, One War

Chapter 7

Getting to Korea

For many soldiers, part of the trauma of going to war is getting there. Going to war for most meant tearful goodbyes at home, followed by hours of homesickness and loneliness while en route. In the Korean War, most Americans traveled by bus, train, and troopship, very much like in World War II. While the GIs going to Korea faced no danger from submarines, unlike their WWII counterparts, they did experience all the other unpleasantries of troopship travel, including boredom, bunks stacked so close together you could turn your body only with great difficulty, KP or other unsavory duties, and worst of all, seasickness. Indeed, for many seasickness is their most enduring memory. The following story, by Second Lieutenant Leslie Davis, describes his journey from his home in Oklahoma to his arrival in Yokohama. While he tends to focus on the humorous side of the voyage, it was nevertheless a most unpleasant experience for the majority of GIs.

Second Lieutenant Leslie R. Davis

Thirty-sixth Engineer Combat Group, Eleventh Engineer Combat Battalion, Eighth Army

I FLEW FROM Ft. Belvoir, Virginia, for a few days leave in Stillwater, Oklahoma, before going on to Seattle, where I would ship out for Korea. Since my buddy Pete Hitt was on leave in Denver, I decided to catch a bus to Denver and ride the train with him to Seattle.

My mother and I decided to say goodbye at the house, so I took a cab to the bus station. In a scene reminiscent of the early morning departure of Jeff Bridges for Korea in the movie *The Last Picture Show,* I, too, started my trek. It was a long bus ride to Denver, but I survived. Youth was on my side.

Pete, his wife, and their brand new daughter met me in Denver. I got to witness another sad farewell when Pete, the ultimate family man, said goodbye to his "girls."

There is humor, though, even at the saddest times. His dear wife baked us both a big stack of homemade cookies to eat on the way. Like so many guys going to Korea at that time, we had purchased lighter fluid–powered hand warmers. While on the train we decided to see if the warmers worked; they did. Then we stuffed them in our handbags. (Incidentally, I never saw anyone use them Korea.) A little later, we decided to check out the cookies, which we found to be "A-one" delicious. Unfortunately, we promptly started burping a "lighter fluid burp." We soon figured out that the fumes had permeated the cookies. We burped lighter fluid from Wyoming to Washington. To this day I hate the smell of lighter fluid. Little did I realize when our train pulled into Seattle that this was nothing compared to the seasickness soon to come.

My trip to the Far East started at Fort Lawton, Washington, near Seattle, which served as one of the two staging areas for the Far East Command, or FECOM. The other was Camp Stoneman, California, near San Francisco. After processing, we were told we could go anywhere we wanted. Of course, we were also told to report to Troop Headquarters every four hours between 6:00 A.M. and midnight for possible immediate embarkation. The area was nice, but it rained almost every day. That was normal, the locals said.

We expected a very short stay. Instead, it lasted on and on, through Christmas. Finally, we were told to grab our duffel bags, and on December 30, 1952, they bussed us to Pier 39, where our ship, the *General R.L. Howze,* awaited us in the harbor. We quickly dubbed this old WWII retread the "*Lowsy Howze.*"

Also there to see us off were the obligatory small army band and the wives and girlfriends of some of the *Howze*'s crew. Some of the ladies were crying and really carrying on. This aroused "great sympathy" on the part of the army troops because we realized the poor babies would not see their guys again until they dumped us in Yokohama and returned—maybe all of *two* months. I'll never forget the day's final bit of gallows humor. As the boat left the pier, the band played "Harbor Lights" and "Now Is the Hour"—honestly!

The *Howze* was an old World War II assault transport ship taken out of mothballs for the Korean War. It was not nearly as large and luxurious as the "dependent-class" ships, such as the *General Walker,* which also carried wives and children.

As a second lieutenant, I had a few privileges but very little respect. I bunked in a "C" deck cabin shared by four other lieutenants and one "old" (about thirty-five) captain. One major bonus—our cabin had a porthole, so we had fresh air. In contrast, my men were crammed in like sardines with no fresh air outlets.

Once on board, most of us were stuck right away with some kind of routine duty. They made me the compartment commander of Compartment 6E, two decks down from my bunk. Half or more of my guys were Puerto Ricans, and many of them spoke very little English. Although it was forbidden, a lot of them spent their time gambling. Several vicious fights took place over small amounts of money in dice or card games.

I was convinced before we left Seattle that seasickness was largely psychological—in a person's head. Shortly after we left the calm waters of Puget Sound for the wild seas of the North Pacific, however, I knew it was in my stomach. I became very seasick and stayed that way for most of the voyage to Yokohama. The trip was supposed to take thirteen days, but the rough seas slowed us down and we were twenty-two days on the water.

Ironically, the best food I ever had in my army days was on the *Howze.* Yet, I practically lived on crackers and oranges provided to those too sick to eat the good navy chow.

Most of my guys in 6E developed varying degrees of seasickness the first day. The cramped conditions, the lack of fresh air, and the inability to shower regularly made the compartment a less than pleasant place to live and keep clean. We had an inspection of the latrine (the navy called it a head) every morning at 10:00 A.M. The old chiefs and swabbies were quite critical and hard to please, as they should have been.

We had a lot of time to kill on the voyage, and boredom was a real problem. The chaplain had a few books, crossword puzzles, chess games, etc., which helped relieve the monotony. Desperation even drove some of us to try our hand at making crossword puzzles. This wasn't easy, but it consumed a lot of time, which is why we were doing it in the first place.

Special Services set up talent shows with some pretty good singers and musicians. One guy had even appeared on the Arthur Godfrey program on national radio (T.V. was still in the wings).

One thing I never figured out was why the mess halls were located in the front part of the ship. Every time we tried to eat we would feel the nose rising and dropping over and over. It seemed so sensible to put mess halls midship, where the rising and falling would be less violent. But then, the navy never asked me.

While at sea we surrendered our greenbacks for M.P.C. (military payment certificates), since it was unlawful to spend dollars in Japan or Korea. This made us realize we were really leaving home. On the voyage back the process was reversed, and the old greenback looked mighty good.

If really truthful, I think most of us on the boat would have admitted that arriving in Korea was a pretty scary thought. At the same time, due to the boredom, seasickness, and cramped conditions, most of the guys on the *Lowsy Howze* were happy to vacate the old tub. Despite all the bad stuff we had heard about Korea, we were anxious to see it for ourselves and see what fate awaited us in this cold, distant land.

The entry dock at Pusan, the first view of Korea for most GIs. (Courtesy of Leslie Davis)

Chapter 8

A Mortar Man's Story

Like many other youths at the time, Bobby Martin decided to join the army and get his service obligation out of the way. Unfortunately, this meant he was trained and certain to be called up during the Korean War. Assigned to an 81mm mortar section in the Eighth Regiment of the U.S. Cavalry Division, the division that had already been hit hard in the fighting at Unsan, Sergeant First Class Martin arrived in Korea around the middle of November 1950. Since this was only a few days before the Chinese committed the main body of their forces, he was just in time to participate in the general UN withdrawal to the south. Sergeant Martin, the reader will notice, has the highest regard for General Ridgway, the new Eighth Army commander.

Sergeant First Class Bobby J. Martin

D Company, Eighth Regiment, First Cavalry Division

SOMETIME BEFORE I turned eighteen in 1948, Congress passed a law that permitted you to fulfill your military obligation by entering the service for one year and then remaining in the reserve for six years. Several of us in Pauls Valley, Oklahoma, where I grew up, thought that sounded better than the alternative, which was to be drafted into the army for two years of active duty. So we decided to join the army for one year and get our service out of the way, or so we thought. Little did we realize a war was less than two years away.

For basic training I was sent to Fort Hood, Texas, and assigned to the Second Armored Division, Forty-first Armored Infantry Battalion. I can't say I enjoyed basic, but I can say we received excellent training, largely because most of the cadre were battle-hardened WWII veterans.

After my year of active duty, I returned to Oklahoma and ended up as the manager of a variety store in Healdton, a small town not far from Pauls Valley. In the meantime, on June 25, 1950, North Korea attacked South Korea, and the Korean War had begun. Since I was trained and in the reserve, I was ripe to be called up. In September 1950, my mother called me in Healdton and said I had received a letter from the army ordering me to report to Fort Hood, Texas, in twenty-one days. That was her interpretation of the letter. About an hour later, however, a friend of mine in Pauls Valley called and told me my mother did not understand military abbreviations. The twenty-one days referred to the minimum length of time I would be expected to serve; I was due at Fort Hood in two days.

After some hurried goodbyes to my family and to my bride of about one month, I left for Fort Hood. When I arrived, people were coming in from everywhere. We spent the first three days processing, getting shots, and all that stuff. Then we took twelve days for training in a refresher course, after which we found ourselves on a train heading west. When we arrived at Camp Stoneman, California, we did more processing, including the preparation of a will. We shipped out on the *General Hase* and spent the next two weeks or so playing pinochle or something to keep from being bored to death. Some guys got seasick, but for some reason I never did. One guy got so sick he just stayed in his bunk, and we took turns bringing chow to him. Finally, we arrived at the port of Yokohama, and from there they trucked us to Camp Drake (near Tokyo) for more processing. Among other things, we saw a film on the prevention of trenchfoot and picked up our M-1 rifles with three rounds of ammunition (to zero our rifles in). We also received our orders. I was assigned Company D, First Battalion, Eighth Regiment, First Cavalry Division. I asked someone at the bulletin board where the First Cavalry was located. The answer—no one had heard from them for two days. I found this a bit disturbing.

A short time later, we again loaded out on a ship, this time for Korea. When we embarked the three thousand of us on board had been given different assignments. By the time we disembarked at Inchon, however, all of us had been assigned to the First Cavalry Division. I reached my regiment sometime around the middle of November, while the division was still in reserve. So, we trained—squad tactics and all that basic training stuff. At the end of each drill our platoon leader would yell, "Bug out," and we were supposed to fall back quickly toward the south. In early November, just before I arrived, the First Cavalry had been hit hard by the Communist forces at Unsan and had been forced into a hasty retreat.

Thanksgiving Day saw the army go all out to provide the troops with a really good meal, a complete turkey dinner. The problem was eating it before it froze. I remember the meal sat on burners in the serving line, but by the time we got it on our trays and sat down to eat, much of the food would be ice cold. By the time I got to my fruit cocktail it had actually frozen.

On November 25, just after Thanksgiving, the war entered a new phase when the Chinese entered in force. This, of course, changed everything, and instead of marching northward toward the Yalu River, the UN forces found themselves in a hasty retreat to the south. During the retreat, our battalion would go into a blocking position and set up, then another battalion would move through us and block for our battalion. Sometimes we set up with two of our mortars facing north and two facing south. That was because North Korean units that had been bypassed earlier attacked from the south, while the Chinese attacked from the north.

By this time, the temperature had really dropped, sometimes to more than twenty degrees below zero. It was a sharp, stinging cold that cut right through to the bone, despite the fact we wore a ton of clothes. We had long-handled underwear, wool pants, wind-proof pants on the bottom, a wool shirt, a sweater, a field jacket, mittens with inserts, socks, boots with rubber soles and leather tops, and overcoats, which we didn't always wear because they impeded our movement too much. It sounds like a lot, but we were still cold most of the time. The cold also made it almost impossible to dig in our mortars, since the ground was completely frozen.

One time during the retreat, when the Second Battalion pulled through us, our 81mm section was ordered to provide the rear guard while our troops withdrew. Our orders were to stay in position until 1:00 A.M. that night and then pull out. They left us with a jeep and a trailer, and somehow we managed to scrounge up a machine gun. We set up the machine gun, dispersed a bit, and waited until 1:00 A.M. Since we heard nothing and saw nothing, we loaded the machine gun into the trailer and started walking out behind the jeep at about four or five miles an hour. We had gone only a short distance when we heard a Chinese mortar firing from the left side of the road. They had gone past us on our flank and were already firing into our forward troops. Somehow we managed to slip past them and rejoin our battalion okay. The next morning we had no sooner set up in our new positions than a runner came by and shouted, "Get ready to move out." So we did, about one hundred miles to the south, to a new defensive position on a little road junction east of the main supply road, where we dug in our mortars and set up.

During the retreat our cooks had become separated from us; we didn't know where they were, and they didn't know where we were. As a result, we didn't get much food, and we got pretty hungry. We did find some rabbits and a four hundred–pound calf in a village. We confiscated both the rabbits and the calf. After butchering the calf, we gave half of it back to its owner. We kept the two hind quarters and cut them into steaks, so we ate pretty good for a little while. Later we moved on down to the 38th Parallel, and again, we ran out of food. This time we found some dried English peas and some chestnuts in a village. We roasted the chestnuts and ate them but couldn't find any water in which to cook the English peas. This crisis prompted one of our old sergeants to do a bit of reconnoitering, and he came back with some coffee and a gallon of Wesson oil. We boiled the peas in the Wesson oil, but they were still hard as rocks when we got through cooking them. Fortunately, late that afternoon the cooks found us. They set up their kitchen and we had biscuits, spam, and cocoa. Some guys were so hungry they ate too much. Because their stomachs had shrunk, some of them threw up on the way back from the chow line.

Like everyone else, the First Cavalry Division kept retreating to the south, and by Christmastime we were near Seoul. To make sure we had a Christmas tree, we climbed a hill and cut down a fir. Then we discovered we didn't have anything to make a stand for the tree, so we took a pickax and dug a hole over a foot deep in the frozen ground. Next, we set the tree in the hole, held it upright, and poured water into the hole. It took only about thirty minutes for the water to freeze, and our Christmas tree was firmly locked in the hole.

To decorate the tree, we took the cans from our beer rations and Cokes and cut them into stars and moons, or whatever, and then hung them on the tree with communications wire. One of our more artistic guys cut out the letters for "Merry Christmas" and "Happy New Year," and we tied them together and wrapped them around the tree. When we left the area, we hung Merry Christmas on the lead vehicle and Happy New Year on the second.

In the days following Christmas, we crossed the Han River and continued our retreat south, finally stopping and setting up our defense near Chungju. But this time we had retreated as far as we would go. Fortunately, the Eighth Army in Korea now had a new commander—Lieutenant General Matthew

Ridgway. He was a wonderful officer, who made a special effort to talk and listen to the men. In my opinion, he performed near miracles in lifting the morale of the GIs and getting the troops ready to take the offensive.

In a matter of weeks the First Cavalry was on the move again, but this time to the north. Admittedly, we were pretty sloppy in carrying out some of these offensive operations, in part because the troops were still in pretty bad shape from months of hard fighting. The night before we started our attack, one man just sat down and cried, asking over and over why were we not getting on the boats, and where were the boats?

One night in early January 1951, we had one of the saddest things that can happen in war happen to us—we shot and killed one of our own men. It was a particularly cold night, with a strong wind blowing. We always had to keep someone on the radio in case someone called for a fire mission. About midnight, the relief man approached our radio position and was shot by the man monitoring the radio. The soldier who fired the shots said he had hollered halt twice but didn't get an answer, and no action was taken against him. Whatever the facts, as could be expected, this event really shook us up. We always wondered if the relief man failed to hear the challenge because of the strong wind blowing that night, or if he just thought he would be recognized anyway. There was no way to know, of course; these things just happen. Our own artillery once mistakenly "fired for effect" on our troops while they were taking a hill. We also had a near tragedy when a soldier on guard duty shot up a poncho that had been hung up at night to dry. When these stories get around, they are pretty tough on morale.

During late January, as we continued our advance to the north, the action picked up. On February 12, the Chinese mounted a major attack on our positions, starting around 1:00 that night. At the time we had our four mortars set up but not dug into the ground, which was frozen. We had been moving so fast there was no time to dig deep enough for a good emplacement. So we just stuck the base plate into the ground as firmly as we could and fired away. Unfortunately, this left the mortars exposed and more vulnerable to enemy fire than if they had been properly set. Because of that, we had four GIs wounded that night when an incoming round hit between the third and fourth guns. I was the gunner on the second gun, and we escaped without injury, but we had to double up on the mortars to make up for those who had been wounded. That night, from the time the Chinese attacked until daybreak the next morning, we fired twelve hundred rounds. The firing was made more difficult by our lack of night-firing devices; we

Preparing to fire a 4.2-inch mortar. (Courtesy of Forty-fifth Infantry Division Museum)

actually lit cigarettes to see the bubbles on our mortars. All night long we kept two cigarettes burning on each gun, because we fired our guns the entire night. I might add that the sergeant who ran the ammunition vehicle was also on the road the entire night bringing us the necessary ammo. Fortunately, by daybreak our machine gunners opened up and brought the attack to an abrupt end.

That same night, a friend of mine who came over with me on the same boat and served as the platoon sergeant for one of our machine gun platoons, Ed Hagadorn, won the Silver Star for his action. Unable to direct fire successfully on an enemy machine gun nest, he knocked it out himself with hand grenades.

Following this action, we moved off the line and into reserve. This was when bitter fighting was taking place at Chipyong-ni, where the Twenty-third Infantry Regiment of the Second Infantry Division was surrounded by the Chinese and was unable to break out. The Fifth Regiment of the First Cavalry Division sent an armored task force to break the encirclement, and a few days later the rest of the division moved up to reestablish the line north of Chipyong-ni. Fortunately, the Twenty-third managed to hang on until the Chinese pulled back, but they suffered heavy casualties for their gallant defense.

During this time, we were driving down the road one day when we noticed a mountain peak in the distance. We kidded each other that our positions would probably be on top of that peak, and we would have to carry everything up to the top. Guess what? When we arrived at the base of the mountain our platoon leader said we would have to put two mortars on the top of the mountain to cover the necessary field of fire. He chose the second section for this honor, because they had screwed up on some assignment. Unfortunately, the first section had to carry up the bedrolls, chow, and ammo for the second section. We told the platoon leader to punish us next time; it was less work. When we moved out of this area, we saw more dead Chinese bodies than ever before. They were piled everywhere.

As the weather became warmer, we made use of a small creek in the area where we could wash our clothes and go swimming. Once, while we were swimming, some women came walking down the road, laughing and jabbering. When someone hollered "white women," we immediately scrambled around trying to get some clothes on as quickly as possible. It turned out to be an American USO show called "Camel Caravan," put on by Camel cigarettes. That evening they performed for us, and they were about thirty minutes into a really good show when the British, on our flank, began firing their artillery. Soon they were firing faster, and then still a little faster, until the firing was almost continuous. About this time someone jumped up on the stage and yelled, "Every man to their units; there has been a breakthrough on our flank." Unfortunately, we never did see the rest of the show.

Around Easter time, we went through Chunchon, a city in central Korea that commanded several important road junctions and had served as a major invasion route for both armies during the war. As a result, there was not a wall standing over three feet tall. It was the worst devastation I had ever seen in any one place; there was only one smokestack standing at the end of the city. In reserve at the time, we set up on a hill on the north side of Chunchon. The next morning, which was foggy and cloudy, "Bedcheck Charlie"[1] flew over our position at a low altitude with a loudspeaker squawking, "Surrender or Die." How we would have loved to shoot that sucker down.

That same day we got mail, and a friend at home had sent me a package that included a bar of Lux soap. It doesn't sound like much now, but when I opened the package and the smell of Lux soap filled the air there were guys twenty or thirty feet away that came over just to get a good smell. I still use Lux soap to this day.

That evening, a Korean man in a black suit, white shirt, black tie, and black top hat came by the mess tent and asked to work in the kitchen for food. With the help of an interpreter, we discovered he owned the factory with the smokestack still standing. He had no idea where the members of his family were. He was simply waiting for the war to end so he could get his factory going again. We gave him some food and he went on his way.

Not long after this we went back on line and moved to the west side of Korea, a little to the north of Seoul. By this time I had been promoted to sergeant first class and was serving as a forward observer (FO). We ended up on top of a large hill, which is where the FOs needed to be for observation and fire direction. But while the hill was good for observation, it was a pain for us in every other way. We had to walk to the bottom for everything, and it was a long hike. When we took the time to clean up, shave, eat, and all of that, we would be gone most of the day. Some of us, of course, always stayed on the hill.

At various times during the spring of 1951, different sections of our battalion were pulled out temporarily to put on firing demonstrations for other units. My part was to demonstrate the use of 81mm mortars. Once we even put on a demonstration for the marines, which became the subject of a lot of speculation and rumors. We were told the marines had been taking excessive casualties because they usually attacked straight into enemy fire, but I don't know if that was the reason. The idea of a bunch of marines standing around watching army guys show them how to fight a war with a "fire and maneuver" demonstration seemed a little strange to me, as well as a little humorous. They did it, but I'm not sure they enjoyed it very much.

In the early part of the summer, I flew to Osaka, Japan, for a few days of R&R (rest and recuperation). While waiting for our plane at Kimpo Airport, I met a Greek lieutenant and we visited for some time. I wondered why the Greeks would come all the way to Korea to fight, and he explained it. He told me about the war the Greeks had been fighting against the Communists in Greece, and how they saw Communism as a real threat. He also told me horror stories about atrocities the Communists had committed in Greece. There were about one thousand Greek soldiers fighting in Korea, all volunteers, and they hated the Communists with passion. Unless ordered to do so, they almost never took prisoners.

Once, just after we had arrived at the south bank of the Imjin River, we smelled an odor as we were eating our evening meal. We weren't quite sure what it was, and when we started looking around we found GIs from the Third Division, long dead, still in their foxholes. One had a hole straight through the center of his skull and all his flesh was gone to his waist, indicating he died with his shirt off. It was all very sad. Naturally we called Graves Registration, which removed the bodies.

We kept moving north, to the Kansas or Wyoming line (I forget which), and established a patrol base about two miles in front of our battalion area. The battalion was set up in a perimeter, with the mortars in the center. During the day, company-sized patrols were sent into no-man's-land, and at night they set up. It almost seemed like we were daring the Chinese to attack. Actually, we were trying to prevent the Chinese from getting close enough to our MLR to attack in force.

At this time, I was serving on the hill as a forward observer, with the mortars nearby. Once, a tank on patrol in no-man's-land was unable to cross a tank trap until a dozer came up and filled in the trap. To protect the dozer, we did our best to silence the enemy mortars, which eventually quit firing. Then, suddenly, an individual emerged from a house out in the middle of no-man's-land. After our tank tried but failed to shoot him, he ran into a cave along the edge of the river. They asked me to burn all the houses in the area, which we did with a mixture of HE and WP shells. I think we burned every house. We also spotted a huge enemy observation post (OP) down in the valley. After some difficulty, we finally dropped enough rounds on the OP to knock it out. In the process, however, we used more charges on the rounds than we were supposed to. As a result, we broke two base plates and weren't able to replace them until we got back to our MLR.

As the month of August approached, I began to think more and more about going home. After all, that was the month I was scheduled to rotate. We were on patrol base and getting ready to return to our MLR when I received the news. While we were loading our mortars and ammo on a jeep and trailer, our platoon leader came down the road to meet us. "Martin, you're going home," he shouted; "you are on the rotation list this morning." Why he came all this way to tell me I don't know, but it was a moment I will never forget. I immediately started double timing down the road. Then a surprise—a Chinese soldier emerged from the side of the road with his hands in the air. It made no difference. I was going home, so I just waved him on to my rear so the other guys could deal with him. At this point no Chinese prisoner was going to hold me up.

When I got back to the MLR, I immediately started gathering up my things, and within hours I was on my way. I rotated through Inchon Harbor and then on to Japan. Strangely, the further away from the front line I went the more I heard about problems and dangers, such as enemy infiltrators and planes in the area. Even after we boarded the ship in Inchon, someone remarked about how the mines had never really been cleared from the harbor.

When we reached Sasebo in Japan, we had a good meal with steak and ice cream, a shower, and fresh clothing. With all of this and no weapons to lug around, we felt like new men. After a few days at Sasebo, we loaded on a ship and set out for home.

After about two weeks on the ocean, we approached San Francisco Bay early on a foggy morning. "Look up there," someone said. We looked up and there it was, the Golden Gate Bridge just ahead of us. What a sight; this was an experience I would never forget. Someone on the bridge waved at us, and everyone on deck started waving back and yelling and laughing. It was truly a happy moment. And that's the way we returned to the good old USA.

Chapter 9

Escaping the Trap

The U.S. Army assigned a significant role to artillery in Korea, especially after the war stalemated and the period of trench warfare began. Since the UN forces had control of the air and roads, equipping and supplying ammunition for the big guns posed fewer problems than it did for the Communist forces. The expenditure of artillery shells in Korea was enormous; UN Command alone averaged 1 million shells a month. Private First Class Nelson, in the following story, was assigned to an 8-inch Persuader howitzer unit, the U.S. Army's heaviest artillery in Korea. Unfortunately, when the Chinese entered the war in the fall of 1950 his unit was cut off and badly mauled. Most of the men in Nelson's unit managed to make it through the Chinese roadblocks, but without most of their big guns.

Private First Class Herman G. Nelson

*Headquarters Company, Seventeenth Field
Artillery Battalion, Eighth Army*

WE LANDED AT Pusan on August 24, 1950, at Dock 5. It was about 4:00 in the morning and still dark. Most of us were out on the deck waiting for the ship to dock. On the docks, we saw our first Koreans; they were putting in place the gang planks we would use to disembark. They had a yellowish complexion, slanted eyes, and wore what we called knee pants.

From the ship's deck we could see part of the city of Pusan, and it looked very crowded. The main part of the city was built along the flat lands close to the docks, but a big part stretched up to the hills and mountains nearby. Most of the people wore white or light clothing, and all seemed to be hurrying off to work or to their daily tasks. A large percentage of these people, we learned, were refugees from Seoul or other parts of Korea who had fled from the North Koreans.

By midday the Seventeenth Field Artillery Battalion had all cleared the ship and were aboard big army trucks that took us through Pusan to an abandoned schoolyard. After we had made camp, we were all given K rations, which I think were left over from WWII. But I was so hungry I stuffed them down anyway.

On September 3, 1950, at 8:00 in the morning, we started for the front lines. We were assigned to the Eighth Army, which attached us to different frontline units as needed. At the time, the front was somewhere north of Taegu, a city about eighty-five miles northwest of Pusan. It took us about five hours in a truck convoy to reach our positions at the front, which were in the same area as the First Cavalry Division. You could hear the sounds of the guns firing long before we reached the front lines. When we got to our positions, we set up our guns and fire direction center and were ready to receive our fire missions. That same night, we fired a few rounds for the first time in the war. And when we fired our guns, everybody knew it for miles around. The Seventeenth Artillery Battalion had the big howitzers, called the Persuader. They had a range of around twenty miles and fired a shell eight inches in diameter and about thirty inches long. The concussion from these big guns was so powerful that on occasions they would blow down pup tents two hundred yards away.

In my case, however, I was not one of the guys who worked on the gun crew that actually fired the weapon. Instead, I was part of a six-man fire direction center (FDC) that coordinated the messages between the forward observer (FO) and the gun crews. My specific job was to operate the radio for the FDC.

At 8:00 the next morning, September 4, UN troops attacked the North Koreans with everything we had. It sounded like every weapon in the Eighth Army was firing at the same time, and the air force did its share of bombing and strafing. Finally, we had the North Koreans on the run. We moved toward Waegwan, just a little northwest of Taegu, where I saw dead enemy soldiers for the first time. Beside a knocked-out North Korean tank we saw three dead North Korean soldiers stretched out on the ground. And that was just the beginning. Further up the road we saw ten GIs on the ground covered with blankets. They had been killed by incoming mortar rounds just two hours before we got there.

We moved into position between Taegu and Waegwan. The next day,

September 5, we surveyed the terrain as we worked our way toward Waegwan to determine if it was suitable for bringing up our big guns. On the way an artillery round (or mortar) landed about fifty feet in front of us on the left shoulder of the road. Although you wanted to turn around and go back, you knew you couldn't, because it was our duty to stand together as soldiers and fight for freedom.

On September 15, 1950, we arrived at Taejon, a city with a prewar population of about one hundred thousand inhabitants, which had been nearly flattened by the war. The Twenty-fourth Division had occupied Taejon briefly back in July, before the North Koreans captured the city. During the five or six days we stayed there, I saw things I will never forget. In an old civilian jail in the heart of the city, we found thirty-two GIs buried underneath the floor. Two of the GIs were still alive, but nearly insane from the experiences they had endured. The North Koreans had made the GIs put on Korean clothing, hoping they would be mistaken for Koreans. Fortunately, an American soldier discovered thirty-two dog tags in the area, and their serial numbers matched exactly the numbers of the GIs in the jail. Later we went to an old prison camp and found two older women kneeling down, clawing the ground, and crying, probably on behalf of their sons and relatives inside the camp. When I saw this, a sense of horror and sickness overcame me as never before in my life. After all, I was only twenty years old and had been in combat only about twelve days.

At the time, we were attached to what was left of the Twenty-fourth Division, the division Major General Dean had commanded before his capture by the North Koreans. As the North Koreans retreated from Taejon, they committed some of the worst murders and atrocities to take place during the entire war. While occupying the city, they had not only imprisoned American GIs, but also most of the Korean men and young boys. Then, when leaving the city, they went by the prison camp and forced the South Korean men to dig two trenches about two hundred feet long. After the North Koreans had made the South Koreans line up in front of the trenches, they gunned them down with Russian burp guns and just left them where they fell. This is where we found the two women kneeling and crying. Some of the bodies had been there for days and were very bloated. And that's not the end of the story. After a GI thought he saw a body in an open well in the prison camp, an American officer ordered the well searched. A total of twenty-nine dead American soldiers were fished out of the well. There were also about three hundred dead GIs discovered in the hills around Taejon, with their hands tied behind their backs, ruthlessly murdered by the North Korean Communist soldiers. If this is what they call a "police action," I would sure hate to be in real war.

The next few days were quite strenuous for all of us—not just because of the war, but also because of the sorrow and concern we felt for the helpless GIs who were murdered in such an unjust and sickening manner. Just when we thought we had found and buried all the people ruthlessly murdered, we discovered more. With the help of a north wind, we noticed once again the strong odor of death. We proceeded to follow the smell to a little red brick church house just north of Taejon. As we approached the churchyard, we noticed a dead woman lying on the ground, and then another one, and still another. We also noticed a lot of empty ammunition shells on the ground from the same Russian burp guns. Then we discovered the church basement full of women slaughtered by the North Koreans. It was the same sickening sight we had witnessed a few days earlier. Apparently, when the women realized the North Koreans were preparing to pull out of Taejon, they went to the church to pray for their husbands and loved ones who were still in the prison camp. When the North Koreans slaughtered the men in the prison camp and the GIs in the hills, the women undoubtedly heard the shots, and the North Koreans decided they too must be murdered. I feel sure that those who committed these cowardly acts will be rightfully punished in eternity.

During the next several days we moved north and supported the recapture of Seoul. By this time we had carried out the Inchon invasion, and everywhere, UN troops were moving northward. My unit moved up to Kaesong, on the 38th Parallel, and stayed there for about four weeks. This turned out to be "resting time" for us. We stayed in an old mission, and since it had a gymnasium we managed to play some basketball. There were lots of Korean kids around, and after the cooks had fed us, they would line up these hungry kids and feed them leftovers. Each kid had his own small tin can that our cooks had given them, and they protected those cans as if they were made of gold.

By this time, I had been assigned to Captain Skelly, our company commander, as his jeep driver. One day Captain Skelly had me drive him along the foothills of the mountains overlooking Kaesong. While we were out driving, we tested our weapons and did a little sightseeing. Looking around, I happened to notice a beautiful pheasant about 150 feet in front of us. We stopped the jeep, and I picked the pheasant off with my carbine. By the time

I reached the bird, however, I heard Koreans talking and getting closer. I soon realized I had shot their pheasant, a "tame" pheasant, not a wild one. I ran back to the jeep with my bird in hand and told the captain we had to get out in a hurry, which we did.

That night I cooked the pheasant in my mess tin, while about six other GIs watched and drooled. When done, I took one of the best pieces for myself and let the other guys divide the rest. It was absolutely delicious.

At the end of October we finally got orders to move out of Kaesong. So we headed north, into North Korea, along with the rest of the American army. Autumn weather had already arrived, and the temperature had dropped to the low forties by the time we left Kaesong. We moved up toward Pyongyang, the capital of North Korea, where we stopped for one night. The next day we moved on to the north, and by this time the temperature had dropped to around zero. We were headed for the Yalu River, the border between Korea and China.

One evening, after we had settled down for the night, a Private Pope came by and asked me to accompany him to the cab of his truck. There he showed me a stack of letters, and he asked me to read them to him because he had never learned to read or write. I agreed and found myself reading letters from his wife back home, most of them quite personal. I soon learned he also wanted me to write his wife, which I did. So I found myself with an extra duty, although one I eventually began to enjoy. Even though I was single, by the time I returned to the United States, about nine months later, I had acquired a lot of experience writing letters to "the wife."

At last the UN forces were advancing north, and we were pretty optimistic the war would soon be over. General MacArthur had said we would all be home by Christmas. Little did we know that thousands of Chinese soldiers had already crossed the Yalu River. They had penetrated deep into North Korea and were hiding in the hills, well behind advancing American units, just waiting for orders to attack. Sadly, the war was just beginning.

On Thanksgiving Day, 1950, we moved to a new location near Kunu-ri, well north of the North Korean capital of Pyongyang. We ate our Thanksgiving dinner there with an armored tank company, and it was really good. We had a turkey dinner and all the stuff that goes with it.

At about 10:00 that same Thanksgiving night, all hell broke loose as the Chinese army attacked in force. We found ourselves firing our eight-inch howitzers into the evergreen trees at point-blank range. The low side of the mountains in front of our position was blazing like a forest fire. All night long everybody fired their weapons, big guns and little guns. The next morning our air force came in at daybreak, strafing and dropping napalm bombs on the enemy positions. Sometimes they dropped their stuff really close to the Second Division positions, the division we were attached to at the time.

At 10:00 the following morning, about ninety men in the Ninth Infantry Regiment came by and ate breakfast with us. They informed us that there was a small roadblock behind us and that they were going to knock it out so we and the rest of the Second Division could bring out all of our heavy equipment. We proceeded to move out, but just before we reached the roadblock that afternoon we learned that all ninety of those men had been killed or wounded. Prior to the Chinese attack, the Ninth Infantry Regiment had been on our left, the Thirty-eighth Infantry Regiment on our right, and a ROK unit held the center. Between fifteen and twenty thousand Chinese soldiers attacked the ROK unit and ran right through it. Then they set up positions in the rice paddies and mountains behind us. Our positions were so infiltrated by the Chinese that when we drew near the roadblock that day we passed a 105mm howitzer company that was firing in three different directions. We pulled up to the entrance of the roadblock about 5:00 P.M. and were stopped by a Chinese machine gun firing down on the road from the mountains, knocking out anything that tried to get through. Finally, someone rolled a half-track down the road with its four .50-caliber machine guns mounted on top. When that baby opened up on the Chinese machine gun, it looked like a dust storm had hit the side of the mountain. After the half-track ceased firing they motioned for a vehicle to move on through. When the vehicle reached the other side, however, more Chinese machine guns opened up, plus some mortars. Once again the half-track fired its quad-.50s and another vehicle moved onto the road, but the Chinese machine guns, seemingly invulnerable to the half-track, kept right on firing. Finally, they backed the half-track out and replaced it with a tank equipped with two twin 20mm gun turrets. The tank promptly silenced the Chinese machine guns, and our vehicles were finally able to move on down the road.

The road was clear, but for some reason the jeep in front of me remained in place. Major Ross, in the three-quarter-ton truck I was driving, told me to check out the situation. I walked up to the jeep driver, tapped him on the shoulder, and told him he needed to move on out. Then a shock. I discovered he was dead. He had his helmet buckled, his winter parka buttoned up, a clean shave, and his hands locked around the steering wheel. Strangely, I could find no trace of where he had been shot. I believe he may

Firing quad-.50s from the platform of a half-track. (Courtesy of Forty-fifth Infantry Division Museum)

have had a weak heart and, under the stress, died from a heart attack. So many times, when I reflect on my experiences in the war, I see that young soldier in the jeep with his hands locked on the steering wheel.

We went around the jeep and through the roadblock, but not without receiving plenty of incoming fire. I promised the Lord that night that if He would get me through that roadblock and home safely I would be his servant for life. About 4:00 A.M. we finally reached an established line where we were able to stop and rest for about three hours. During this rest, the Lord assured me I would make it home okay, and although I went through more campaigns, I never feared death again.

During our retreat to the south, we spent one night in an old schoolyard. Right in the center of the yard we noticed some freshly dug up earth. We carefully removed the loose dirt with our hands and discovered a round piece of metal about the size of a land mine. Very slowly, I lifted up on the metal with a knife, which we removed with surprising ease. Underneath we

Lieutenant Leslie Davis, Eleventh Engineer Combat Battalion, extending an arm to a Korean orphan boy. The GIs have just presented the boy with some warm clothes and a gift, Kumhwa, 1953. (Courtesy of Leslie Davis)

found a fifty-gallon barrel of rice buried. We just put the metal top back on the barrel and left everything the way we found it. While we were busy checking for a land mine, about a half dozen young kids had gathered nearby and were watching us with great interest. That evening I went over to see what the kids were doing. To my surprise, the oldest little girl, who must have been about eight, had seated all the other kids around a table. She had retrieved some of the rice and prepared a meal for all of the kids. It was a scene that nearly broke my heart, and I have never forgotten it. These kids were probably all orphans, the tragic losers in war, as kids always are. I have often wondered what happened to them.

After this, we retreated all the way back to Pusan to reequip our battalion. This was necessary because during the retreat we had lost a number of our guns and part of our other equipment. By this time General Ridgway had taken over command of the Eighth Army, and by the end of January 1951, UN troops were again marching north. We provided support for the recapture of Seoul, which fell to UN troops in March for the second time.

While we were camped in the Seoul area, I learned that we were scheduled to support a drive to the north that included the Seventh Division. This was good news for me, because my brother, Captain Teddy Nelson, commanded a company of 105mm howitzers in the Seventh Division. When our two units came together, I happened to be in a jeep on a mission to our command mission center. I was parked on the road waiting for the convoy so I could help guide it to their camping area when I noticed an artillery unit from the Seventh Division. I got out of my jeep and walked up to the soldier who was directing the unit to its campsite. Guess what? About ten feet from this soldier I saw my brother, Teddy. So I decided to play a little game with him. I went up and asked him for a cigarette. Without looking at me he took out a pack and told me to take one. Then I said, "Soldier, do you have a light?" Only then did he turn around to see who was bugging him. It was a happy occasion, and we saw each other on and off for about a week. After this, our units went their separate ways, and we didn't get together again until after the war.

About this same time we were dispatched to help the Twenty-third Infantry Regiment of the Second Division, which had been cut off at a place east of Seoul called Chipyong-ni. After helping to relieve the Twenty-third, we remained in the area for about a week. During this time, I ran into an old school buddy of mine from Southward, Oklahoma, Bobby Joe Kopf, who was in the Forty-fifth Division. One day he came over to my unit, and while we were sitting around talking we happened to notice a large number of empty cartridges down the side of the mountain, obviously left over from previous fighting. We walked further down the mountain and came across about seven dead Chinese soldiers, their bodies arranged in a circle around a barrel. It looked like one of our units had dropped a mortar round right in the middle of the barrel. Most of them were still clutching pencil and paper, as if they were writing letters. It was one of the strangest things I ever witnessed in Korea, and I still remember it vividly.

After the lines stabilized, we moved back into Seoul. In June, I went on two weeks of R&R to Tokyo. We went through Sasebo in southern Japan, and from there were bused to the Meiji Hotel in downtown Tokyo. While riding through Tokyo on the bus our eyes fell on the many young Japanese girls wearing split dresses. They really looked nice, and the guys on the bus did not pass by these young beauties without comment. The first morning after arriving I ate breakfast at the hotel, and it tasted so good I ate twice. We had everything in that hotel—a movie theater, a restaurant, a bowling alley, and dance clubs. The room only cost seventy-five cents a day. While staying there, I met some very nice Japanese families and young girls. It was almost like coming home. The hard thing was going back to Korea after all the fun and easy living.

I went back, but only for about a month. Toward the end of July 1951, I rotated back to the States, having served one year in Korea. I had seen Korea all the way from Pusan in the south to near the Yalu River in the north. I have both good and bad memories of my experiences in Korea, but I sure wouldn't want to go through all of that again.

Privates First Class Herman Nelson (right) and Bobby Joe Kopf (left), Seventeenth Field Artillery Battalion, on a guard post near Chipyong-ni, early 1951. (Courtesy of Herman Nelson)

Chapter 10

A North Korean Officer's Story

When North Korea attacked South Korea on June 25, 1950, more than eighty thousand soldiers of the North Korean People's Army (NKPA) crossed the 38th Parallel and engaged the ROK Army and the United Nations forces (UNF). Since North Korea is still one of the few closed Communist states in the world today, the North Korean soldiers' experience in the Korean War has been largely inaccessible to the West. Colonel Lee, a Korean who lived in China, fought in a Korean unit but as a part of the Chinese Communist Army. He fought first against the Japanese, then in the Chinese Civil War, and finally in the Korean War when his unit was placed under the command of the NKPA. Colonel Lee offers interesting insights about life in the NKPA during the early part of the war.

Colonel Lee Jong Kan

Thirty-third Regiment, Twenty-sixth Division, North Korean People's Army

IN 1928, I was born into a Korean farmer's family in Hailin County, Heilongjiang Province, Northeast China. Let me tell you a little bit about the Korean immigrants to China. There are about 2 million Korean people living in China today as one of the fifty-six Chinese minorities. Most of the Korean Chinese live in Northeast China, including Heilongjiang, Liaoning, and Jilin Provinces. Most of them work on their farms in the countryside. We are Chinese citizens, but we speak Korean, celebrate our holidays, and keep our traditions, just like the Mexican immigrants living in America.

As the first generation of an immigrant family, my parents left North Korea and moved into Northeast China during Japan's occupation of Korea

(1895–1945). China and Korea share a land border longer than seven hundred miles. After the Chinese-Japanese War started in 1937, more Korean people crossed the Chinese-Korean borders, including many Korean Communist Party members and their guerrilla forces. They continued their resistance movement in China against Japan and received strong support from the Chinese Nationalist (Kuomintang, KMT) Government, the Chinese Communist Party (CCP), and the Chinese people.

My parents sent me to a Korean-Chinese elementary school and then to middle school during World War II. After my graduation from the middle school in Hailin in 1944, I couldn't find a job in the town. I had to move back to my parents' farm and help them with their farming for eight months. In the spring of 1945, a Chinese Communist Army recruiting team visited our village. They promised city employment for each Korean soldier at his retirement from the service. "We are finishing the Anti-Japanese War very soon," I remember one of the CCP representatives said in Korean at our village meeting. "We are going to take over many cities from the Japanese. We need you to win the war and run our cities!"

It seemed a good opportunity for me. To live in a city and use the knowledge I learned in my school was all I wanted. As a middle school graduate, I was considered a "degree-holder," or as they say in Chinese, "*xiao zhishi fenzi*," a "junior intellectual." This was an important improvement in social status, which meant a lot to me and to my family. I am the first middle school graduate in my family. Listen to this, less than 20 percent of the Chinese people had a middle school diploma at that time. The war could help me move out of the countryside and land a job in the city. I was so excited after the meeting, I was ready to sign up.

But my parents said no. They had five boys. Three of them had already joined the CCP armed forces, later called the People's Liberation Army (PLA). My parents still hadn't heard from them since they left home. My parents were so happy to see me coming back home to their farm. "You are only seventeen," my mother yelled at me with tears in her eyes. "Don't leave. You don't even know how to take care of yourself."

Two days later, however, everything changed. The recruiting officers told us that Japan was preparing a final battle against an imminent Soviet invasion of Northeast China in the summer of 1945. Our hometown would soon become a major battleground and could suffer very heavy civilian casualties.

Moreover, the Japanese Imperial Army had a zero-tolerance policy against any family whose members served in any anti-Japanese force. Our entire family would be executed if they found out my older brothers served in the Communist forces. It was not safe for us to stay at home. My parents couldn't leave, but I could. The Chinese Communist Army seemed a safer place for me to survive the war.

My parents finally let me go when they learned that a large number of adult males in this Korean village had signed up, including my uncles and cousins. They felt even better when I told them that the Chinese Communist Army would keep us together in the same unit by organizing Korean companies, Korean battalions, and Korean regiments.

After two weeks of training in a Communist infantry training camp in Heilongjiang, I was assigned to the Forty-sixth Korean Regiment of the Sixteenth Division. My middle school education in my record surely caught the eyes of the regimental officers, who appointed me an assistant political instructor in the Seventh Company. Having adopted the Soviet Red Army system, the CCP established a political instructional system in its army. We had a political instructor and an assistant instructor for each company, a political commissar and a deputy commissar for each battalion, and a commissar and a political department in each regiment, division, and army. This chain of political control parallels the chain of command.

As an assistant political instructor, my job was to receive political instructions, educational booklets, and propaganda materials from our battalion political commissar's office. Then I visited the four platoons in our company, plus each of the eight squads, and read these political propaganda materials to our soldiers. Most of our 120 soldiers couldn't read. I had to talk to some soldiers individually if they did not quite understand the concept or terms like "communism," "capitalism," "class struggle," or "international imperialists."

I did not quite understand the ideas in Marxism, Leninism, and Mao Zedong's thoughts myself. Sometimes I was confused. To keep the job, I had to keep reading in order to be able to explain them to the soldiers who had a lot of questions. They seemed more interested in learning how to read and write the Chinese characters than in understanding Communist principles. As poor peasants' sons, most of them never had a chance to go to school. The Communist army became a huge primary educational institute for the Chinese masses. The word "*gongchan zhuyi*" (communism) was the first Chinese character they learned to read and write. If I had a teaching problem, I always talked to the company political instructor. If I found a morale problem among the soldiers, I needed to report to the captain of our company.

We aimed to promote revolutionary spirits and high morale in our company through political propaganda, mental and psychological education, and individual consultation. We believed that we could defeat any enemy with superior weapons and technology and win any war by virtue of not only our superior numbers, but also our soldiers' superior fighting spirit.

The army recruiting officers who visited my village were right about WWII. The Pacific war suddenly ended on August 15, 1945. As a CCP member and a WWII vet, I thought I could retire from the army and get a city job.

I was wrong. The Chinese Civil War between the CCP and KMT broke out in 1946. Instead of demobilizing, the army fought another nationwide war, which continued until 1949. Our Korean regiment was enlarged into the 118th Korean Division, Fortieth Army, Fourth Field Army of the PLA. Our army fought the KMT troops all the way, about three thousand miles, from North China to the southern end of China, Hainan Island.

On October 1, 1949, Mao Zedong, CCP Chairman, announced the founding of the People's Republic of China (PRC) in Beijing, following the PLA forces' conquest of the mainland and the KMT's withdrawal to Taiwan Island. Finally, the Chinese Civil War was over. By the end of the year, I was promoted to battalion political commissar. I was looking forward to a more comfortable retirement and a better job in Guangzhou, the largest industrial and commercial city in South China, just like Los Angeles in America.

I was wrong again. When we were preparing a massive PLA demobilization in February 1950, we heard some rumors about the conflicts between North Korea and South Korea. In the North, the Korean Workers' Party, or the Korean Communist Party, had established a Communist state, the Democratic People's Republic of Korea (DPRK). In the South, the Korean Nationalists founded the Republic of Korea. Kim Il Sung, North Korea's Communist leader, wanted his fellow Communist Korean-Chinese soldiers back home to complete the Korean revolution. Kim intended to defeat South Korea's Nationalist army and extend his Communist regime over the entire Korean peninsula. It seems that the Chinese Communists' victory over the Chinese Nationalists encouraged Kim to unify his country under the Communist government by force.

In April, our Korean division received an order to leave Guangzhou and move all the way from the south to Northeast China. After a long railway trip, about twenty-five hundred miles, we were back home in Heilongjiang Province and prepared for a "return" to North Korea. I didn't know why they called it "return," since I had never been in Korea. Neither had most of the Korean soldiers in my battalion.

My parents were so glad to see me when I visited them in May 1950. They were even happier to know I was going to Korea to fight my third war. Well, they believed the Korean War was not supposed to be a bloody one among the Korean people themselves. My new journey seemed to ease their homesickness. It had been more than twenty-four years since they left Korea. They missed their hometown and my grandparents so much. They even hoped I would find a Korean girl there and bring her home to get married. (To tell you the truth, they didn't want to have a Chinese daughter-in-law in the family.)

In June 1950, the Korean War broke out. The battlefield situation seemed in favor of the North Koreans until mid-July, when their southward offensives stopped and they faced a strong defense by the ROK Army and the American troops at Pusan.

On August 25, 1950, our division entered North Korea. There were two Korean divisions in the Chinese army, about fourteen thousand soldiers of Korean origin, both of which were transferred into the North Korean People's Army (NKPA). We kept our weapons and equipment, and the same formation, unit, and commanding officers when we were incorporated into the Thirty-third Regiment of the NKPA's Twenty-sixth Division. Like the Soviet military system and the PLA, the NKPA had a dual system with a chain of command and a chain of political control.

The NKPA, however, was a more Russianized army than the PLA. First of all, they had a Soviet officer ranking system that the Chinese did not have until 1955. Although I still served as a battalion political commissar, I was now ranked as a Korean army colonel. Second, their weapons and equipment were better than ours. Before the Red Army withdrew from North Korea, the Soviets re-armed the NKPA with Russian-made tanks, heavy artillery pieces, and automatic rifles, which we did not have. Our Korean comrades were so happy to see us entering the Korean War and hoped we could win the final offensive battle at Pusan.

In late August, our battalion participated in the NKPA's fourth offensive campaign. We broke the enemy defensive line and pushed ROK and UN troops into a small area east of the Naktong River in South Korea. By the end of the month, the NKPA had liberated 90 percent of the country and had control of 92 percent of the population.

On August 31, Kim launched his last offensive campaign against the enemy stronghold at Pusan. At that point, even though our troops' morale was high, the NKPA had suffered fifty-eight thousand casualties in its four southward offensive campaigns. It had also lost 120 of the 150 Russian-made tanks and one-third of its artillery pieces in the past two months. Most important, our transportation line had been extended more than two hundred miles. Our supply became more and more difficult. Our defense at the rear, if any, became weaker and weaker, which did not seem to worry Kim at all. The faster we could win the last battle, the less opportunity the enemy had for a counterattack. However, we couldn't break the enemy defense at the Pusan perimeter during our offensive campaign.

After our failure at the Pusan perimeter, the NKPA could not launch another major offensive campaign. On September 10, we went on the defensive when the ROK and UNF launched their first major counteroffensive. Our situation became especially serious after MacArthur landed twenty thousand U.S. troops at Inchon on September 15. We pulled out from the south and rushed back to the middle of the peninsula to defend Seoul, the capital city of the ROK, which had been occupied by the NKPA since June 28.

The defense of Seoul on September 21–28 was our last major battle. I told my battalion that the NKPA had concentrated more than twenty thousand troops at Seoul, and that Comrade Kim was in the city with us. We had to stop the enemy offensive right here. Our battalion took up defensive positions in a tractor factory on the south side of the city. Our job was to stop any retreat from our front line and then reorganize a second defense.

I also remember that our Thirty-third Regiment Commissar recommended to other battalions my approach to a civilian mobilization. I held a meeting with about two hundred workers remaining in the factory and asked them: "Who are the Communist Party members?" "We are," they shouted, and about three dozen workers stood up. I asked them to join our defense. We showed the workers how to shoot and armed them with our extra rifles.

The NKPA mobilized the entire population in the city, even arming and training the women and children. NKPA-occupied Seoul was ready for its final battle.

On September 21, MacArthur launched an all-out attack against Seoul. Our position was bombed and shelled heavily by superior UN air and artillery firepower. Instead of fighting, many factory workers dropped their weapons and left. I didn't stop them. Later that day, some NKPA soldiers began to withdraw from our first defense line, passing us and moving northward. I didn't stop them either. Most of them were wounded. Next evening, UN troops broke our first defense line.

About 4:00 A.M. on September 23, the enemy began to shell our position again. It was so heavy, I realized that the enemy troops were going to attack our second defense line soon. At 4:30, the enemy charged our position with about three hundred infantry troops led by ten light tanks. Our battalion commander ordered anti-tank teams to go out there one after another. But they couldn't stop the tanks. Some of the tanks ran over our trenches. We had to stop shooting and hide ourselves from tank firing power. We waited until the enemy troops came close and then opened fire. Some of my soldiers had a hand-to-hand fight. A few factory workers who stayed with us lit up several gasoline barrels and rolled these fireballs toward the tanks, finally stopping the tanks.

After we defeated the enemy's second attack around 9:00 A.M., our commander called the Thirty-third Regiment Headquarters for reinforcement and supplies. We had lost half of our men. Many wounded needed medical care. We had almost run out of ammunition. But the Thirty-third Headquarters did not send anything. They had the same situation, having asked the Twenty-sixth Division Headquarters for reinforcement and supplies. They never came.

We managed to hold our position until 4:00 P.M., when we were ordered to withdraw after dark and "carry on our defense in the city." We left the factory about 9:00 in the evening, leaving many comrades' bodies behind.

Our fight in the streets of Seoul, which continued for three more days, was no longer an organized, effective defense. Kim and the NKPA Command had fled to the North, and our divisional and regimental communications had collapsed. We were pretty much on our own. Our men just tried to find a way to get out of there. The UN troops were well trained for a house-to-house battle. And the ROK troops were familiar with their capital city and its population. I was so surprised to see the same residents who warmly welcomed us a week before now welcome the ROK troops back into the city with cooked food and the ROK national flags.

During the night of September 27, the battalion commander, two of his staff, six soldiers, and I broke through the enemy lines and headed north, through the woods. We had no radio, no ammunition, and no food.

Fortunately, we ran into the NKPA Twenty-seventh Regiment around the Kaesong area two days later. By that time, we also heard Kim's new policy, issued on September 27 to all the North Korean troops, party members, and people. Our new task was to slow down the enemy offensive, save

North Korean soldiers defend their position, October 1950. (Courtesy of the Center for Archives and Information, Heilongjiang Provincial Academy of Social Sciences)

the main part of the NKPA, organize a strategic withdrawal, and build up a new reserve for a future counteroffensive.

The NKPA defense was put to rout all along the line by the end of September. We retreated north all the way to Pyongyang, the capital city of North Korea. After a one-week defense, the UNF took over Pyongyang on October 19. There was not much room left in North Korea for our further withdrawal.

Some of our soldiers thought we might pull out and go back to China. Kim, however, wouldn't let us go. After Pyongyang fell, we were ordered to break up the battalion into several guerrilla groups. According to the new order, we would fight on our own behind the lines by harassing the enemy troops, attacking their communication and transportation, and recruiting for the NKPA.

As a group leader, I led fifty men to the eastern coast and established a small base in a mountain. We hit and ran at night and rested in the daytime. Without any supplies and local connections, we had to hunt small animals to feed ourselves and capture enemy ammunition and medical supplies for our needs. That winter (1950–1951) in Korea was extremely cold. We didn't even have winter clothes, blankets, or tents. Some of our comrades survived the battles but did not make it through the long, cold winter.

Finally, we were able to move off of the mountain in April 1951, when the Chinese armies launched their fourth offensive campaign against the UN forces along the eastern coast. We were reorganized back into NKPA regulars in May 1951.

But I could no longer keep up with my unit in the night because of my poor sight. I got night blindness due to the lack of nutrition and medicine during our mountainous guerrilla warfare. I was sent back to China for treatment in the summer of 1951.

After a few weeks in a PLA hospital, I was retired from the NKPA first, and then from the PLA as a disabled war veteran. An officer asked me in his office where I wanted to retire to, China or North Korea? "Here, China, of course," I told him without even thinking about it. China is my homeland, and the war was still going on in Korea. I was so tired after six years' service through three major wars in East Asia: the Pacific war, the Chinese Civil War, and the Korean War.

Eventually, I got a city job as the principal of the Twenty-fourth High School in Harbin, the provincial capital city in Heilongjiang Province. I moved my parents into the city with me. Two years later, at the age of twenty-five, I married a high school math teacher. Like me, she is Korean-Chinese.

Chapter 11

China's Crouching Dragon

The first encounter between Chinese soldiers and an American regiment in the Ko-rean War was accidental. In fact, the Chinese armies made every effort to avoid U.S. troops during their early intervention. On the night of November 1, 1950, the Chi-nese Thirty-ninth Army attacked Unsan, believing the town was held by the ROK First Division. Only after sighting much taller and heavier soldiers did the Chinese realize that it had engaged the Americans (the Eighth Regiment of the First Cavalry Division, which was taking over the defense of Unsan from the ROK Fifteenth Regiment). As a captain, Zhou Baoshan led his Fourth Company and engaged the Eighth Cavalry Regiment near Unsan. Badly wounded in action, Captain Zhou suffered permanent injury and was forced to transfer to an engineering unit, where he lacked the necessary education for advancement in rank. Because of his failure to win promotion, during the Chinese Cultural Revolution some of his coworkers labeled him a "deserter of the Korean War."

Captain Zhou Baoshan

Fourth Company, Second Battalion, 347th Regiment, 116th Division, Thirty-ninth Army, Chinese People's Volunteer Force

IN 1922, I was born into a peasant family in Leting County, Hebei Province. During the Chinese Civil War (1946–1949), I joined the Chinese Liberation Army (PLA), and the Chinese Communist Party (CCP) in 1948. At twenty-eight I became a captain in the 347th Regiment of the PLA Thirty-ninth Army. In late July 1950, our army moved one thousand miles from Henan Province in Central China to Liaoning Province in Northeast China.

We were told that American troops had invaded Korea. Some soldiers asked me during our long, northward railroad journey if we were going to Korea to fight Americans. I had the same question myself and didn't have a clue at the time. As a civil war veteran, I just followed my orders. Many soldiers in my company had the same attitude; they would fight as ordered, and it did not matter where or when the fight took place.

When our train approached Hebei, a soldier made a joke to me by saying: "Hey, Captain Zhou, we are getting close to your hometown. Don't you want to get off the train to see your wife?" "Don't worry," I told him. "I won't leave my company. I will be very happy just to see my village from the train."

It was the middle of the night when our train passed through Hebei, and so dark outside that I couldn't see anything. I couldn't sleep for thinking of my wife and our two young daughters. I didn't know at the time that it would be more than four years before I could see them again.

We arrived in Liaoyang, Liaoning Province, in early August, and received an order to prepare for a possible war with America. Thereafter, some of our soldiers (about 20 percent) became worried.

Some of them were the "liberated soldiers." They had served in the Kuomintang army and fought against the Communist army during the civil war. In the final battles of that war, these KMT soldiers either surrendered or were captured by the Communist forces. The PLA wasted little time in incorporating these soldiers into their own forces. During the Communist offensive campaign against Beijing (Peking) in late 1948, the PLA took in about 200,000 of these Nationalist troops. Between February and April 1949, more than 150,000 Nationalist troops were incorporated into the PLA units in Beijing. These "liberated soldiers" knew very little about the PLA or Communism. The others were usually young "volunteers" from the newly liberated regions. They were reluctant to leave their peacetime life behind and wondered why they had to fight over a foreign country.

To deal with these unsettled minds, our army's political department launched a timely campaign of ideological education in early September, emphasizing patriotism, internationalism, and revolutionary heroism. During the political education campaign, first of all, I told the men some historical facts about American invasions of China in the past and its recent occupation of Taiwan. We were the victims of American imperialism. I argued that if we didn't stop Americans in Korea now, we would have to fight them later in China. To assist Korea was the same as defending our homeland. Then I tried to explore the nature of the American imperialist "paper tiger" and its strategic weaknesses. Even though the U.S. military had modern weapons, the American troops were fighting an unjust war and suffering from low morale. They were short of manpower, and their support had to come from a great distance. Our army was dedicated to a just cause. We had the brilliant leadership of the CCP and Chairman Mao, and the full support of our people, the Korean people, and peace-loving peoples all over the world. Our weapons were not as advanced as those of the Americans, but we enjoyed a numerical advantage.

In September, the new commander of the Thirty-ninth Army's 116th Division, General Wang Yang, organized an intensive training program with two phases. (Our old commander, General Wu Guozhang, was then serving as a Chinese military advisor in the Vietnamese Communist forces, who were fighting the French forces in the First Indochina War.) Completed by mid-September, General Wang's first phase focused on the exercises of small-group combat tactics, including rifle, anti-tank, demolitions, and anti-aircraft training. His second phase was new to us, stressing large-group cooperation tactics. I remember our battalion participated in one of his group attack exercises on a very small hill with two other battalions. We felt very crowded when hundreds of soldiers charged the same point at once. Wang also brought in WWII veterans who had once fought alongside the American troops in Burma (now called Myanmar). They gave us talks about American soldiers, their training, and their characteristics.

On October 15, our army became part of the Chinese People's Volunteers Force (CPVF). This reorganization resulted from the order issued by the CCP Central Military Commission and Chairman Mao on October 8. In fact, the CPVF troops were exactly the same PLA troops. We were the Chinese troops assigned to the Korean War. We still wore the same PLA uniforms, but no Chinese badges, no Red Star cap insignia, no PLA rankings, and no Chinese names.

After the reorganization into the CPVF, a rocket artillery battalion and an anti-tank battalion were added to our Thirty-ninth Army. Our 116th Division established a headquarters security battalion, an anti-aircraft artillery battalion, and a medical battalion. Our 347th Regiment also organized its own medical company.

After two months of preparations, our regiment crossed the Yalu River, the boundary river separating Northeast China and North Korea, during the evening of October 21. We crossed the Yalu at Andong. Under its light-control and curfew, the city was both quiet and dark when our trucks rolled through its streets. I saw the local troops guarding each intersection and patrol vehicles everywhere. I could feel the war.

While still on the Chinese side of the Yalu Bridge, our troops got off the trucks and marched across the bridge. A great many artillery vehicles, trucks, horses, and soldiers crossed the bridge that night. To keep China's intervention undetected, we could only cross the bridge at night. Though the traffic was unbelievably heavy, nobody yelled, complained, or even talked. All the faces looked so serious because they knew they were entering the Korean War.

When we marched to the middle point of the bridge, we saw a sign both in Chinese and Korean, "China–North Korea," which divided the two countries. One of the soldiers asked me in a very low voice, "Captain, what time is it?" "Eight-thirty," I told him, as I continued to count my steps on the bridge. "Fifteen hundred steps," I told myself when I put my foot on the soil of North Korea.

The first Koreans I saw were the security troops of the NKPA, stationed on the Korean side of the Yalu Bridge. They lined up and cheered in their broken Chinese: "Welcome the Chinese People's Volunteer Forces coming to Korea to fight!" I was impressed by their Soviet-made automatic rifles and brand-new heavy machine guns. We had a mix of single-shot Japanese rifles from WWII and old American rifles captured from the Kuomintang army in the Chinese Civil War.

Our regiment kept marching twenty-five miles southeast into Korea through the first night and stopped at dawn. For several days, we moved full speed in the same pattern, marching at night and resting during the day.

I was surprised when I saw my soldiers became so excited after we entered Korea. It was the first time for all of us to enter a foreign country. Everything seemed different, but interesting. We talked to the Korean people when possible, and we tried to read the Korean signs, even though we didn't understand them at all.

We marched southeast toward the Kusong area. On October 25, our regiment passed Kusong. Then we moved into the Kumchon area before the dawn of the 26th. The same day, we were told that the Fortieth Army had engaged the ROK Sixth Division. It was the first battle for the CPVF after it entered the Korean War.

We kept moving fast in the same direction toward Unsan. Having reached the area north of Unsan on the 28th, we were ordered to get ready to engage the frontline ROK units.

The battalion commander told us that the ROK First Division was garrisoned at Unsan, about twenty miles from our positions. The Thirty-ninth Army planned to encircle Unsan and establish roadblocks in case the ROK First Division tried to withdraw. The army would employ its 115th Division to attack Unsan from the southwest, its 116th Division from the north, and its 117th Division from the east. We were told not to engage the American or British units during this offensive campaign. We should avoid the superior firepower, attack only weak enemy units and gain some successful experience in our first battle.

During the night of October 30, we moved into our position near Hill 626.6, where my company was supposed to launch an attack at 1930 hours the next evening. Next morning I could see the ROK soldiers moving in and out of their bunkers, and I could hear them yelling to each other on the hill.

Through the whole day of the 31st, sitting in the trench with cover at the bottom of the hill, I had a mixed feeling of excitement and nervousness. As a war veteran, I was excited to have a chance to fight again. As a captain, however, it was my first time to command a company and fight enemy soldiers who didn't speak Chinese. I practiced a few Korean words we had just learned, such as "*jung ji*" (don't move) and "*hanbok animyun juknunda!*" (Surrender or die!). I may need to use these words when we launch our attack on the ROK troops that evening, I thought.

That afternoon, one of our outpost watchers reported to me, "Captain, the enemy is moving out!" I looked out and saw a couple dozen ROK soldiers packing their stuff, walking out of their bunkers, and disappearing toward the other side of the hill. Without knowing that they were going to be replaced by the Americans, I reported the ROK troops' withdrawal immediately to the Second Battalion Headquarters and suggested that we launch an attack as soon as possible. Dong Wencai, our battalion commander, called me back and rescheduled the attack for 5:00 P.M.

At 4:50 P.M., our supporting artillery began shelling, and Hill 626.6 was soon covered with heavy smoke. At 5:00, four CPVF companies, about five hundred Chinese soldiers, charged the hill together. We met only light resistance. Commander Dong ordered us to continue our charge on the next enemy position at Hill 96.9. We captured three hills in less than two hours and moved close to Unsan. The ROK soldiers seemed to have just disappeared, and we only had a few casualties. I didn't expect that the first offensive battle would be such an easy job.

We learned later that after the ROK troops pulled out from their frontline positions, the American troops who replaced them had neither enough

The 347th Regiment, 116th Division, CPVF Thirty-ninth Army, charges a UNF position at Unsan, November 1950. (Courtesy of the Center for Archives and Information, Heilongjiang Provincial Academy of Social Sciences)

men nor enough time to fill in all the ROK defensive positions. The U.S. Eighth Cavalry Regiment, which had replaced the ROK First Division, deployed its troops only at key positions outside Unsan.

We did not know the situation that night. When we reached a hill north of Ryongpo-dong, a small village outside Unsan, we met a very strong defense. Commander Dong employed the Fifth and Sixth Companies to charge the hill several times. They failed and suffered very heavy casualties, losing most of their men and both captains.

"The Fourth is up next," Dong shouted to me on the phone. "They are not Koreans. They are Americans!" He hung up before I could ask a question. I somehow became excited. After running around all evening without a serious fight, we were now facing a real challenge—the American troops.

It became completely dark when we moved out and forward to the bottom of the hill. But the hill soon lit up because of the heavy enemy bombing and shelling. American firepower was so strong that it could hit every part of the hill.

At that point, I realized that there was no way for us to take the hill before the enemy artillery and machine guns wiped out my entire company. I wanted to persuade Dong to halt the next charge until our supporting artillery units and regimental reinforcements could take part in the attack.

Slightly wounded and desperate, Dong began organizing the next assault formation. Without even looking at me, he shouted: "Ten minutes! Get ready!" I understood his decision and the situation he faced. The night was on our side, and the enemy dominated the daytime. If we could not take over Unsan and destroy the garrison troops tonight, the enemy would reinforce their troops and secure Unsan tomorrow with their superior air power. Our Thirty-ninth Army's entire offensive campaign would fail.

I followed Dong's order without saying anything. I asked my soldiers to get rid of all their blankets, food, and water bottles in order to run faster. Our only chance was that some of us might be able to run fast enough and reach the top of the hill before the enemy fire got all of my company. I tried to talk to as many soldiers as I could. This could be the last time I would see them.

We were lucky. The regimental commander, Li Gang, arrived with the First Battalion as reinforcement just before we launched the next charge. Li reorganized our assault formation. He added two more companies (from the First Battalion) to our two remaining companies as the frontal attacking force. He ordered a mortar company to move forward to the bottom of the hill in order to increase the covering fire. Li also ordered the deputy com-

mander of the First Battalion to take one of his companies around the hill
and flank the enemy defensive position.

It took about one hour for Li to prepare the next assault. We were now
in a much better position. At midnight, Li gave the order for the attack.
"Good luck! See you in Unsan," Commander Dong said to me. "In Unsan!"
I saluted him. I didn't know at the moment that it would be the last time we
would see each other.

Running, I led my company up to the hill. This was a race between our
soldiers and enemy bullets. I saw some of them get shot and fall. But I kept
yelling loudly and pressing them hard. "Charge!" "Faster!" "To the top!" The
faster they could run, the better chance they had of surviving. I kicked several men who had slowed down. I pushed those who were looking for cover
from the enemy machine guns. The hill was pretty flat and totally stripped
by the constant firing and shelling from both sides. There was no tree or rock
left to hide behind.

Suddenly I felt like somebody had kicked me on my leg and I almost fell
down. Somehow I managed to balance myself and continue running, but at
a slower pace, and many soldiers passed me.

After a short man-to-man fight at the top of the hill, the enemy troops
gave up and withdrew to Unsan. "We made it!" I cheered with the other
soldiers, but I could not help but sit down on the ground.

"Captain Zhou, you have been shot," one of my soldiers said to me. I
reached for my knees and felt warm blood all over my left leg. A terrible pain
in my left leg suddenly hit me, so strong that it almost knocked me out. A
couple of my soldiers helped me lay down on the ground and tried to stop
my bleeding. I stayed on the hill all night waiting for medical units. I never
made it to Unsan. Nor did my soldiers. My company stayed on the hill
because we had so many casualties. In fact, Commander Li ordered the Second Battalion to rest in the Ryongpo-dong area and wait for reinforcements
since the battalion had lost more than half of its men during the first night of
battle. Commander Dong did not make it to Unsan either. He suffered
multiple wounds and died a couple of days later in a field hospital.

I was sent to a CPVF field hospital in a mountain near Sinanju. Three
months later, I had recovered, but I could not return to my company. Even
now my left leg is not normal. In late January 1951, I was reassigned to the
Fourth Bridge Regiment of the CPVF First Railroad Engineering Division.
I was assigned as a captain for the Sixth Company, Fourth Railroad Bridge
Battalion, Fourth Bridge Regiment.

I never had a chance to visit the 347th Regiment, which was actively engaged on the front while I repaired the railroad bridges in the rear areas. I missed my comrades. With their help and support, I had survived two wars in the past three years. I missed combat. Only combat action could ease the pain of not seeing my wife and daughters. I heard that the 347th had a new regimental commander and that most of my soldiers in the Fourth Company were gone. Three months in the Korean War seemed a long time for all of us.

At that time, I did not know our engineering troops would have to stay in North Korea longer than the Chinese combat troops. After the cease-fire agreement in July 1953, most of the CPVF armies returned to China, but not us. We continued to work on the South River Bridge outside Pyongyang for the rest of 1953, and repaired the Sinsongchon Bridge and then the Chongchon River Bridge in 1954. Finally, our railroad engineering division was ordered to return to China in the fall of 1954. After we left, there were still two Chinese engineering divisions in North Korea working on airport constructions.

After returning to China in 1954, our division participated in the Tibetan Railroad construction in Northwest China, and the Ying-Xia Railroad construction at Xiamen, Fujian Province, South China, as part of the PLA Railroad Construction Corps. I retired from the PLA in 1956 and worked as an engineer at the Provincial Institute of River and Water Conservancy Engineering and Design, Harbin, Heilongjiang Province, North China, from 1957 to 1982.

During the Chinese Cultural Revolution, between 1966 and 1976, some of my coworkers questioned my service during the Korean War. They asked me why I did not get promoted during the war and why I transferred from combat troops to an engineering corps. During the Korean War, most of the commanders received promotions quickly because of the CPVF's heavy casualties. If you were a captain when you entered Korea, you should be a major or colonel by the time you left Korea.

What they really wanted to know was whether I had made any serious mistakes as a commander in the war. They wanted to know if I had been disciplined, and if I had found a way out of a combat unit because I was scared of death. I tried to defend myself by explaining that I was wounded in the first battle. After my recovery, I was transferred to the engineering troops, which did not have as many casualties as frontline troops. And I did not finish my elementary school. It was very difficult, if not impossible, for someone to get a promotion in engineering units without basic algebra and geometry. Unfortunately, nobody believed me, and I was labeled a "deserter of the Korean War." I did not give any further explanation. I did not complain. Having thought so many times about my many dead comrades, I considered myself lucky to be one of the survivors in the Korean War.

Part Three

Chosin Accounts

Chapter 12

The Chosin Reservoir

A Marine's Story

Some of the toughest fighting in the Korean War took place at the Chosin Reservoir, where the unexpected entry of the Chinese into the war caught the First Marine Division and the Seventh Division unprepared as they were driving north toward the Yalu River. Badly outnumbered and frequently cut off by Chinese roadblocks, the marines and GIs battled cold, hunger, and fatigue as they fought their way back to the coast. While forced to retreat, they fought tenaciously, and they emerged badly battered but with their pride intact. Today, many of those who took part in the Reservoir fighting still meet from time to time as members of "The Chosin Few." Corporal Harold L. Mulhausen, a marine assigned to a 3.5-inch rocket section, arrived in Korea in November 1950, just in time to become a member of "The Chosin Few."

Corporal Harold L. Mulhausen

A Company, Seventh Regiment, First Marine Division

IN DECEMBER 1948, I joined the Twentieth Infantry Battalion, USMC Reserve, in Oklahoma City. Like many others, I became a marine largely because so many of my friends had already joined. When summer came, we climbed aboard a military transport plane and flew to Camp Pendleton, California. This was my very first ride in an airplane. After two weeks of marine training I returned to Oklahoma City, where a short time later I married my girlfriend, Betty Baker.

Little did I realized when I joined the Marine Reserve that I would be just in time for the Korean War, which began on June 25, 1950. Sometime in July our battalion was activated. I really didn't want to go to war, but I was pretty excited about being a marine. The war, I figured, probably wouldn't last very long anyway.

We left Oklahoma City, and after a long train ride we ended up at Camp Pendleton. On July 28, I began my active duty in the Marine Corps. We prepared for combat, and the training was intensive. One of our officers was a tall, thin, square-jawed lieutenant we called "Snake Face." He was tough as nails.

One time when Snake Face was lecturing on how we should pull guard duty, he walked over to a poor, helpless marine, yanked him out of the company, and yelled, "You are now on guard duty. Son, let me have your rifle." The dumb guy handed him his rifle as ordered. Lieutenant Snake Face promptly wheeled around and threw the rifle out to the recruits. Then he just chewed that poor kid up one side and down the other. "When on guard duty," he roared, "you don't *ever* give up your rifle to *anybody.*"

When our training was over, we boarded the USS *General Walker* in San Diego and shipped out. The crossing was mostly smooth, and I never really got seasick. We disembarked at Yokohama and climbed on a waiting train that took us on a night journey to some base I cannot remember. After more training we moved to another base I can't remember, and then on to a base near Osaka, a staging area for troops going to and coming from Korea. This base had been used as a military academy to train Japanese officers, and was really nice. When rumors spread that we were going to remain on the base and process troops we got pretty excited.

The rumors proved to be just that—rumors. One morning they piled us into trucks and hauled us over to Kobe, a seaport about twenty miles away. There they put us on a Japanese-owned but American-made WWII Victory ship, and we set out for Korea. The sea was rough, and the ship bounced up and down on the water like a cork. And that hellhole where I was sleeping stunk to high heaven with vomit from seasick marines.

I finally started feeling sick myself. When I realized I was about to vomit, I headed for a garbage can not far from my bunk. When I got there I pulled off the lid and found the damn thing already completely full of vomit. I slammed that thing down and looked for another place to throw up. I made my way through the toilet and shower area, where the stink from vomit and crap was unbelievable. I went up on deck, where I seemed to recuperate with the cold, fresh air, but a guard ordered me below. Retracing my steps, I made my way back through the toilet and shower area. Every shower stall seemed to have somebody in it, but I finally found an empty one. Then I plopped down on the floor of the stall and vomited over and over. I was so sick that I didn't care whether I lived or died.

Sometime in early November, we pulled into Wonsan Harbor, with most of us sick as dogs. Then we trucked to an airfield, where we boarded C-47s and flew to a mountainous area somewhere in the north. Another truck took us to Koto-ri.

Along with Whitney McClain, from Oklahoma City, and Oscar Noriega, from San Antonio, I was assigned to a 3.5-inch rocket section in A Company, First Battalion, Seventh Regiment, First Marine Division. We were replacements for the members of the previous 3.5-inch rocket section that had been wiped out about a week earlier by an enemy tank.

That night, my first in A Company, we had 50 percent watch, one hour on and one hour off. Fortunately, nothing unusual happened, because I had not even seen a 3.5-inch rocket launcher before, let alone operated one. The next morning our section leader, Glen Nolan from Roanoke, Virginia, taught us how to use it. Actually, it was an anti-tank weapon.

The same day, the Chinese pinned down one of our patrols in a gully about a half mile away. A sergeant ordered several of us to grab some stretchers and get the wounded out. To reach them we had to walk down a steep hill, and on my way down I kept hearing funny noises around me—popping, buzzing, and cracking noises. When we reached the gully, I asked another marine what the noise was all about.

"You've just been under fire," he replied. "The enemy is over there about six hundred yards away and shooting at you."

That was my baptism under fire. We got the wounded marines out okay, but when it was all over, I was pretty shook up thinking about it.

By this time, mid-November, the weather was turning cold. The wind was blowing, the sky spitting snow, the rivers and streams freezing, and we still hadn't been issued our cold weather gear. We couldn't even build a fire, except on rare occasions. Just before Thanksgiving we did receive our parkas and cold weather clothing, but by this time, the temperature had already dropped to around twenty degrees above zero. And we were headed north. To this day, I cannot think of Korea without also thinking about the intense cold.

On Thanksgiving Day, 1950, the marines continued to move north toward the Chosin Reservoir. This meant, of course, my 3.5-inch rocket squad had to move out, and we were pretty upset over the thought of missing our Thanksgiving dinner. This appeared to be a certainty when we reached our assigned area, somewhere near Koto-ri, and dug in for the night. To our great joy, next morning the cooks brought the kitchens up to our positions, and we had our Thanksgiving dinner after all—turkey, dressing, pumpkin pie, and all the goodies. It was delicious, and I ate until my belly nearly popped.

On November 25, just after Thanksgiving, about two-thirds of our company went on a patrol, led by Lieutenant Frank Mitchell, from Roaring Springs, Texas. The patrol returned about 2:00 the next morning, all shot up. They had run into a major concentration of Chinese Communists, who had now officially entered the war. Those guys did some really hard fighting, and they fought like heroes. Lieutenant Mitchell earned the Medal of Honor for his part. They managed to bring back all their wounded but had to leave their dead behind. This was tough on them, because marines are trained to return with their dead if at all possible.

We kept driving northward, into the Chosin Reservoir area, finally passing through the little town of Yudam-ri. There wasn't much there but a few shacks, and we saw very few inhabitants. By the time it became dark, we had set up a perimeter just outside of town, with our 3.5-inch rockets positioned on a creek bed. The ground was frozen and so full of rocks it was nearly impossible to dig, but we finally managed to set up a half-assed defensive position.

With fighting in the hills all around us, we remained on 50 percent watch. At about one o'clock that night we were ordered to move back about two hundred yards. This time we set up our 3.5-inch rockets in a field next to the road. We tried to dig in again, but the ground was frozen so hard we had little success. There were firefights everywhere, so they put us on 100 percent watch. Somehow we managed to avoid contact with the enemy that night, but we sure as hell didn't avoid contact with the cold. By morning, the thermometer had dropped to thirty degrees below zero, with a strong wind blowing.

They gave us three days worth of rations and told us we were moving back. They also ordered A Company to take a hill, which we did after a full day of hard fighting. We were helped by air strikes, but unfortunately, one of the F-51 Mustangs hit one of our men in the ankle during a strafing run. He lost his foot as a result.

That night we set up a perimeter around the top of the hill and stood watch in the bone-chilling cold. Everywhere we looked we could see firefights. Clearly, the Chinese army was all around us. The marines in the valley began to burn huge piles of supplies to keep them from falling into enemy hands.

Under cover of darkness, we moved off the hill—very quietly. My sergeant came by and checked us for anything that rattled; if it did, we had to tie it down or throw it away. We moved down the hill slowly, slipping and sliding. Then we just walked and walked, sometimes in snow that came up to our knees. Those poor devils in the front column got the honor of breaking the path for the rest of us.

At times, the Chinese were so close we could hear them talking. When that happened everybody got super quiet and made no noise at all. Nobody had to tell us how serious the situation was. We walked by one foxhole that contained three dead Chinese soldiers—all frozen to death at their posts.

All night we walked, with just an occasional rest. When we did stop to rest we were so tired we would go to sleep immediately, and that's when the danger of freezing to death was greatest. Sometimes we punched and kicked each other so no one would die a frozen death.

Shortly after daylight we relieved Fox Company at the Taktong Pass. Fox had been badly cut up in several days of bitter fighting and had wounded men all over the area. They had wrapped their dead in parachute cloth and stacked them in piles. It was not a pretty sight. There were also hundreds of dead Chinese scattered around the area.

My platoon was ordered to set up a roadblock on a small hill overlooking the road. We sat and watched while hundreds of battle-weary marines moved down the road, with the wounded and the dead piled into vehicles.

Miraculously, during all of this we managed to get some hot food. The cooks set up a field kitchen, and we were allowed to go down the hill two or three at a time. We got sausage, bacon, scrambled eggs, hot cakes, and a big old cup of coffee. Boy, did it taste good. This was my first hot meal in about two weeks. I stuffed myself, but my stomach had shrunk so much I could not eat everything I had taken.

We moved on to Hagaru-ri, where the engineers had built a small airstrip. Under very difficult conditions, planes brought in much-needed supplies and took off with the dead and wounded.

When we left Hagaru-ri, one of our tanks intentionally ran over our 3.5-inch rocket launchers so they would not fall into enemy hands, and we ended up in a rifle platoon. We walked on past the airstrip, then along a ridgeline in the mountains. Eventually we reached Koto-ri, where the fighting just got tougher. When leaving the town, we received steady fire from the hills on both sides of the road.

Once, when under sniper fire, I ran like hell for a ditch. About twenty yards from the ditch I suddenly tumbled headlong into the snow. I got up and dove into the ditch, where I joined about a half dozen other marines already there. I was still mad over falling when I noticed the heel of my boot; it had been shot clean off. I fell down because a bullet had hit my boot.

We moved out again, sometimes able to see no more than thirty feet ahead of us because of the snow and fog. While we ran into several firefights along the way, just about dark we managed to move forward to a big hill overlooking a pass. That night we dug down into the snow as deep as we could to get out of the stinging wind, but the bitter cold went right through us. A lieutenant told me to help a wounded man get down the hill and onto the road, which I did. Then I got lost trying to find my way back in the dark. I ended up crawling into my sleeping bag beside a tank with its track knocked off, but still occupied. I was not only freezing cold but starving as well, so when the tank crew gave me a can of Beanie Weenies I savored every bite.

Somehow I managed to doze off, when—BLAM—the cannon on the tank went off. It was morning and we were under attack by the Chinese. They finally withdrew, but not until we had a dandy firefight.

We continued walking down the road and finally came to an assembly area where trucks were waiting to take us to a train station. There we boarded a train that took us to the port of Hungnam for evacuation by sea. At Hungnam, I actually got a good night's sleep, ate a good breakfast, and began to feel halfway warm.

A landing craft carried us out to a ship named the USS *Sultan*. I went below, found a bunk, got a clean set of clothes, and took a hot shower. Boy, did it feel good. I thought I was in heaven. It had been fifty days since I had taken a shower. After shaving, I hardly recognized myself in the mirror. When we had left Japan for Korea I weighed about two hundred pounds. Now, I weighed 143, fully clothed.

On board the *Sultan* I ran across Bill Burkett, a kid I went to high school with back in Oklahoma City. The ship was so crowded he didn't even have a bunk, so I shared mine with him until we disembarked at Pusan. There we boarded LSTs for a short voyage to Masan, where the First Marine Division was reassembling. When I rejoined A Company, only sixteen people were left from the original company. But soon replacements started coming in, stragglers returned, and people were getting out of the hospitals. As a result, we were soon able to form a pretty good company. In the next several weeks we did some training, updated our shots, checked out our clothes, recuperated, and shared a lot of experiences with each other.

Private First Class Harold Mulhausen, First Marine Division, waiting to board a ship at Hungnam following the Chosin Reservoir fighting, December 1950. (Courtesy of Harold Mulhausen)

Sometime in February 1951, I'm not sure exactly when, we climbed aboard trucks and headed north. The UN forces were mounting an offensive once again, and after so much retreating, it was a good feeling to be pushing the Communists back. It was still winter, however, and we nearly froze to death riding over mountain passes in those open trucks.

At some point we stopped and set up a perimeter, partially to destroy enemy forces that were interfering with our supply lines. Everyday we went on patrol, with patrols ranging from platoon to company size. As a member of a 3.5-inch rocket section, our primary job was to knock out enemy tanks and bunkers. Our services were not always needed, however, so the Marine Corps found other uses for us, such as going on patrol and assisting the medical corpsmen as stretcher bearers. At other times we served as ammo carriers, radiomen, or just plain riflemen. When there were no targets for our 3.5-inch rockets, we just filled in as needed.

Going on patrol meant walking, and plenty of it. Often we kept going until we made contact with the enemy. Then, after a brief skirmish, we would hike back to our company area. Every night we stood 50 percent watch, and it seemed like we never got any rest. To make matters worse, the chow was the sorriest I had ever experienced in Korea, perhaps because our supplies were not getting through regularly. As a result, the combination of terrible chow and lack of sleep seemed to deprive all of us of the energy to do anything. Maybe this was a carryover from the fighting at the Chosin Reservoir.

One day on patrol we came across an army convoy that had made a wrong turn and had been ambushed by the Chinese and North Koreans. Almost all of their vehicles had been destroyed, and dead soldiers were everywhere—Chinese, Koreans, and Americans. We did not find one person alive, and all the valuables, including weapons and ammunition, were gone. It was a very sobering experience.

Once, when we were moving into a new area, we found ourselves running low on water. Naturally this called for a "water patrol," so off we went, scouting for water. We heard a noise that sounded like running water, but it turned out to be flies circling above a dead animal, so thick they formed a solid black cloud. Then we caught a whiff of the dead carcass, and it was something unbelievably awful. So we went back to the company and reported that we couldn't find any water.

Gradually, with help of air support, we managed to disperse enough of the enemy forces to allow our supply lines to operate smoothly again. On occasion, when we were lucky, we even brought back prisoners.

As the days grew warmer, and winter turned into spring, we were involved in a strange incident, one that I never read about in the history books on the Korean War. One morning, between two and three companies of marines climbed on trucks and we took off down the road. We finally stopped on a big plateau area about twelve to fifteen miles in front of our MLR. We set up with heavy machine guns, 81mm mortars, 3.5-inch rockets, artillery, a field kitchen, and two tanks, with concertina wire placed around the entire area. Everything considered, we formed a strong defensive position.

Every day, ten or fifteen infantrymen would load up on top of each tank and head down the road toward a little village in the valley. Often they would make contact with the enemy, have a brief skirmish, then turn around and come back. Helicopters quickly evacuated the wounded. We followed this routine for ten to twelve days.

One night all hell broke loose behind us. Our artillery let loose with an awesome barrage and kept it up for most of an hour. We immediately went from 50 percent watches to 100 percent, but nothing happened except we lost a lot of sleep.

Early the next morning we packed up our gear, got on the trucks, and headed back to our MLR. After we had gone eight or nine miles, we came around a big bend in the road that opened onto an area of huge rice paddies. Littered across these rice paddies were the bodies of dead Chinese—about five or six hundred of them. They were stacked in piles, some up to ten feet in height. Army engineers had already moved in with bulldozers and, after digging huge trenches, were rolling these bodies into mass graves. I had never seen so many dead people in my entire life.

Later we learned what had happened. Known as Operation Mousetrap, our group, way out in front of the MLR, provided the bait. When the Chinese tried to sneak into our area under the cover of darkness, our artillery, mortar, and rocket fire absolutely annihilated them. We set a trap, and the Chinese fell for it.

Following this strange battle, we went back into battalion reserve for a few days. Even then, our company sent out daily patrols as a precautionary measure to prevent ambushes. One day, Chinese mortars wounded a number of our guys on patrol, and about ten of us were told to get some stretchers and go after them. After a hike of about a mile and a half, we reached the patrol and proceeded to put the wounded on stretchers and evacuate them. One guy had an arm wound that didn't appear to be serious. When we stopped to rest, a marine came along helping a guy unable to walk because he had been hit in the ankle. So we said to our guy on the stretcher with the arm wound, "Hey, why don't you get up and walk along beside us and let us carry this guy who's got his foot shot off?" He said, "Fine," and got off the stretcher. We got both of them to an aid station at the bottom of the hill, where they waited for a helicopter to evacuate them. Then we went back to our units.

What followed was nothing short of tragic. The poor guy with the arm wound was repeatedly passed over while the helicopters evacuated the "more seriously" wounded. When they finally got around to putting him on the helicopter, they found him dead. With no one to help him, he just went into shock and died.

Rain can be a real problem in Korea, especially in the spring. One night, after we had pitched our pup tents in a rice paddy, we ran into a big problem. We were all snug in our sleeping bags on top of air mattresses when I rolled over and my hand fell into a puddle of water. When I got up, I discovered the water inside the tent was about three inches deep. I dressed, went outside, and discovered the problem. Up above us on the hillside, marines were busy with shovels cutting holes in the irrigation dikes to let the water flow through. That's where our water was coming from.

To solve the problem, we dug a ditch across our rice paddy about one foot deep and two feet wide so we could drain the water. But the rain continued, and so much water flowed through that ditch that by the next evening it had grown to about eight feet wide and ten feet deep. It was a real "gully washer," as we would call it in Oklahoma. As a matter of fact, they eventually brought in some engineers to build a bridge so we could get from one part of the camp to the other.

About the same time, our sergeant grabbed six of us early one morning and said, "Come with me." Naturally we all volunteered; we thought it must be some emergency. He did not seem particularly bothered by the fact we had not yet eaten breakfast. We followed him to the motor pool, where we climbed into several trucks and took off down the road. About 10:30 A.M. we pulled into a big army supply base.

When we complained about not having had breakfast, one of the army guys took us to the mess hall for some chow. This was the first time I had ever eaten army chow, and I was impressed. They served cafeteria style, with fried eggs, scrambled eggs, boiled eggs, poached eggs, fresh sausage and bacon, biscuits and gravy, hot cakes, fresh juice—anything we could possibly want. I mean, those army guys really had it knocked. They even had table-cloths. And the food tasted great. We ate until we were about to bust.

Soon our sergeant came back, and he put us to work. That's when we discovered the nature of the "emergency." One of our trucks backed up to a railroad car, and we filled that sucker clear to the roof with Pabst Blue Ribbon beer. Unfortunately, we couldn't sneak away with any extra beer because the old boy at the door counted every can. The other trucks loaded up with C-rations, mail, and a bunch of supplies, and we drove back to our company area. Then we had to unload all that junk. This was typical of the kind of jobs we found ourselves doing while in reserve. The Marine Corps did not intend for *reserve* to mean *rest.*

Reserve also meant *inspection,* and we had a big one while we were set up in this area. As a reward for being the best company, our battalion commander came down to our area and told everybody in A Company we could have a day off to do anything we wanted, but we had to be back by midnight. About two-thirds of the company took off for a small Korean town about four or five miles away. The guys I ran around with didn't want to do that, so we messed around the camp for awhile, got bored, and finally decided to go into town and join the others. While three of us were hitching a ride, an army truck came by and offered to take us to another, bigger town, where we could have a "helluva time." This other town was about twenty-five miles away, but they promised to bring us back, so we accepted. They were right; it was a nice town with an open market, shopping stalls, and a pleasant little restaurant where we had a nice meal. We enjoyed ourselves and caught our ride back to the company area with the army guys, arriving at about eleven o'clock that night.

Very quickly we saw that just about everyone in the area was drunk. The beer we had brought back earlier had been intended as the beer ration for the entire company. Since most of the guys had gone into town, the handful of people who stayed behind had access to the entire company's ration, and they took full advantage of the opportunity. They drank the beer that really belonged to the guys who went to town. Moreover, the corpsmen had picked up a couple of jugs of grain alcohol to spike the beer. The result was "drunk city." I'd never seen anything like it in my life.

When I woke up about 8:30 the next morning, I kept hearing a noise out in the company street. I raised the flap on my tent and saw a sergeant trying to pick up a guy passed out in the middle of the street. He actually belonged to another company but had found the beer flowing when he came over to visit a buddy and drank until he passed out.

Our time in reserve soon came to an end, and we went back on the line. It began very badly. We were about two hundred yards past battalion headquarters when we heard a humongous explosion. We turned around in time to see parts of a jeep flying off in all directions. The jeep had run over a land mine, and all three of its occupants were killed. How and when that mine got there, nobody knew. A minesweeping group was called in, and they found six more. When stuff like this happened in rear areas, we understood better why we sent out patrols and had guards on duty around the clock.

We continued four or five miles up the road, and when we reached a rice paddy incoming artillery shells began to fall. I dove into an irrigation ditch that snaked in and around the paddies, along with fifteen or twenty other marines. The barrage wasn't particularly heavy, but it was enough to keep us pinned down. Suddenly, I heard a thud and looked up. About three feet in front of me a round had hit the bank on my right side but failed to explode. It was a dud. If that shell had gone off, there would have been a bunch of dead marines—myself included.

Fortunately for us, the Chinese used quite a bit of ammunition that failed to go off. Often, their hand grenades would just lay there and fizzle, like a firecracker. Artillery and mortar rounds were often duds as well. When it happens, however, and you realize how close you came to being killed, it really eats away at your mind.

After we had been on the line for three or four days, work trains (i.e., Korean laborers) would arrive carrying the nonessential stuff we had left in the rear, such as shaving gear, writing material, etc. And when we left the line they would show up and haul it back to the rear.

Once, when we had completed our tour of duty on the line and were ready to move out, the work train didn't show. After we had waited several hours, the company commander came by about 11:00 A.M. and told me to take a couple of guys and remain with the gear until the train came, then join the rest of the company. He showed me our new position on a map, and then pointed to it with his hand. It was about one thousand yards away. He left the map and a walkie talkie with us and went on his way. "We'll see you later on this evening," he said.

We waited and waited, and finally about 5:00 the work train arrived and loaded up our gear. Then we took off to find our company. We walked and kept walking, but with no success. I kept trying to contact the company with the walkie talkie, but got no answer. By this time, it was around midnight, so we decided to set up for the night in a clump of trees nearby.

Just as we got to the edge of the trees, however, we heard a noise. We froze. Suddenly we heard an American voice demanding to know the password. Hell, I didn't know the password, so I tried to identify myself while cussing and bitching at the same time. Finally, a marine emerged and proceeded to tell us where we were. Our company lines extended up to the top of a long hill, which we proceeded to climb. When we reported to the company commander, he apologized for the sorry map he had given us. According to the map, we were supposed to have traveled only about a thousand yards to the new lines, but we had actually hiked closer to seven thousand yards.

It was not a good feeling to wander around in the middle of the night lost, with a worthless map. We could have easily stumbled into an enemy patrol. When we saw our friends in A Company again, they never looked better.

It was not unusual for our maps to cause us serious problems. Made by the Japanese before World War II and translated into English, they were terrible—but they were all we had. About the only thing they attempted to show were roads and rivers, but many of the roads we encountered weren't even built when the maps were printed. Other roads shown on the maps no longer existed.

One time, while on line, we were ordered to advance about a thousand yards up to a big horseshoe ridge to link up with another company. We started out in the morning and walked all day, trying to follow our map. Finally, about 9:00 that evening and well after dark, we reached our objective—the horseshoe ridge. It was the longest one thousand yards I ever walked. Nevertheless, we finally got the line set up. We positioned my 3.5-inch rocket section in the midst of a bunch of rocks, some as big as automobiles.

That night, we lay amongst the rocks, looking out toward the front as usual. Unfortunately, the night was so black we couldn't see a damn thing. After standing my watch, I crawled in the sack and went to sleep. But not for long; I soon woke up to the sound of a burp gun, and it was close. For the next few minutes we had a helluva firefight, with hand grenades, burp guns, rifle fire, and people hollering for corpsmen. Then it ended just as quickly as it started.

When daylight came, we were surprised to learn that the high horseshoe ridge we had finally reached had a big meadow in the middle of it, probably a mile in diameter. It appeared that the Koreans used this meadow for grazing their cattle during the summer months. We also figured out the Chinese apparently came up behind the company by chance, using a road that happened to lead to our mortar section. Then they found themselves in a firefight, and they were probably as surprised as we were. We killed several Chinese soldiers, but four or five marines were wounded.

Daylight also brought another revelation. Right out in front of the area my section was set up to defend was a sheer cliff that dropped off some two hundred to three hundred feet. If during that dark night I had walked just ten or fifteen feet straight forward from my position, I would have fallen off this cliff to my death.

One day we were ordered to assault a hill about a thousand yards from our position. While we were waiting for the artillery to begin its barrage in preparation for our assault, we watched the Chinese moving around on the side of their hill. Just then, a marine with a sniper rifle walked up to where I was standing. After surveying the scene, he said, "You know, I think I'll see if I can't just scatter those guys." For his target he selected two Chinese soldiers sitting on the edge of a foxhole, eating. He laid down on the ground, propped up his rifle on a sleeping bag, got his windage, and fired. The bullet hit low and to the right, but the two Chinese soldiers just kept right on eating. The marine adjusted his sights and cranked off another round. The bullet was high, but this time he got their attention. The Chinese soldiers dived into their foxhole and disappeared from view. Finally, after a long wait, the two Chinese emerged again, and the marine took aim and fired another shot. This time one of the soldiers fell over backwards and just laid there. Later, a corpsmen told me the bullet severed the spinal column of the Chinese soldier. He probably died instantly.

At about the same time, our artillery began to soften up the hill in preparation for our assault. After a forty-minute barrage, the assault platoon launched its attack on the hill, while my 3.5-inch rocket section sat on our side of the hill and watched. Our guys took the hill without a fight; for some reason the Chinese had hightailed it out of there when the artillery hit. We never understood why. When we moved up, we discovered the Chinese foxholes were actually outlets to a large bunker and tunnels on the back side of the hill. Their positions were strong, and they could have put up a vigorous defense.

Another time, we assaulted a large wooded hill and ran into some real problems. When our troops reached the top of the hill, they were pinned down by heavy enemy fire. At the time my section was providing supporting fire. About forty yards from our position, three marines were taking cover in a depression and were calling for a corpsman. A corpsman jumped up and tried to reach them, but he got hit about halfway there. Then another corpsman, a big black guy about six-foot-six, took off running and dodging bullets while we gave him cover fire. He made it to the three marines, and after giving first-aid he stood up and shouted, "Hey, I'm coming back. Cover me." So we laid down another field of fire.

The corpsman then grabbed two of the wounded marines by the collar, one in each hand, and started moving back to our lines. Somehow he made it and dove over the edge right beside us. He stood there talking while we checked the wounds of the two guys, and all of the sudden this big corpsman just collapsed. He had been shot three times and still managed to drag those two guys back to our positions. It was an amazing act of courage. Unfortunately, I never saw the big guy again or heard what happened to him.

While all of this was going on, we started receiving a heavy barrage of 120mm mortar fire, and a guy standing right next to me got hit in the neck. I immediately put a battle dressing on his neck, and then we started receiving rifle fire. One of the new recruits ran up to me and shouted, "Muley, Muley, what are we going to do?" I turned to him when—CRACK—a bullet hit right above his eye and blood gushed everywhere. He fell right flat on his back. A corpsman pitched me a battle dressing, and I wrapped it around his head as well as I could. I really figured he was dead, however, having been shot in the head like that.

A rifle team was dispatched to clean out the Chinese who had been shooting at us, and then a strange thing happened. When the team got into position, for some reason the Chinese just threw down their weapons and surrendered. So now we had prisoners, about five of them.

After this, things began to quiet down, and the choppers came in to fly out the wounded. We helped carry them down the road for evacuation. Unbelievably, the kid who had been hit in the eye was still alive; the projectile had gone between his helmet and eye and lodged in his skull. He not only survived, he later rejoined our company.

When I reflect back on that incident, I find it amazing that the human body can be so fragile at one time and so resilient at another. On the one hand, there was this kid who survived after being shot in the head. On the other hand, there was this other kid who was shot in the arm—a seemingly minor wound—and died. It doesn't make any sense. But then, war doesn't make any sense. Combat is very difficult on the individual and totally un-natural. You're always waiting for your turn, wondering when you're going to get it or when your friend is going to get it. You worry about getting wounded, especially the kind of wounds that handicap you for life. It seems like you're always busy, always nervous, and always tired because you never really rest properly. Even in reserve, you don't really rest; you're still waiting for something to happen.

One thing never changed in Korea—the hills. They all looked about the same, and there was always one more we had to take. Once, when trying to take a hill and the assault platoon got pinned down about two-thirds of the way to the top, my 3.5-inch rocket team was called to take out an enemy bunker set up with a machine gun. We made our way up the hill and through the trees to a position about five hundred yards from the bunker. We fired one round, and it landed about twenty feet short. We reloaded and prepared to fire again when a mortar shell hit in the tree directly over my head and showered my rocket team with shrapnel. The man directly in front of me was hit in the throat, and another man was hit in the arm real bad. I held a battle dressing tightly against the throat of the one guy to slow down the bleeding. Then a corpsman removed the battle dressing and had me hold the guy's jugular vein with my fingers while he applied a clamp. After he tied the two ends of the jugular vein together with stitches, the bleeding stopped, and the corpsman went on to the next guy. Meanwhile, the assault platoon managed to take the hill and the firing stopped. We helped evacuate the wounded down to the road, where a chopper could pick them up. Some-how, the guy who had been hit in the throat survived.

Fortunately, we did not experience combat everyday. We had good times in Korea as well as bad. When we were in reserve, we frequently played catch, wrote letters, read books, and rested. We usually had a couple of hot meals a day, and when the PX truck came by we could buy gum, candy bars, shampoo, writing tablets, and stuff like that.

One afternoon, when returning from a patrol, we came across an army jeep a mile or so from our company area. Since the engine was cold, and we couldn't get any response when we yelled, we all piled in the jeep and drove it down the hill to our company. We showed it to the captain, who told us to take it to battalion headquarters. First, however, he told us to use it for a water run, which we did.

We had filled up the water cans and started back when three soldiers came walking up the road. They were madder than hell; we had their jeep.

They had been on a reconnaissance patrol and had driven the jeep as far up the hill as they could go before striking out on foot. We explained the situation as best we could, and they agreed to our request to take the water back to the camp before returning the jeep. So we unloaded the water cans and returned the jeep as promised. They took off in it but had only gone a few hundred yards when the damn thing ran out of gas. Those army guys were really pissed off; if there hadn't been so many marines, I think they would have come after us.

Another time, we were returning from patrol when a Korean, dressed in civilian clothes, jumped out from behind a tree. We held a gun on him, but the Korean turned and ran away, so one of our guys shot him. Then we made an interesting discovery—the Korean was not a "he" but a "she." She also had an American-made walkie-talkie with her, wrapped in a baby blanket, which she dropped before trying to run away. She could easily have been calling in artillery or reporting troop movements. This is a good example of why we went out on patrols, even when in reserve.

Not long before I left for Korea, my father sent me a .38 caliber pistol, but without bullets or a holster. I tried to buy bullets in the PX, both in the States and in Japan, but with no success. So I arrived in Korea with this beautiful pistol but no bullets. Finally, our air officer, a big red-faced Irishman, gave me six rounds. I loaded that sucker and carried it in my pocket all the time I was up in the Chosin Reservoir area. When I got to Masan, I found an old .45 holster that I modified to fit the .38 so I was able to carry it on my hip. Then I wrote my wife and asked her to find a way to send me some bullets. She did it by sending me a goodie box and wrapping each bullet in a piece of candy or a cookie. I might get six or eight rounds with each package. The other guys all knew they could eat my candy, but if they came across a bullet, the bullet was mine.

I slept with that pistol every night I was in Korea. It became a bed-partner for me, just like a teddy bear for a kid. I couldn't go to sleep without my pistol, even when we were in reserve. The pistol provided me with comfort and warmth. I brought it home with me, and I still have it. And it still gives me comfort and warmth.

We could never get enough mail from home, but unfortunately, it generally came in bunches. One time, the seven guys in my section received a total of twelve packages from home all on the same day. The cookies and cakes were a bit crumbly, but we feasted on them anyway.

One new guy in our unit corresponded with eleven different girls at the same time. Naturally, he was the envy of everyone because we all thought he was a real lover. He would write one letter, then copy it ten times, perhaps changing a date or an incident. He mailed at least one set of letters a week, and sometimes two. After about six weeks in the company, however, he started receiving "Dear John" letters. And after about two months, the only letters he wrote were to his mother and father. He actually became the joke of the company.

Toilet paper was almost always in short supply. A few sheets came with our C rations, but generally not enough to meet our needs. One guy must have said something to his wife about the shortage, because he started receiving letters written on toilet paper. Very practical. If he carried his letters around with him, they could serve a very useful purpose in the end.

Nobody likes to talk about "friendly fire," but we worked so closely with the aircraft, artillery, and tanks that it was understandable that accidents occasionally happened. I once saw a tank shell kill two marines and wound three or four more trying to knock out an enemy machine gun bunker. Apparently the tank commander didn't know some of our troops were holed up in a depression near the bunker. We tried to take every precaution to prevent this sort of thing, but sometimes it still happened.

About a month before I was scheduled to leave Korea, the company sent me and a couple of other combat veterans back to the rear area for safekeeping. Our primary job was to direct the Korean work trains carrying food and supplies up to the lines and back. Normally it took about a day to make the round trip, and we did a trip every other day. Sometimes we had as many as 150 Koreans in a group. We usually had one marine at each end and a couple in the middle to keep the group together.

On our days off, we would write letters, play cards, toss the football, or whatever. I spent hours sanding, cleaning, and polishing a Russian carbine I had taken from a captured Chinese soldier. When I finished it, the rifle was absolutely beautiful, but I never got home with it. Somebody stole it from my tent the day before I was scheduled to rotate. I was really pissed.

On November 11, 1951, I started for home. The day I left the battalion, I went around and shook hands with everybody I knew. Five of us from the company were all leaving at the same time. When we got to division headquarters, we discovered there were a number of fellows going home from the first replacement draft, many of whom we knew. My friend Bill Burkett was there, the guy I had gone to high school with back in Oklahoma City. We also served in the reserve together, and we were on the same ship coming back from the Chosin Reservoir fighting. He had been promoted to sergeant and didn't even know it until someone read his name from the rotation list as "Sergeant" Bill Burkett. Then he was put in charge of the group because he held the highest rank.

They drove us down to the coast in trucks, put us on board a landing craft, ferried us out to a Victory ship, and carried us back to Japan. There must have been six to seven hundred of us going home at the same time. When we arrived at the dock in Kobe, Bill and I learned that our seabags, which had been placed in storage while we were in Korea, had been lost. The only clothes we had were those on our back and a few changes of socks and shorts. Fortunately, we got enough stuff from the other guys to get us home with changes of clothing everyday.

We came home like we went over, by ship. The trip was supposed to take about eleven days, but it took fifteen. We finally docked at San Diego. There was no fanfare; the only people at the dock to see us come in were families and girlfriends. My wife, Betty, couldn't come because she didn't have the money to travel.

We were taken from the ship to the Marine Corps Recruit Depot in San Diego, where we received new orders and new uniforms. We filled out forms that gave us three choices for our next assignment. I don't know why they bothered with this because the orders were already made out.

Bill and I were both assigned to Camp Lejeune in North Carolina. I got sixteen days travel time and thirty days leave. We also got all our back pay the day before we left San Diego, which in my case was $517. Since Bill's folks had driven out to see him come in, I was able to ride back to Oklahoma City with them. We arrived on December 3, and my birthday was on December 4. What a wonderful birthday present it was for me to be home.

Betty had managed to save some money while I was in Korea, so we were able to buy a car—a 1951 Chevrolet. When it was time to leave, we drove it to North Carolina.

On January 16, 1952, I reported to Camp Lejeune, and they assigned me to a weapons company. A short time after I arrived the major called me into his office and tried to persuade me to reenlist. After noticing I was eligible for promotion, he asked, "If I got you a sergeant's stripes, would you stay over?"

My reply could not be misunderstood. "No sir! I've had all the Marine Corps I want, and I don't want any more."

At that point, the major became real hostile. "Then get yourself out of my office! I don't ever want to see you again," he snarled.

A few days later, about twenty of us due to get out were called to attend a meeting, where two staff sergeants harangued us about reenlisting. They told us about how difficult life would be on the outside; unemployment was high, jobs were hard to find, prices had gone up, and people didn't care anything about the GIs coming back from Korea. Then they talked about how great life was in the Marine Corps and all the advantages we'd have.

When the sergeants were finished talking, they announced, "All of you that's going to reenlist, we want you to go over to this next room. The rest of you, we want you to stay right here."

The group split about fifty-fifty. One of the sergeants then came around and asked each one of us individually why we were not going to reenlist, and then he'd give his little spiel about the mistake we were making.

When he got to me, I said, "I've had all the Marine Corps I want. I don't want anymore. There's not any living way I would reenlist!" After that, he didn't ask me any more questions.

About January 29, 1952, after receiving my orders, it was time to head back for Oklahoma City and civilian life. I joyfully packed my bag, said my goodbyes, and Betty and I hit the road in our new 1951 Chevrolet. We drove straight through, arriving in Oklahoma City around February 1. We're still here.

Chapter 13

The Chosin Reservoir

A Chinese Captain's Story

During the CPVF's second offensive campaign, between November 25 and December 24, 1950, its Ninth Army Group, which included the Twentieth, Twenty-sixth, and Twenty-seventh Armies, attacked the UN forces led by the U.S. First Marine Division and U.S. Seventh Infantry Division. Although the Ninth Army Group scored a major victory of the CPVF during the three-year war in Korea when it wiped out the entire Thirty-second Regiment of the Seventh Division, it suffered a terrible toll both from the battle and from the cruel Korean winter. Consisting of about one hundred thousand frontline troops, the Ninth suffered more than forty thousand casualties, and about one-half of these were from frostbite. The following story by Captain Wang Xuedong describes several CPVF engagements with the First Marine Division and the hardships endured by the soldiers, which so characterized the fighting in the Chosin Reservoir.

Captain Wang Xuedong

First Company, 172nd Regiment, Fifty-eighth Division, Twentieth Army, CPVF Ninth Army Group

THE PLA NINTH Army Group became the CPVF Ninth Army Group in mid–October 1950. It was stationed in Southeast China as the CPVF reserve. In early November, the army group received its order to move north. It began to transport its three armies, the Twentieth, Twenty-sixth, and Twenty-seventh, by railway from Southeast to Northeast China on November 7.

The CPVF situation in Korea became critical in November. After the CPVF's first offensive, in late October, the UN forces prepared an all-out counteroffensive scheduled for late November. General Douglas MacArthur promised his soldiers they would be "back home for Christmas" after this largest and final offense.

The UN Command positioned its Eighth Army on the western front with 130,000 troops. The CPVF had 230,000 men there, and clearly outnumbered the UN forces in the west by a ratio of 1.75 to 1. On the eastern front, the UN forces consisted of 90,000 men in its X Corps. The CPVF, however, had less than 20,000 men (two divisions of the Forty-second Army) in this part of North Korea.

In November, the X Corps rapidly advanced north along the eastern coast toward the Yalu River and Kanggye, the wartime capital of North Korea after Kim Il Sung withdrew his government from Pyongyang on October 19. It appeared the X Corps would drive Kim and his government out of North Korea and cut off the CPVF from behind.

On November 5, Chairman Mao approved the request for reinforcements by Marshal Peng Dehuai, CPVF commander in chief. Mao ordered the Ninth Army Group to enter Korea immediately. The task of the Ninth Army Group, 150,000 strong, was to stop the X Corps on the eastern front. During the army group's long railway journey from the Changjiang (Yangtze) River to the Yalu River, General Song Shilun, commander of the Ninth Army Group, gave his orders to the army commanders on the train.

Following General Song's orders, on November 17 the Twenty-seventh Army crossed the Yalu River from Ji'an (Chi-an) as the first wave of the army group. On November 19, the Twentieth Army crossed the Yalu River from Linjiang (Lin-chiang) as the second wave. The Twenty-sixth Army temporarily stayed at Linjiang as the reserve and waited for promised Russian weapon and equipment shipments in order to replace the army group's old Japanese-made weapons.

The Twentieth Army included the Fifty-eighth, Fifty-ninth, and Sixtieth Divisions. On November 19, my division, the Fifty-eighth—the army's vanguard—began to march at full speed across North Korea from west to east toward Kanggye. By November 21, after we had marched about sixty miles, we reached Kanggye. The division's three regiments, the 172nd, 173rd, and 174th Regiments, continued our southeastern movement toward Chosin (Changjin) through the mountains.

There were some unexpected problems during our first week in North Korea. We were clearly not adequately prepared for such a huge offensive assignment.

First, the logistic services failed to keep up with the movement of our

combat troops. We were hastily thrown into combat without good preparation, and had serious breakdowns in our supply and transportation systems.
We had to take with us whatever we needed, or whatever we could carry on
our shoulders. When our regiment ran out of food, we had to trade our
blankets, towels, and even medicines with local Koreans for their rice, corn,
and vegetables.

Second, the cold winter hit our troops very hard. The commanders did
not have any idea about how cold the weather would be in North Korea. We
had not been issued our winter clothing when we entered Korea; we lacked
gloves, caps, and even winter shoes. We came from Southeast China, where
the average annual temperature is about 72 degrees Fahrenheit. When we
left our homes in early November, the temperature was about 60 degrees.
Two weeks later, in North Korea, the temperature had dropped to below
zero. Many soldiers caught colds and could not keep up with their regiments. Our division lost seven hundred men during the first week due to
severe frostbite.

Third, transportation became another serious problem. To conceal the
southeastern movement of more than one hundred thousand men, the two
armies marched 120 miles through mountains and forests in the cold winter
with heavy snow and without trucks. In these conditions, it was impossible
for the army to move with any kind of speed. The division's artillery battalion, for example, had some horses that refused to walk on the snow-covered
narrow pass along the cliffs. It was just too slippery and dangerous. The men
came up with the idea of laying down their comforters on the cliffs to cover
the snow and ice. The idea worked, and they led their horses safely through
the pass.

We were behind schedule. On November 25, the CPVF General Head-
quarters ordered the army group to launch its attack in the east, when the
CPVF began its second all-out offensive campaign. But the Ninth Army
Group Headquarters had to ask the General HQ for a two-day delay since
its armies were not yet in position to attack. The General HQ approved the
Ninth HQ's request for a delay.

Two days later, during the evening of November 27, the Ninth HQ
ordered a general attack, which centered on the Chosin Reservoir along the
eastern front. The attack force consisted of eight infantry divisions which
made use of some very successful tactics during the first night attack.

First, the Ninth Army Group achieved a big surprise since its entry into
North Korea had remained undetected for ten days. The U.S. First Marine

Chinese commanders plan an attack on the UNF at the Chosin Reservoir, November 1950. (Courtesy of Wang Xuedong)

and Seventh Infantry Divisions, the main strength of X Corps, were traveling in one column along one small mountain road and stretched out over fifty miles. Surprised and unprepared for such a large-scale attack, X Corps had been broken down into five sections by the next morning. They were separated by the CPVF troops at Ryutam-ri (Yudam-ri), Sinhungri (Chinhung-ri), Koto-ri, Hahwaok-ri (Hagaru-ri), and Sachang-ri.

Second, in order to destroy as many enemy regiments as possible—rather than to simply push them back into South Korea—the Ninth Army Group purposely concentrated a total of one hundred thousand men. The UN forces engaged in the Chosin Reservoir fighting consisted of about forty thousand troops.

Third, we were able to surround the separated UN units. The Twentieth Army surrounded part of the First Marine Division at Hahwaok-ri from three directions.

To our surprise, however, superiority in numbers and quick encircle-

ment did not bring us a victory. Even though we were able to trap the First
Marine Division and cut it into smaller pieces during the first night, we
could not destroy the division.

On November 28, the Fifty-eighth Division employed its three regiments to attack the divided and surrounded U.S. Marines at Hahwaok-ri.
The battle turned out to be extremely fierce and difficult. The marines were
indeed the toughest fighting unit among the UN forces. After being divided
and surrounded, they immediately formed defensive perimeters at three places
with the help of their tanks. They also constructed a makeshift airstrip for
resupply of ammunition and winter equipment, as well as for shipping out
their wounded. They were able to hold their ground with their superior
firepower and air cover. They exhausted our repeated attempts to annihilate
their companies and smaller units.

On November 29, the marines launched counterattacks in order to break
our encirclement and to connect their scattered units. Our 172nd Regiment
held the highest hill, the key point of the Fifty-eighth Division's line. The
regimental commander gave me an order to position my First Company on
the middle of the hill.

Shortly after noon, the marines attacked our first line of defense at the
bottom of the hill, which was held by the Third Company. I never saw
anything like the marines' combat moves before. When our defense stopped
their charge, the marines just dug in instead of retreating all the way back to
their original positions. They stayed wherever they were stopped, waited for
reinforcements, and then charged again. With each charge they came closer
to our position, until they were no more than two dozen meters away. After
nearly four hours of heavy fighting, the Third Company lost its position, its
captain, and most of its soldiers.

My company now held the first defense line. About 5:00 P.M. the American artillery began to shell our positions, followed by a charge in the center
of our line by more than two hundred marines. Thanks to the hill and the
rocks, we had strong positions in the middle of our line and we defeated the
marines' charge. And thanks to the early darkness of the winter, at about 7:00
P.M. the marines retreated. They did not intend to charge the hill again that
night.

Night at the Chosin Reservoir belonged to us. On November 29, our
172nd Regiment launched a night attack against the marines. Our regiment
recovered some of the positions we lost to the marines during the day, but
we were unable to break through their lines before dawn. Next morning,

The 172nd Regiment, Fifty-eighth Division, CPVF Twentieth Army attacks the First Marine at the Chosin Reservoir, November 1950. (Courtesy of Wang Xuedong)

the marines retook the positions with well-organized counterattacks, strong firing power, and air support.

The battle at Chosin swayed back and forth, but the fighting was always intense. During the three days of fighting, the 172nd Regiment suffered very heavy casualties. Our battalion ran out of ammunition, and we received less than half of our daily ration of food. Also, the temperature dropped to 20 degrees below zero. My company was nearly disabled due to combat casualties and frostbite.

On November 30, the Ninth HQ changed its plan. Instead of attacking the First Marine and Seventh Divisions at the same time, it decided to concentrate its attacks on the Seventh Infantry Division first at Sinhungri. This time the offensive force was much stronger. The Ninth Army Group organized all of its own artillery units and two divisions of the Twenty-seventh Army (the Eightieth and Eighty-first), about twenty-five thousand strong, to attack the three thousand men in the U.S. Seventh Division's Thirty-second Regiment at Sinhungri.

Having suffered heavy casualties and exhausted our supplies of food and ammunition, our Twentieth Army was supposed to be relieved by the Twenty-sixth Army, which had been in reserve. The Twenty-sixth Army, with fresh troops, was assigned the job of eliminating the U.S. First Marine Division at Hahwaok-ri.

But the Twenty-sixth Army never made it to Hahwaok-ri. On December 1, when the Twenty-sixth Army was still about fifty miles away from Hahwaok-ri, the marines broke through our Twentieth Army's encirclement and began their retreat to the south. Unable to stop the marines, our Twentieth Army was ordered to slow down their retreat and stay with them until the Twenty-sixth Army had a chance to catch up and destroy them.

For the next eleven days, the remnants of the Twentieth Army harassed the marines with small-scale attacks. We would ambush them, hit them hard, and then run. During the night, we set up roadblocks in order to stop or delay their southward withdrawal. During the daytime, however, the marines broke our roadblocks and moved south about five to ten miles every day. They traveled on the road while we stalked them in the mountains along both sides of the road.

I had only eighteen men left in my company. On December 5, my company had to combine with two other companies to make a new company. Even though we did not know each other very well, the tough fight and hardships brought us closer together quickly. We shared our food, and we cut up our blankets and gave them to those who suffered from frostbite. The men wrapped their cold, injured hands and feet with our blanket pieces. We thought we could get some supplies, at least some food, left behind by the marines when they pulled out of Hahwaok-ri. But they burned everything before December 7, the day the last marine unit evacuated Hahwaok-ri.

On December 12, the U.S. First Marine Division met the U.S. Third Infantry Division at Hamhung. The Chinese Twenty-sixth Army never managed to catch up and engage the marines, who kept moving southward until they reached the coastal city of Hungnam. On December 24, the First Marine Division left North Korea at Hungnam Harbor and sailed for Pusan.

Following this setback, the CPVF General HQ ordered the Ninth Army Group to disengage and stop the fighting with X Corps. Since the northern mountains end near Hamhung areas, the UN forces could take advantage of their tremendous firepower and mobility on the plains. They also had better air and artillery cover and uninterrupted supplies along the coastal areas. We had to give up our hard pursuit.

We had our own problems. First, we were unable to pursue retreating UN troops because of our unmotorized infantry and lack of supplies. The Twenty-sixth Army delayed their movement because they had to wait for their food and ammunition. We had thought we could collect grain from the local Korean people and ammunition from retreated enemy positions. We were wrong. The Chosin Reservoir area was very lightly populated and could not feed a large force with more than one hundred thousand men.

Second, the Ninth Army Group from South China was not prepared for a cold winter battle in North Korea. The Ninth had more than forty thousand casualties (out of one hundred thousand frontline troops) during its first battle (from November 17 to December 21, 1950). One half of the casualties were from frostbite. For the next three months, the entire Ninth Army Group became a giant field hospital for its wounded and severe frostbite soldiers. The army group was virtually disabled and unable to fight a major engagement until the late spring of 1951.

Third, as the CPVF began to strike south, the tactics of "divide, encircle, and destroy" began to lose effectiveness. Although successful at first, the UN forces rapidly adjusted to these tactics. Also, as our supply lines became extended, the damage to our logistical efforts caused by UN air strikes became increasingly heavy.

For all of these reasons, the Ninth Army Group managed to drive the X Corps south of the 38th Parallel, but it fell short of the original plan of annihilating two divisions of X Corps. By the end of 1950, the badly depleted army group was ordered to return to the Chinese–North Korean border for its replenishment and reorganization.

Part Four

On the Front Lines

Chapter 14

The Hwachon Reservoir Fighting

In early June 1951, only a few weeks before the beginning of the peace talks, General Van Fleet ordered the Eighth Army to advance on a limited front to consolidate the UN positions (Operation Piledriver). A squad leader at the time, Staff Sergeant Charles Bielecki describes the fighting that took place in the Hwachon Reservoir area. At one point, when he felt a push from behind during the fighting, Sergeant Bielecki discovered he had been hit by the body parts of a Chinese soldier. During the action on June 5, the company's first sergeant, Master Sergeant Ben Wilson, won the Medal of Honor for killing thirty-four Chinese soldiers. Sadly, when the fighting concluded a few days later, Sergeant Bielecki was the only member left from his original squad, which had fought in the Chosin Reservoir. All the rest had been killed or wounded.

Staff Sergeant Charles M. Bielecki

I Company, Thirty-first Infantry Regiment, Seventh Infantry Division

ABOUT 3:00 P.M. on June 5, 1951, I (Item) Company was ordered to attack in the Hwachon Reservoir area, which was located in central Korea, north of Chunchon and a little south of the 38th Parallel. Our mission was to take a hill, the largest hill in the area. We began our attack in a valley and started the long climb up the hill.

At the time of the attack, I was the squad leader for the Third Squad in the Second Platoon. We started up the hill while our artillery bombarded the enemy positions. After we had gone about a quarter or perhaps halfway up the hill, the order came down the line to fix bayonets and, moments later, to open fire. By this time our artillery fire had lifted, but we still had not received any enemy fire. It looked like the attack might be a cakewalk.

When we approached the Chinese trenches, however, the real battle began. The fighting was hard, but somehow we managed to take the first line of trenches. We found dead and wounded Chinese all over the place; it was very sad. Most of their wounds were head wounds, because the trenches protected other parts of their bodies from our fire.

When we passed beyond the first line of trenches, members of my squad suddenly warned me about an enemy soldier nearby, one that I didn't see. I turned to my left and, sure enough, there was a Chinese soldier about fifty to sixty feet away. I fired and hit him eight times. When we came to a second line of trenches the fighting became even more intense. The Chinese hit us with everything they had, especially hand grenades, which they threw by the buckets. Fortunately for us, many of their grenades were duds, or I probably wouldn't be around today.

As we approached the second trench, heavy fighting continued, but we did force the Chinese to retreat. During the battle, I looked up at the horizon and saw a rugged-looking figure coming over the top of the ridgeline. When I raised my rifle to fire, the soldier yelled out, "Don't shoot, it's me, Monterosso, don't shoot." Fortunately, I did not. Corporal Monterosso, who was in the Second Squad, had an amazing story to tell. He told us that somehow his entire squad got up on the hill ahead of the rest of us and found themselves surrounded by Chinese soldiers. All of the other members of his squad, including his squad leader, were killed. His squad leader, he said, had his head blown apart by small arms fire. As for himself, he had been literally blown into the air, probably by a grenade. When he landed, he had lost his rifle, his helmet, and didn't have the foggiest idea which direction to run. Fortunately, Monterosso chose the right direction, toward our lines, but he was in pretty bad shape. He had been shot in the leg, he was scared to death, and his clothes were torn and just hanging on his body. The medics evacuated him, and he returned to duty several months later.

While we had reached the crest of the hill and had driven the Chinese back, we soon discovered we had not finished the job—there were Chinese soldiers all around us. That's when Master Sergeant Ben Wilson went into action. Sergeant Wilson was our first sergeant, and normally first sergeants hang around the company commander a little behind the front line. Ben, however, was not the kind of soldier to hang back when fighting was going on; he had to be in the middle of it. Once the fighting started, he became another Sergeant York and took on the entire Chinese army. He shot Chinese, he bayoneted Chinese, and he picked up Chinese grenades and threw them right back at the enemy. Later, another soldier told me he even killed seven Chinese soldiers with a trenching tool, an amazing feat. Altogether, Master Sergeant Wilson was credited with killing thirty-four Chinese soldiers on June 5. Fortunately, his heroic efforts did not go unrewarded, and he later received our nation's highest award, the Medal of Honor.

Another soldier, Staff Sergeant Frank Monfetti, the Fourth Squad leader, was badly wounded on the hill when he got caught in an open area with no cover. The first medic who attempted to save him was fatally wounded. The second medic, after crawling on the ground, finally reached him and managed to drag him back to our line while we gave covering fire. After we got Monfetti to a safe place, we discovered he had been hit sixteen times. Unfortunately, Frank died about 10:30 the next morning. He was a good friend of mine and a very nice guy.

We also lost our platoon leader, Lieutenant Tally Bugs Sheppard, another nice guy. Lieutenant Sheppard was a small town boy who, with his family, had a general merchandise store in Ohio. He was always talking about going back home to his business and his family. Another soldier, Private First Class Barney, received a nasty head wound and had to be evacuated. Somehow, Platoon Sergeant Bill Rowland managed to keep us all together, which was essential, because there were still plenty of Chinese on the hill.

One time, during the fighting, I had an experience I will never forget. Suddenly, I felt as if someone had come up behind me and pushed me, or put a forearm in my back, but when I turned around there was nobody there. Then I looked on the ground. I saw the arm and shoulder of a man; this is what had "pushed" me in the back a few seconds earlier. I don't know how this happened, but I assume the soldier received a direct hit by an artillery or mortar round. I am sure he was Chinese.

The fighting on the hill went on, with much of the combat being hand-to-hand, or at distances of no more than fifteen or twenty feet. At times it was total chaos; we were confused, and I think the Chinese were equally confused. The fighting on June 5 cost us a number of good men, including most of our officers and NCOs.

About one hour into the battle, a ROK unit arrived on the hill to give us some much needed support. The ROK soldiers all wore yellow scarfs, and each had a big yellow insignia on his helmet. Unfortunately, before the ROKs reached the crest of the hill and got into position, the Chinese sent up four red flares, their signal for a counterattack, and started blowing their bugles. When the ROKs saw the flares and heard the bugles, they just took off down the hill, all of them. Fortunately, we had just been supplied with ammunition, which we desperately needed. Most of us had either been out or very nearly out.

Captain Smick, our company commander and a WWII veteran, was severely wounded during the fighting, along with his runner, and First Lieutenant Willard took over the company. Incoming artillery and mortar fire continued to pound the hill while a strong Chinese force attacked our positions. Lieutenant Willard decided that if we tried to hold the hill we would only be slaughtered, especially since the ROKs had bugged out. He gave the order to "back off the hill," but added, "I don't want anybody turning and running." So we backed off the hill as masses of Chinese soldiers poured over the ridgeline and took over our positions. Some of the guys actually did turn and run, despite Lieutenant Willard's order, but most of us kept firing our weapons as we retreated. That same evening we dug into a hill nearby. We remained there for the night, very quiet, because none of us were in a talking mood.

For the next several days we just held our positions, rested, and got ready for the next attack. We also received supplies and replacements. The attack came four days later, on June 9. By this time, I had been promoted from squad leader to assistant platoon sergeant. Sadly, I was the only one left in the squad I had served with in the Chosin Reservoir. The others had either been killed or were wounded and had to be evacuated.

Again we attacked, and again Master Sergeant Ben Wilson took on the entire Chinese army by himself. On June 5 he had been just warming up for June 9. This time, he took out about forty-two Chinese soldiers, using nothing more than his rifle, bayonet, and grenades. Somehow he managed to do all of this without receiving a serious wound. Since no one can receive the Medal of Honor twice, he received the Distinguished Service Cross for his action on June 9. Incidently, we did finally take the hill on the second day. Most of the hard fighting took place on June 9; the next day it rained pretty hard, and the Chinese just took off.

Reflecting on these events years later, I think we could have used more artillery support before we attacked, and perhaps an air strike would have been helpful. But there was no way the Chinese were going to give up that hill without some serious man-to-man fighting.

Chapter 15

Life on the MLR

This marine, Private First Class Bruce Lippert, provides few details about combat operations in Korea; yet, he was wounded twice. He does, however, provide a glimpse of what frontline soldiers had to endure, such as the cold and the rats. Once, while on guard duty and physically exhausted, he pulled the pin on a grenade and held it in his hand to keep awake.

Private First Class Bruce D. Lippert

C Company, Fifth Regiment, First Marine Division

ON MARCH 2, 1952, we left San Diego for Korea on the *Rego*. We arrived in Korea and disembarked on March 27. Almost immediately we found ourselves on a train headed for the front, and then on a truck to our unit. I was assigned to Charlie Company, Fifth Regiment, First Marine Division. My job—machine gunner.

By the time I arrived in Korea both the Communist forces and the UN forces had dug in, and the lines had stabilized in what had become a war of the trenches. This was supposed to be a quiet war, just a "police action," as President Truman called it. For a quiet war, there seemed to be a lot of mortar and artillery shells dropping on us from time to time. On occasions, like when we were at Bunker Hill, the fighting was really tough, and we found ourselves engaged in hand-to-hand combat. We lived in the trenches with the rats, which were some of the largest I had ever seen. Most of the time we spent on guard duty or some work detail. We slept in bunkers made of timbers and sandbags, which were built right in the middle of the trenches.

Back slope of the MLR, Punchbowl, early 1953. (Courtesy of Richard Peters)

Only our shoes came off when we slept; we kept our clothes on night and day, for weeks at a time. Bathing consisted of washing with warm water in a helmet liner, except when we were trucked back to the rear for "Little R&R." On those occasions, about once a month, we could take a shower, get clean clothes, and even do a little shopping at the PX.

Like everyone else who served in Korea, I have a lasting memory of the cold. We wore heavy parkas, thermal "Mickey Mouse" boots, and all kinds of other stuff, but I still couldn't get warm during the winter months. At the same time, I found the summer heat oppressive, mostly because of the high humidity.

During the night, the Chinese repeatedly blew their bugles, even when they had no intention of attacking our lines. It was just one of their gimmicks to make us jumpy. At Christmastime in 1952, they even played Christmas carols over their loudspeakers, to make us homesick I presume. We heard "Silent Night" and all the other well-known carols drifting out over no-man's-land while freezing our butts off thousands of miles from home.

A view from the American MLR looking toward the enemy lines, Punchbowl, early 1953. (Courtesy of Richard Peters)

One thing never changed—we were always dead tired. If we weren't on guard duty, we were repairing bunkers or doing some other damn detail. There were times when I think I would have given six months' pay for one night in a soft, warm bed. Once, when I was totally exhausted and afraid I would fall asleep on guard duty, I actually pulled the pin on a grenade and held it in my hand. I don't really recommend it, but I didn't fall asleep.

I was wounded twice in Korea, the last time in the chest. After a helicopter ride and some emergency medical attention, they put me on a hospital ship and sent me home. I arrived at Treasure Island in March 1953, delighted to be home. I'm proud to have served my country, but this was not an experience I would want to repeat.

Chapter 16

A BAR Man's Story

It is generally recognized that one of the most dangerous jobs in the infantry was to operate a Browning Automatic Rifle (BAR). The following soldier, Sergeant Albert Snyder, did just that prior to becoming a squad leader. Arriving in Korea in April 1951, he saw action during the final months of UN offensive operations, just before the conflict became a stalemated war of the trenches. He also witnessed the implementation of the army's new policy of integrating all black units into regular army units, a policy that sometimes led to racial incidents. After returning to the U.S. in 1952, Sergeant Snyder experienced a warm welcome from a perfect stranger, a contrast to the indifference experienced by most Korean War veterans when they returned.

Sergeant Albert Snyder

I Company, Thirty-first Infantry Regiment, Seventh Infantry Division

IN 1950, I was a twenty-three-year-old single man living in Cumberland, Maryland. In the eyes of my draft board, that made me just right for the army. I entered the army in November 1950, and after training at Camp Pickett, Virginia, I found myself on the USS *General A.E. Anderson* headed for Korea. When the ship pulled out of the harbor near Camp Stoneman, California, an army band on the dock played "So Long It's Been Good to Know You." When we arrived in Yokohama another army band on the dock played "If I Knew You Were Coming I'da Baked a Cake." After processing at Camp Drake, we took a train to Sasebo in southern Japan, then some type of ferry to Pusan, where we disembarked. Next, we climbed aboard a Korean train with straight-back wooden seats that took us north to Chechon, and we were practically at the front. After a truck ride, I wound up in I (Item) Company, Third Battalion, Thirty-first Regiment, Seventh Division. It was early April 1951.

At the time I arrived, Item Company was about 75 percent of its regular strength, due to the terrible losses it suffered at the Chosin Reservoir in late November and early December 1950. Only about 20 percent of the men that had been on the Item Company roster in mid-November 1950 were still with the company. When I got there in April, the company consisted of Regular Army (RA) personnel transferred from the First Battalion, WWII reservists (ERs) that began arriving in late December, and draftees that were just beginning to arrive.

I was assigned to the Second Squad, Third Platoon, which at the time consisted of only three members—Sergeant Ortiz, the squad leader; Corporal Harold Newcombe, the BAR man; and Private First Class Glenn Black, a rifleman. Ortiz and Newcombe had transferred from the First Battalion. Private First Class Black had been wounded in the Chosin Reservoir fighting and had just returned from a hospital stay in Japan.

In mid-April, a few days after I arrived, two men in Item Company were seriously wounded during a firefight with enemy troops. I wasn't involved in the firefight, but Harold Newcombe and I were assigned to accompany the two wounded men and four Korean litter bearers as an armed escort against enemy guerrillas operating in the area. Actually, to expedite the trip to the battalion aid station, we became litter bearers when the Koreans bearers became exhausted. One of the men had a very visible back wound, and the company medics had lashed him face down on the litter. The terrain was very rough, and I found the job of serving as a litter bearer utterly exhausting. About halfway to the aid station, one of the wounded men kept moaning and muttering, "Please, please, please." When we finally arrived at the aid station both men were still alive, but unconscious. I didn't know either man, but to this day I wonder if they made it.

By mid-May 1951, enough replacements had arrived to bring Item Company up to almost full strength. Sergeant Ortiz had the luxury of commanding a squad consisting of eight men (a squad at full strength had twelve). The new men in the Second Squad were Private Andrew McLaughlin, Private Donald Queen, Private Jasper Tobey, Private Arthur Lancaster, and myself.

In early June, Item Company was engaged in heavy fighting in the Punchbowl area at Hwachon-Myon, near the Hwachon Reservoir. We managed to drive the Chinese out of their first trench line, but unfortunately, a

Corporal Albert Snyder, I Company, Thirty-first Regiment, Seventh Division, operating the BAR on Hill 1073, October 1951. (Courtesy of Albert Snyder)

member of my squad, Private McLaughlin, was killed in the fighting, and Privates Queen and Lancaster were wounded. I didn't fare too well myself. At the time, I was the BAR man for the squad and was carrying a ton of ammunition. When I jumped into one of the empty Chinese trenches, my foot accidentally landed on an unexploded American grenade. Somehow, perhaps because I was so weighted down with ammo, I severely sprained my ankle and had to be evacuated. After hobbling down to the aid station by myself, they took me by ambulance to a MASH unit, and eventually to an army hospital in Japan. I returned to Item Company in late July, after an absence of about seven weeks, but with no Purple Heart. No skin was broken, so I guess I didn't qualify.

In late September 1951, Item Company occupied a hill we knew as "Hill 1073." Frankly, I don't even remember where we were at the time; the hills in Korea all looked the same to me anyway. When we started up the long trail to the top, we discovered enemy mortars had zeroed in on some parts of the trail, which received incoming rounds periodically. About two-thirds of the way up, a barrage came in about two hundred feet in front of the Third Platoon. We all dove for cover, and when the barrage lifted, we got up and ran forward. Everyone in the Third Platoon made it okay, but we passed two dead soldiers that were caught standing up by the first rounds. One, I learned later, was an artillery forward observer.

On October 4, our company commander, Lieutenant McGuire, led the entire company on a combat patrol near Hill 1073. Suddenly there was a loud explosion and someone hollered, "Look out for that log." When the "log" landed near our squad, we discovered it was Sergeant Richardson's leg. He was walking ahead of us and had stepped on a box mine, which blew off his entire leg from the thigh down. His boot was still on his leg. A mortar blast killed Sergeant Drouillard as well, a squad leader in the Third Platoon. Several others were also wounded on the patrol.

Not long after I arrived in early April, we began to receive our first black soldiers in the company. This was in keeping with the new policy of eliminating all separate black units and integrating the men into regular army units. While the process generally went pretty smoothly, there were some problems. We had one with our assistant platoon sergeant, a bigot (who shall remain nameless) from Atlanta, Georgia. While we were in reserve a black man, Sergeant Williams, was promoted to platoon sergeant. In November, when we moved up on Heartbreak Ridge for the second time, our assistant platoon sergeant had to share the Third Platoon Headquarters bunker with Sergeant Williams, and he made it clear he wasn't happy about the situation. He would "rather go over and sleep with the Chinese," he said. When word of this got back to Sergeant Williams and went up the chain of command, our "assistant platoon sergeant" became an "assistant squad leader." He did manage to hang on to his rank, but it was still a demotion.

On October 26, 1951, the entire Third Platoon, led by Lieutenant Culver, went on a patrol about eight or nine hundred yards in front of the MLR, which was strung out along the top of Heartbreak Ridge. Sergeant Telly served as our squad leader (Sergeant Ortiz had rotated home), and I still operated the BAR. As we approached a suspected fortified enemy outpost, the point man, Private First Class Clyde Rampart, was hit by hail of grenades and wounded. Lieutenant Culver sent him back to the MLR and made Private First Class Willie "Frenchie" De Herrera from Colorado the new point man. We had advanced about ten yards when De Herrera and a black soldier who had just arrived, Private Peters, were struck by small arms

Preparing to fire a 57mm recoilless rifle. (Courtesy of Forty-fifth Infantry Division Museum)

fire and grenades. Both fell seriously wounded. To bring supporting fire on the outpost, Private First Class Roland Wakenight and his assistant gunner, Private First Class Freed, set up the machine gun on a small knob about fifty yards from the enemy positions. At the same time the platoon came under rifle fire from enemy snipers.

While the platoon was pinned down by enemy fire, Private James Sevier, who was only seventeen years old and married, exposed himself to enemy fire by making three attempts to reach Private First Class De Herrera, who lay wounded just over the crest of a hill. On the first attempt Private Sevier was beaten back by heavy small arms fire; on the second attempt he was thrown back by a concussion grenade. Finally, on the third attempt, he made it over the hill and found De Herrera, but he had already died from his wounds. Private Sevier lifted De Herrera's body over his shoulder and carried him back over the crest of the hill, where he got help from others. For his bravery under fire, Lieutenant Culver recommended Private Sevier for the Distinguished Service Cross. It never came through, however, and I never learned the reason.

After our machine guns and 57mm recoilless rifle had silenced the snipers, the rest of us in the platoon stormed the hill and took the enemy outpost. Then we recovered our dead and wounded and pulled back to the MLR. In addition to De Herrera, we lost Wakenight, Freed, and West, and a number of others were wounded.

In late January 1952, the Thirty-first Regiment was deployed on a series of connected ridges in the very rugged mountain terrain near Heartbreak Ridge. By this time, I had been promoted from BAR man to squad leader (the sergeant's stripes came a few weeks later). There were rumors that the regiment was going to be relieved shortly. When this happened, it was the usual procedure for the relieving unit to send an advance party a few days before the switch took place. My two-man bunker was located in a position that commanded a strategic view of the enemy positions about fifteen hundred yards away across a valley.

One sunny afternoon, when the temperature warmed up to about fifteen degrees above zero, the Third Platoon leader, Lieutenant Kleinfield, escorted what I assumed was an officer from the rumored relief unit to my bunker and adjoining trench. While the "officer" didn't have any bars or insignia on his outer garment, that wasn't at all unusual for officers on the front lines. They remained in the trench for about forty-five minutes observing the enemy positions, which at the time were receiving fire from our 75mm recoilless rifle team. I also noticed that the soldier without insignia seemed unusually relaxed and nonchalant for an infantry officer or a high ranking noncom. He needed a shave, wasn't wearing a helmet, and wasn't carrying a weapon—all very unusual.

The next day, while I was in the chow line on the reverse slope, I saw the sloppy "officer" again, about four or five men ahead of me. Only then did I learn from one of the other guys in the line the name of this mysterious person. It was Bill Mauldin, the famous World War II cartoonist and creator of "Willie and Joe." Two or three days later Mauldin accompanied Lieutenant Kleinfield and a reinforced squad from the Third Platoon on a routine night ambush patrol. I guess he wanted to get the feel of combat for his cartoons and stories.

In January 1952, a patrol from Item Company was ambushed and several men were killed and wounded. Two bodies were left out in no-man's-land until the next night, when they were recovered by a patrol of volunteers, including Jim Sevier and Clyde Rampart from the Third Platoon. Later, Rampart told me the dead GIs had been stripped of their boots and most of their outer garments, and were frozen stiff in awkward positions. As a result, they were very hard to handle, and there was a lot of slipping and falling before they got the bodies to the MLR.

Finally, after about ten months in Korea and thirty-six points, on February 4, 1952, I left Item Company on rotation back to the States. I went home the way I arrived, by boat. We started at Inchon, disembarked at Sasebo, then boarded the *Pvt. Sadao S. Munemori* for Seattle. I flew by commercial airline from Seattle to Camp Meade, Maryland (now Fort Meade), which was close to my hometown of Cumberland, Maryland. It was great to be home again.

While I think most Korean veterans were generally received with indifference by the public when they came home, I did have one very pleasant experience. Not long after arriving at Camp Meade for processing, some of us with passes decided to go into nearby Baltimore and visit Baltimore's famous "Block." After spending some time at the Hi-Ho Club, someone unknown to us picked up our bar tab. I figure it was probably some old vet who recognized our ribbons and knew we were Korean War veterans. Regardless of who the person was, it was a nice gesture, and it left us with a good feeling.

Chapter 17

First Combat

This story is about a WWII veteran sergeant, experienced and knowledgeable in all forms of small arms combat, and a totally green private first class (one of the authors of this book), who faced an enemy attack for the first time. The story reveals the value of combat experience as the sergeant calmly tries to tell the nervous private what he should do in reacting to the attack. This brief firefight is also typical of the kind of fighting that took place after both the Communist and UN forces had ceased major offensive operations. In this skirmish the Chinese aimed only at getting into the UN trenches, killing as many GIs and ROK soldiers as possible, and returning to their own lines; it was not their intent to capture and hold the UN positions permanently. Nevertheless, such minor engagements, when repeated many times across the peninsula over a period of many months, claimed thousands of lives on both sides.

Private First Class Richard Peters

A Company, Fifth Regimental Combat Team

SOMETIME LATE IN March 1953, we received our orders to go back on the hill, somewhere in the Punchbowl area. I was in the Fourth Squad, Third Platoon, A Company, Fifth RCT, and had been in Korea only since January. While I had been on the front line before, I had yet to see a Chinese soldier or experience any real combat.

We reached the top of the hill after a tough climb, and Corporal Boucher, our squad leader, showed us our guard positions. I stood guard on the last post on our right flank, only about fifteen or twenty yards from the next unit. The next unit, however, was a ROK unit. At the time I attached no particular significance to this, but Sergeant Riewe, our platoon sergeant,

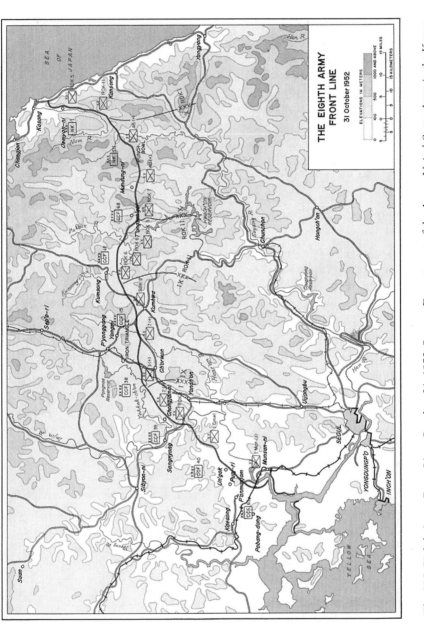

The U.S. Eighth Army Front Line, October 31, 1952. Source: Department of the Army, *United States Army in the Korean War: Truce Tent and Fighting Front* (Washington, D.C.: U.S. Government Printing Office, 1988), Map V.

certainly did. He knew our positions before we left for the hill, and had predicted that we were likely to take a hit this time.

In general, I was never very fond of sergeants, but Master Sergeant Riewe was an unusual and remarkable sergeant in many ways. He was totally in charge of the platoon, and while he could roar like most sergeants, he seldom found it necessary. Even if he spoke softly, his voice exuded authority. He commanded much fear from those below his rank, and respect from those both below and above him.

Normally, as a private first class, I would have had little contact with a platoon sergeant like Sergeant Riewe. We had just finished about six weeks in reserve, however, where we trained, dug drainage ditches in the company area, and all the other pleasantries reserved for army privates. By chance, Sergeant Riewe chose to bunk with the Fourth Squad, and my cot happened to be very near his in the squad tent. For this reason I came to know something about him as a person, as well as a sergeant. He liked to chat, which we often did at night before slipping into our sleeping bags. He frequently talked about his experiences in WWII, the army in Korea, and sometimes just life in general. He was better read than most sergeants, and enjoyed conversing about history and similar subjects. This appealed to me since I was a bookish person with some college, but I was also totally unencumbered with the slightest trace of soldierly qualities, and furthermore, had no particular desire to acquire them. Sergeant Riewe, I think, saw me as something of a challenge; if he could make a soldier out of me he could make a soldier out of anyone.

In every way, Sergeant Riewe was the epitome of the ideal combat soldier. Physically tough, tall and straight as an arrow, he carried not one ounce of fat. His knowledge of small arms weaponry was so thorough he frequently gave demonstrations in training sessions for other units. Trained as a paratrooper, he had seen action during many of the major battles of WWII, including Bastogne. Highly decorated, he had received every major decoration awarded by the army except the Medal of Honor, plus a number of decorations from foreign governments. He was actually a German, but fortunately he fought on the Allied side. We used to joke that if he had fought on the German side the Allies might have lost the war.

Sergeant Riewe saw soldiering as a necessary and noble profession, one that required courage and a deep commitment. Career soldiers who lacked these qualities, and who took advantage of their rank to ensure their personal comfort, were often the targets of his sharp tongue. Soldiers were

Private First Class Richard Peters, Fifth RCT, Punchbowl, early 1953. (Courtesy of Richard Peters)

supposed to fight, not perform some cushy job well behind the lines. I always suspected Sergeant Riewe was one of those rare individuals who actually enjoyed the thrill of combat, although that might be going too far. He expected much from the officers, and he could be very critical of them if they failed to live up to his standards. One evening he told the story of how he once went all the way through Officer's Candidate School, graduated at the top of his class, and then informed his superiors on graduation day he had decided to remain a noncom. It's a crazy story, but somehow it kind of fits Sergeant Riewe.

Even more than the others, I think Sergeant Riewe had a real problem adjusting to the "limited" war in Korea. He wanted to fight to "win," like in WWII, but by 1953, the Korean War had become a stalemated war of the trenches, fought according to rules made in Washington. He also disliked the rotation system, which permitted soldiers to return home just about the time they had learned to perform their jobs with proficiency. Sometimes he would compare the army in Korea with the army in WWII, but always with a melancholy tone in his voice.

All of this chitchat ceased, however, once we went back on the hill in late March. Everything went pretty smoothly the first night on line, although I do remember pulling about nine hours of guard duty, which was a record for me. Very quickly, however, we discovered a problem, especially to Sergeant Riewe. The ROKs on the right flank of the Third Platoon frequently moved back and forth in the trenches between their positions and our positions, apparently for no particular reason. Sergeant Riewe would have none of this, and he had barbed wire stretched across the trench between our last guard post and the first ROK guard post. It served its purpose, and the ROKs remained in their own sector.

Life in the trenches for the next ten days or so was pretty routine. We received incoming mortar rounds on occasions, but nothing very heavy. The Fourth Squad bunker, however, built right in the trench, was a disaster. It leaked like a sieve, the commo wire beds were too short for us to stretch out fully, we couldn't stand up without bending, and the place was lousy with rats. Sergeant Riewe immediately proclaimed the facility unacceptable and ordered the construction of a new bunker. Since the Fourth Squad would occupy it, we got to build it. Unfortunately, all the trees in the area had been cut down or blasted away by shell fire, so we had to haul our timbers from the main supply road, a considerable distance away. We needed the new bunker, but we didn't find building it a whole lot of fun, especially after standing guard duty at night.

The rat problem was not so easily solved; rats were naturally attracted to the bunkers for warmth and food. They were both numerous and huge, and they scurried about the bunker as if they owned the place. Whenever we saw a rat we grabbed our bayonets and tried to stab it, but we were arguably more dangerous to each other than to the rats. Only Junitz, a steeplejack from Chicago, had success. While on guard duty one day, I heard a piercing yell. It was Junitz; he had just stabbed a rat and wanted everyone in the battalion to know it. I think this was our only kill, making Junitz a kind of local hero.

Since all the action was at night, daytime guard duty was about the easiest duty we pulled. There really was little to do except to stare out into a bleak and treeless no-man's-land and wish we could be somewhere else. Frequently, air force jets provided a nice show and helped relieve our boredom by dropping napalm bombs on the Chinese MLR. Once in a while, I pulled a paperback out of my pocket, but only rarely. Sergeant Riewe had no appreciation for this sort of thing.

After about two weeks on line, we still had not received the hit that Sergeant Riewe had predicted, but we did have plenty of noise. Our artillery fired day and night, the ROKs rattled their machine guns incessantly for no particular reason, and the Chinese in the valley blew their bugles during the night, but did not attack. So far the Fourth Squad had even escaped going out on patrol, although the same could not be said for some of the other squads in A Company. Then, about 3:00 one night in early April, the Chinese attacked.

At the time of the attack I was on guard at my usual post, the one next to the ROKs. I thought I saw movement, directly to my front, but I wasn't certain so I didn't report anything. There had been a number of false reports of attacks called in, and I didn't want to test Sergeant Riewe's patience with another false one. It also concerned me that neither Junitz on my left nor the ROKs on my right gave any indication that they saw anything. Perhaps I had been wrong.

After waiting and watching a few more minutes, however, I saw more movement, around forty yards directly to my front. Fortunately, there was a good moon that night, and this time I clearly saw four or five men dressed in white snow suits moving slowly up the hill. They would crawl forward, pause for a short time, then move forward again. They were headed straight for my post, and I began to get pretty nervous.

As instructed when we saw enemy soldiers, I called the Third Platoon

CP and talked to Sergeant Riewe. At first he seemed dubious, and asked me if I was certain about the Chinese. When I convinced him they were real, he proceeded to give me instructions in a very clear and calm voice. When I suggested throwing grenades, he even reminded me to get the grenades ready by squeezing the pins together. Then I saw more movement and I told Sergeant Riewe I had to hang up. He promised to be in the trenches promptly.

By this time the Chinese had moved closer to our MLR, probably no more than twenty-five yards from my guard post. I thought that was close enough, especially since no one else seemed aware of their presence, so I threw an HE (high explosive) grenade. It landed on target, exploded, and the Chinese dropped to the ground. For the next several minutes they remained in place, or at least I didn't see any more movement. The grenade, I thought, would surely alert Junitz, only about fifteen yards to my left, or the ROKs on my right, but it did not. I remember trying to warn Junitz in a kind of loud whisper, but he never heard me. (He had a hearing problem, probably the result of his job as a steeplejack.) And the ROKs, who normally fired at everything, were as quiet as church mice. I felt very alone.

More than anything else, I wanted to "light up" the area so that I could share my problem with the others. I could have tossed a flare for that purpose, but instead I threw a WP (white phosphorous) grenade. At that moment I could not actually see any Chinese soldiers, so I just threw it where they had dropped to the ground a few minutes earlier. The WP grenade worked well, and for a few precious seconds the area lit up nicely.

Then came the big surprise. Instead of the four or five Chinese soldiers I had reported to Sergeant Riewe, about twenty to twenty-five suddenly jumped to their feet. They moved up the hill and to my right, toward the ROK positions, but not unnoticed. Now everyone saw them and the entire front opened up. Both Junitz and the ROKs blazed away with their machine guns.

My first instinct was to throw more grenades, but then I messed up. I had not yet taken the time to squeeze the pins together, as Sergeant Riewe had advised me to do only minutes earlier, and the pins didn't pull out as expected. Instead of fighting the problem, I grabbed my M-1 rifle and emptied two clips before they were out of sight. The heavy firing lasted only a minute or two, and then it was all over. By this time Riewe had arrived, and he immediately called in mortar and artillery fire as the Chinese fell back into the valley. I heard later he was pretty upset that no one had set off the napalm drums placed in front of the MLR.

Nothing really happened during the remaining hours of the night, but I think we were all pretty jumpy and afraid that something might happen. I actually learned nothing from the other guys until I got off guard duty, about daylight. Even then I got only brief reports because my squad leader, Corporal Boucher, told me I was going on Little R&R and must leave immediately. This came as a total surprise because another guy in the squad had been scheduled. As a result I spent the entire day several miles behind the line, where I showered, loaded up on candy and cookies, and just took it easy. The war suddenly seemed far away.

On the way back, we ran into a late snowstorm, and the truck driver slowed down to a crawl. It was about 10:00 P.M. before I rejoined my squad. Only then did I learn the details of what had really happened the night before. Altogether we had recovered the bodies of only three Chinese soldiers. I had expected more, but they may have taken some of their dead or wounded down the hill, especially after the first grenade exploded. A map that Boucher removed from one of the dead soldiers indicated they had intended to hit the ROK positions on our right, but had missed by a few yards. They knew, however, the ROK and American units joined together at this point, which is why they chose it to attack.

What I learned next came as a shock. The Chinese had actually penetrated the ROK trenches and killed a ROK machine gunner. More serious, from my perspective, one of them was cutting on the barbed wire Sergeant Riewe had installed near my guard post that separated the American and ROK positions. Although the wire was only about fifteen feet from my guard post, a bend in the trench prevented me from seeing it. Besides, I was concentrating on the Chinese in front of me. It really hadn't occurred to me some of them could have made it into our trenches. Fortunately for me, a ROK soldier shot and killed the Chinese soldier while he was cutting on the wire. Had the wire not been there, the Chinese soldier would have moved quickly through the trenches and almost assuredly surprised me from behind. I suddenly found myself grateful both to the ROKs, for killing the Chinese soldier, and to Sergeant Riewe, for having the foresight to install the wire. He may have intended it as a barrier for the ROKs, but it also worked for the Chinese. Sergeant Riewe may very well have had this in mind as well.

Although I remained in Korea until after the truce, I never again fired my rifle at an enemy soldier. A short time after this action took place, I was unexpectedly transferred to First Battalion Headquarters Company (probably because I could type), and my life as a frontline soldier came to an end.

At the time I was pleased with the transfer, but in the weeks ahead, I felt an unexpected sense of guilt over leaving a line company for the relative safety of a job at battalion headquarters company. I attribute most of this to Sergeant Riewe, whose lectures on soldiering still rang in my ears; he thought everyone should be in the trenches. I never felt quite guilty enough to volunteer for a line outfit, however, although I did think about it from time to time. Perhaps it's just as well. On June 12, just a few weeks later, A Company suffered nearly 60 percent causalities in one night defending Outpost Harry.

Chapter 18

Outpost Harry

Between June 10 and June 18, 1953, just weeks before the end of the war, the Chinese made a determined attempt to take Outpost Harry, one of a series of outposts in the central section of the front. The defense of the outpost was assigned to the U.S. Third Division and its attached units, the Fifth RCT and the Greek Expeditionary Force. Although the battle is unknown to most Americans, the intensity of the fighting equaled the most bitterly fought battles of the war. Each night a single company defended the outpost but suffered such high casualties (59 percent average) that on the following night it would be replaced by another company. The battle is typical of the kind of fighting that took place toward the end of the war, when the Chinese increased the frequency of their attacks, mostly against outposts, primarily for the purpose of strengthening their bargaining position in the peace negotiations. In the following story, Private First Class James Davis arrived in Korea just in time for the fighting on Outpost Harry, a battle in which he was severely wounded. The reader will notice he has nothing but praise for the doctors and nurses who cared for him during his recovery.

Private First Class James "Red" Davis

E Company, Fifteenth Infantry Regiment, Third Infantry Division

IN MAY 1952, I graduated from a small country high school near the town of Mount View, in southwest Oklahoma. At the time, I had lived my entire life in a farming community with my mom and dad, plus my three brothers and three sisters. I had no idea how much my life would be changed in the next two years by the war in Korea.

I spent the summer working on the farm as usual, but by fall, I was ripe

Evacuating a wounded soldier, Punchbowl, early 1953. (Courtesy of Richard Peters)

for the draft. Then one day I received my draft notice, and on October 23, 1952, I was inducted into the army. After basic training at Camp Roberts, California, the army shipped me to Korea, where I arrived in May 1953. I was assigned to the Fifteenth Regiment in the Third Infantry Division.

Actually, the Korean War was nearly over, although there was no way we could have known this at the time. For the past year or so, both sides had pretty well stayed in their trenches, and the fighting was seldom on the front pages of the newspapers. The truce negotiations had been on and off so much nobody paid much attention to them. As it turned out, the negotiating teams were actually getting close to an agreement by the time I arrived in Korea. At the same time, the fighting had actually picked up. Most of this fighting took place on "outposts," ugly, treeless hills and mountains located well in front of our Main Line of Resistance (MLR). While the Communists lost thousands of men trying to capture these outposts, we also lost of lot of men trying to defend them.

Outpost Harry was typical of these outposts, and the Third Division was assigned to defend the hill. I arrived in Korea just in time for the battle, which was one of the most intense of the entire war (even though the war had only a few months to go).

Outpost Harry was located pretty much in the middle of Korea, in the area known as the Iron Triangle. The hill is nearly 1,300 feet high, greater than any of the other hills we controlled in the area, and commanded a good view of the enemy terrain and attacks on our frontline positions. Unfortunately, the Chinese forces held the highest ground, called "Star Hill," about 350 yards from Outpost Harry. So when we were on Harry, the Chinese were looking right down our throats.

When I arrived at the Third Division MLR in May 1953, I could easily see the outpost to the north of our line. A short time after I arrived, I was assigned to one of the units on Outpost Harry. Right away I met my sergeant and my lieutenant, a Lieutenant Brown. I will never forget what Lieutenant Brown said to me that night: *"We will hold this hill at all costs, even if this means your life. If you run, I will shoot you or someone else will."*

That was my introduction to Outpost Harry. At the time, I thought this was pretty strong talk on the part of the lieutenant, but I wanted to live and stay around awhile, so there was nothing to do but listen and obey orders.

My first stay on Outpost Harry lasted about ten days and nights, just before the Chinese attacks began. During this time, I remember the Chinese playing loud western music over their loudspeakers, and some gal in a sexy voice pleading for us to come over to their side, where, she promised, "We have beautiful girls and maids and you will never have to work again." We had no hot meals, only C-rations from tin cans, but I did learn to like fruit cocktail. Sleep was hard to come by, maybe two hours out of twenty-four, and then only during the day. And since it rained day and night, the trenches were full of mud and water. While the Chinese made no major effort to take the hill during this period, as they would a few days later, they dropped plenty of artillery and mortar rounds on us. I had two lucky near misses. One Chinese mortar round left two holes in my helmet and another tore up my flak jacket. But since my skin was barely nicked, no Purple Heart. I didn't complain.

After ten days on Outpost Harry, I went back to our MLR, where duty was more routine, working on trenches and stuff like that. But we did manage to get a little more rest. I also remember we got fried eggs for breakfast—what a treat!

The real battle for Outpost Harry began during the night of June 10, 1953, when the Chinese mounted a major attack on the hill. At the time I was still on our MLR, but not for long. Within hours I found myself and about a dozen other GIs in a half-track headed for the hill. It was only about a mile from our MLR to the backside of Harry, but it seemed much longer. Perhaps the incoming mortar rounds had something to do with this.

Once we had reached the top of Outpost Harry, we were thrown immediately into the battle as a part of E Company. Earlier that night, huge numbers of Chinese soldiers had attacked the hill, and some of them had managed to get into our trenches. The fighting was bitter hand-to-hand combat, and it went on all night long. There were wounded and dead bodies everywhere—a very chilling experience. I remember hearing one of our wounded men calling for "Mom" in a low, weak voice, but we couldn't help him because the place was crawling with enemy soldiers.

Finally, by daylight on the morning of June 11, we had managed to push the Chinese off the hill, or so we thought. Then suddenly, I saw an enemy soldier emerge from a bunker, probably no more than fifteen feet away. Fortunately, I got off a quick shot with my M-1 and he dropped to the ground. But we knew there could easily be other Chinese soldiers nearby. So, with three other GIs, all volunteers, we searched the trenches and bunkers looking for more Chinese still on the hill. Mortar shells landed all around us, but somehow none of us were hit. Finally, we came to an old bunker that seemed to be secure. But we were wrong; the Chinese opened up with an automatic weapon. Bullets went everywhere, and some of them hit the femur of my right leg two times and ricocheted around the bone. Miraculously, the bullets did not break the bone. The doctor told me later that he couldn't understand how I managed to take the hit and escape without a broken leg.

While I was lying on the ground bleeding and hurting, my buddies tied a tourniquet on my leg and at the same time watched out for enemy soldiers. Although the Chinese kept dropping mortar rounds, some of which landed very close, the guys never left me until a medic had arrived. This took awhile, because the first medic who tried to reach me got hit and didn't make it. Later, two other medics were sent to pick me up, and they finally reached me, despite having to go through heavy sniper fire. They put me on a stretcher and began the tough job of getting me to a safety zone. On two different occasions the sniper fire was so heavy I begged them to put me down and run for cover. They actually did this at times, but they always came back to pick me up. Finally, the medics got me down the hill and put me in a jeep for transportation to an aid station. As the jeep pulled away I remember seeing a tank that had been knocked out with dead crew members

Medics carrying stretchers and dressed in white outer clothing, commonly worn when snow covered the ground. (Courtesy of Forty-fifth Infantry Division Museum)

scattered about. Mortar rounds kept coming in as we moved along, some hitting the road, but we finally made it to a safe place behind the hill. When they lifted my stretcher from the jeep I heard a captain tell the medic who had brought me out not to go back to the hill; it was just too dangerous. What followed I will never forget. The medic, without hesitation, ignored the captain's orders, climbed back in his jeep, and headed back to Outpost Harry to bring out more wounded soldiers. I never knew him nor learned what happened to him; he could very easily have been killed. But I hope with all my heart that he made it out of Korea okay. To me, he was a hero.

Next, they piled a bunch of us who were wounded into a truck and hauled us off. After a short ride, I remember finding myself in a tent surrounded by wounded soldiers and medical workers of all types. The doctors looked over my wounds, gave me medication and emergency help, and put me on a hospital train for treatment at an army hospital somewhere in Korea. By this time I had lost consciousness, so I really don't remember much about anything.

At the army hospital the doctors discovered I had gangrene in my leg. "Get this man to a hospital in Japan—now!" one of the doctors said. So the army moved me again, this time by air, to another hospital on one of the islands south of the Japanese mainland. I had emergency surgery almost as soon as I arrived. I recall how much my body was beginning to stink as a result of the gangrene. Fortunately, the surgery went okay, and I recovered in the peaceful environment of a hospital. During the month or so I spent in the hospital, I saw dozens of doctors and nurses work many long hours to take care of the sick and wounded. They were very dedicated people, and they proved their love and kindness toward their patients many times and in many ways.

While in the hospital I had lots of time to think, and many thoughts entered my mind about the war and my experiences. Why is it, I wondered, that young men in the prime of life have to die fighting wars in far-off places trying to kill people they don't even know. I thanked the Lord for His presence through it all and for delivering me safely.

When I finally recovered from my wounds enough to return to duty, the army sent me to Sendai, Japan. There I was assigned to a military police unit and placed on limited duty. I spent the remainder of my army time there, mostly answering the phone and keeping a log book. The job was pretty routine and even boring at times, but after Outpost Harry, I didn't complain.

Chapter 19

A ROK Lieutenant Survives the Bloody Ridges

Lee Chan Shik was born in Gansuh-gun, Pyongannam-do Province, in northern Korea. He emigrated to South Korea after the liberation in 1945. After the Korean War broke out, he joined the ROK Army as a student volunteer and was commissioned a second lieutenant in 1951. During the war, he served as a platoon leader in the Fifth Infantry Division of the ROK Army. He retired from the army in 1981 as a brigadier general and is one of South Korea's most decorated war veterans. Lieutenant Lee's story is notable for its emotionalism, his eagerness for combat, and his absolute determination to set an example of bravery for his men.

Lieutenant Lee Chan Shik

Eleventh Company, Third Battalion, Fifth Infantry Division, ROK Army

IT WAS AUGUST 1951, the second year of the war. The regiment would move to Yanggoo for an operation to drive the Chinese troops off the strategic Hill 983 (the Sooribong). The roar of artillery in the distance was becoming louder by minutes as if it foretold the coming battle.

Captain Jung addressed his officers. His words were simple and direct. "Until now we undertook operations in tandem with the U.S. Army units. But this operation is for the Thirty-sixth Regiment alone. We should remember that how we do in this battle will reflect on the honor of the entire ROK Army.

"Lieutenant Lee, I know this is your first battle as a platoon leader. The first battle is most important to any officer. If you are not successful in the first battle, you are likely to experience more frustrations later." Most likely, the CO's advice was based on his own experience as a rookie.

"The PLA unit we are facing is known to be one of the best," Captain Jung continued. "We believe that its position is well fortified and surrounded by extensive minefields. In combat, you can't afford to be timid, but neither can you afford to be too reckless either. Don't put your men in danger unless it is absolutely essential. Remember the simple fact that they are all precious sons to their parents." After stating more details of the operation, he embraced each of us one by one.

On August 16, 1951, the company moved to the regiment's main line of resistance (MLR) to undertake preparations for the attack. The main hill, Hill 983, was connected by ridges to a number of other hills (731, 773, 852, 935, and 940). The formation was highly advantageous to the defenders but posed a major challenge to an attacker.

For the last two months, Chinese troops had worked hard to fortify their position on the ridge. The Chinese considered the ridge strategically important, and placed a high priority on defending it. The loss of the ridge would allow us to put their main supply routes under our effective surveillance. The defense of the hill was the joint responsibility of the Chinese troops, who had established their field of fire at the middle point between Hills 983 and 940. We estimated the Chinese had deployed five battalions in the area. Our Sixth Division (a reserve of the ROK Fifth Corps) moved to the rear with orders to be ready for immediate intervention when needed. The Chinese had built a fan-shape system of trenches and bunkers. Some feed trenches and bunkers had covers of large logs. For key locations they built bunkers fortified with concrete.

At the MLR, Captain Jung maintained his customary calm and confidence. After conveying to us the encouragement of Colonel Hwang, the regimental commander, the captain took all of his platoon leaders to a low ridge that faced Hill 983 directly. There he further discussed our assault methods.

"We must take that hill!" the captain told us. When I first saw the Sooribong on August 16, I couldn't help but think how dignified it looked. I even thanked God for giving us such a good-looking hill. Inevitably, my thoughts drifted back to my hometown. . . .

My hometown is Pyongannam-do Province, Gansuh-gun, Bansuk-myun, Hasa-ri in northern Korea. My family was fairly well-off and one of the best-known Christian families in the region. Both my grandfather and father were active in their church and the independence movement. Naturally, the family had to endure harsh treatment from the Japanese colonial government. When the Communists replaced the Japanese after the national liberation in 1945, we suffered even worse oppression. My father chose to move to Seoul in South Korea and start anew.

After the war broke out, I fled along with ten high school classmates to the south and voluntarily joined the ROK Army. On August 1, 1950, I entered the army's noncommissioned officer's school in Gujeri. Within a few weeks I was a squad leader for the Sixth Company, Thirteenth Regiment, Eleventh ROK Division. As a leader of an eight-man squad, I fought virtually nonstop against Communist guerrillas in the southern provinces. Around the end of October, a guerrilla force attacked the Sixth Company. The captain immediately ordered the company to counterattack. I led my squad to the enemy position against heavy small arms fire. Our relentless dash eventually forced the enemy to retreat. Pursuing the guerrillas, we killed sixteen and captured two, while we suffered only two light injuries. From this early encounter, I learned that the best way to defeat the enemy is a bold, focused attack. During the next few months, my squad scored many small and large victories, which made me quite well known in the battalion.

In early March 1951, Major Rho, the battalion commander, summoned me to his office. I had no idea what he had in mind.

"You have good potential for an officer. I believe you are too good to remain a squad leader. I want you to report to the divisional headquarters in Namwon and take the examination to become an officer."

I was surprised by Major Rho's official recommendation because it was so sudden. Nonetheless, I had no objection whatsoever. After passing the examination, I was transferred to the Army Comprehensive School, a wartime service academy for the ROK Army. I knew well the reason why platoon leaders were called cannon fodder. Yet, I was superbly confident of my own ability in combat.

The Army Comprehensive School's training was rough and hard, which could be expected, because we had so much to learn about becoming a field officer in such a short period of time. It was so demanding that even I struggled, although I had a larger and stronger body than the others as a result of my high school boxing career. The program included rifle and weapon training, and various combat courses. On July 21, 1951, after four months' training, I was commissioned a second lieutenant in the ROK Army.

After receiving my commission, I made the following resolutions: (1) I will lead in front of my men whenever an assault is made; (2) I will command at the weakest point when we are in defense; (3) I will never abandon the position unless ordered to do so; (4) I will carry out the mission objective no matter what; (5) I will never abuse my men; (6) I will never forget that a victory requires an act of close fellowship. These resolutions were based on my experiences as a squad leader.

Twenty classmates and I were ordered to report to the Fifth Division. By this time the front lines were pretty well fixed and the war had become more stationary. The fighting had become much more intense, particularly for platoon leaders. There were rumors that officer candidates were to be called up for duty even before their training was completed. While it might appear that a mobile campaign was more costly, in practice a stationary war was more dangerous. When the armies were fighting over a hill rather than an entire front the casualty figures became much higher. Also, the introduction of more powerful weapons by both sides meant heavier casualties.

"We are fighting with everything we have to recover one more hill," General Min Ghi Sik, the division commander, addressed us. "We can't surrender a single square inch of land to the enemy, even if we have to fight hand-to-hand. The division will soon move to the front for such operations."

I was appointed leader of the Third Platoon, Eleventh Company, Third Battalion. My senior noncommissioned officer, Master Sergeant Han, and my platoon guide, Sergeant Sul, were experienced combat soldiers. All of the others in my thirty-two-man rifle platoon, however, were new conscripts with no combat experience. I tried my best to become one of the platoon members during the training period. I made a resolution and rigidly followed it. I did everything that my men did; I dined, slept, and trained with the men. All my platoon members except one private were older than me. So I had to be an officer with exemplary behavior and had to enforce the orders and regulations strictly and fairly. After one week, I could feel that the men were gradually opening their hearts to me.

One day, Master Sergeant Han advised me that I should listen to him if I wanted to avoid becoming cannon fodder. He stressed that he had seen many young lieutenants get killed in action because they did not follow his advice.

"You must be the only one worrying about my safety other than my parents," I replied. "I really appreciate that. But you should know one thing. I will not become a commodity lieutenant.[1] Moreover, I will prove that the terrible nickname for our new commissioned officers is unjust and untrue. I will make sure that no one utters those dreadful words again by showing everybody that new second lieutenants have the guts and knowledge to beat the enemy just like more experienced officers. Even if I become a casualty, I will not die like a commodity. I will die like an officer and brave leader of my platoon. You will soon find out what I am saying."

On August 16, 1951, I faced my first battle as a platoon leader. From their positions on Hill 983, the enemy could easily observe our activities around the town of Yanggoo. Their artillery observers would have no difficulty finding our positions. On August 17, I spent the whole day preparing for the imminent assault. Although it rained hard all day long, U.S. bombers still flew sorties dropping bombs over the enemy positions. The explosions vibrated through the entire valley until it seemed the mountain would disintegrate. The odor of the explosives was strong and offensive. After the air raids, U.S. X Corps artillery commenced their tremendous barrages on the enemy positions; it appeared the Americans were trying to kill the hill itself, piece by piece. Trees, rocks, and debris flew everywhere. Nothing, I thought, could survive such an intense shelling.

"What do you think, Lieutenant Lee?" the captain asked me. "It may appear that the barrage killed all the enemy soldiers, but I assure you the SOBs are waiting for us in their bunkers. Please remember that.

"Don't ever underestimate the enemy," the captain continued. It is bad to be afraid of your enemies, but much worse to slight them." I had no doubt he had learned that lesson by fighting in many battles. The artillery barrage continued during the evening.

On August 18, our own artillery barrage commenced, using every artillery unit in the corps. The shells dropped like a summer shower, not only on Hill 983 but also on Hill 940. The artillerymen adjusted their guns to cover the whole upper half of the hill. The enemy shells, however, kept exploding all around us, and I began to pray earnestly. I had spent more than six months fighting against the Communist guerrillas. But this was the first time I had witnessed such an intense artillery duel.

Around 6:30 A.M. on August 19, with the Ninth and Tenth Companies leading the attack, the regiment's assault on Hill 983 was finally under way. My company, the Eleventh, remained in reserve at the MLR in full readiness for any order. We carefully observed the progress of our two sister companies, which was much slower than expected. They had to overcome the rough terrain and the intense enemy fire.

By 2:30 P.M., the Ninth captured Hills 710 and 731, intermediary points to Hill 983. Since the captured hills were only observation posts and not their main defensive positions, enemy resistance in the area was relatively light.

The enemy fired 82mm shells all over our area. Although we remained in our foxholes, we still suffered casualties. I heard some faint moaning coming from the First and Second Squad sectors. I ran to their positions under the falling shells and found Private Lee badly wounded. He had been hit by a shell fragment in his belly. Although part of his intestine was visible, he somehow recognized me and tried hard to say something.

"I'm sorry," I said. "Be strong! Don't worry about anything here. We will take care of it." Then I summoned a medic and ordered Private Lee's immediate evacuation. In the Second Squad sector, Private Kim had been hit in his upper thigh and was bleeding heavily. I used a pressure bandage on his wound, but it didn't work well.

"Lieutenant! Lieutenant!" His screams sounded terrible. But there were no more medics available, and I had no way of evacuating him. I thought of using my squad members to take him to the rear, but I needed all of them for the attack. Still, the enemy's relentless shower of mortar barrages continued unabated. The smell of gunpowder was oppressive, and my view was obstructed by gun smoke and flying dust. I tried hard to be calm, but I had difficulty focusing and felt a sense of helplessness.

"Lieutenant . . ." Again an urgent distress call came amid the chaos.

It was Private Park, the guy who swore he would return safely to his family. He was married, with a son. His face was badly wounded. I pushed back one of his exposed eyeballs and then applied a pressure bandage.

"Don't worry, Private Park! They can fix you good at a hospital." I summoned Sergeant Han to explore ways to evacuate the wounded, but to no avail. I reported the casualties to the CO using the wireless. Captain Jung rushed to us, calm and poised, in the midst of the shelling.

"Don't worry, Lieutenant. I will evacuate them in no time. Shells don't have eyes, so they fall anywhere. The best way to save ourselves is to dig holes better and deeper." With this encouragement, the CO returned to his post. Shortly afterwards, civilian workers brought us some food and took the wounded to the rear.

The powerful defense of the enemy not only held up the Eleventh Company but also the Ninth and Tenth Companies. They captured a few guard posts, but were unable to reach Hill 983. Major Lee, the CO of the Third

Battalion, encouraged the troops to continue the assault, but both companies were pinned down. As the offensive lost all momentum, fear and frustration swept the entire regiment. To reverse the widespread fatalism, I decided to visit my men in their holes.

"Look at me! I am neither dead nor wounded. I walk amid the enemy shells as you can see. I am not scared at all. Just hit the ground when you hear the shells coming. If you are scared, you can't hear the shells coming in time. So, just relax and be ready to move quickly when shells come to you. Only the Maker knows our fate. Be brave!" I went to every hole and said the same thing to my men. I could see that it had an impact on them very quickly. At dusk, the enemy ended its daylong barrage.

"Lieutenant," Master Sergeant Han yelled. "I am worried about your safety. You don't seem to understand the danger of what you are doing. You shouldn't forget that there are many men you have to lead."

Then Staff Sergeant Sul said to me, "Lieutenant, aren't you scared? I know you are an officer, but shells are coming down in showers and you don't seem to care. I have survived many battles, but I'm very scared. When shells fall, you must lie down and not move. That's how you survive a mortar barrage. We will soon attack their bunkers. If you do what you have been doing, you will certainly get killed. Please do what we do, then you will make it."

"I am grateful for your advice," I replied. "But as you observed, the platoon is terrified when the shells are landing. How can these men fight against the enemy's concrete bunkers? How can we cure their battle phobia? If we're going to handle this problem, we have to do it while we are still in reserve. To tell you the truth, I'm scared as hell, but I'm also determined to eliminate the men's battle phobia. Please understand my intention."

"But it will do no good if you get killed by exposing yourself to the enemy's fire," Staff Sergeant Sul said. "It is our simple wish that you should pay more attention to your own safety."

"Thank you for your concerns," I replied. "I promise I will remember your kind advice."

After I saw the two sergeants back to their posts, I felt content and happy. I was lucky to have two such experienced and considerate leaders in my platoon.

On August 20, the second day of the offensive, the Eleventh Company was scheduled to take part in the attack. We would take the central sector, the Ninth the left, and the Tenth the right. The three companies were to attack Hill 983 in a parallel formation. Our preattack barrage was as intense as that of the first day. I thought the enemy truly remarkable to survive such a heavy barrage.

After the barrage, our company's assault finally got under way. The terrain was rough and the enemy responded with machine gun fire. In addition, anti-personnel mines slowed our advance, and mortar shells fell everywhere. Screams came from every direction, indicating that our casualties were getting heavier. I led my platoon to the front.

"Follow me!" I shouted.

In spite of my lead, intense machine gun fire slowed the advance of my platoon. It was very frustrating. But the slow advance was not limited to my company. Both the Ninth and Tenth had difficulty in advancing. When I was not able to advance, Captain Jung came to me. He remained calm and confident. He did not blame me at all.

"Lieutenant Lee, we could capture Hill 983 if we could neutralize those three bunkers. Why don't you consider organizing a special assault team?" It sounded more like asking a favor than giving an order. I thought it was worth a try.

"Captain, I will try it."

The CO nodded his head with satisfaction.

Then I crawled about halfway up Hill 983. About fifty meters up from my position, I could see a machine gun window. It looked like the threatening mouth of the devil. There was another machine gun window about one hundred meters from the first one, and a third one about 80 percent of the way up the slope. It looked obvious to me that the first machine gun position presented the greatest problem; it would be extremely difficult to take the other two without taking the first.

The ridge was like the edge of a knife, thin and very steep. The approach to the ridge was extremely narrow, allowing only one or two men at a time a chance to climb the forty- to fifty-degree slope. In addition, the Ninth and Tenth Companies were in danger of being attacked from the ridges. I returned to my post and formulated the mission plan.

"Lieutenant Lee," Captain Jung asked, "can you do it?"

"Yes, I can," I answered pleasantly but with confidence.

"You may consider the regular approach for this attack," the CO suggested. "You will need three squads, an assault squad, a support squad, and a clean-up squad."

I accepted the CO's suggestion. Master Sergeant Han would lead the support squad, Staff Sergeant Sul would lead the clean-up squad, and I would lead the assault squad. It was fair because I was the most physically fit in the platoon. I could throw a grenade farther and climb a steep slope better than any of the others. I assembled the entire platoon and issued the assault order.

"This victory," I told the men, "will ensure the success of not only the platoon, but also the company, the battalion, and even the regiment. It is a matter of honor for the ROK Army. Let's not forget that."

I found a rock large enough to cover my body about thirty meters from the enemy machine gun window. From this position, I thought, it should be possible to hit the enemy bunker with a grenade. I immediately ordered my assault squad to advance.

"Advance forward!"

While the squad advanced in parallel formation, Master Sergeant Han's support squad provided precision cover fire. At the same time, Staff Sergeant Sul's clean-up squad did the same to the second bunker and to the ridges on both sides. I jumped down to the cliff on my left and climbed the front slope like a mountain climber. After about an hour of hard climbing, I was able to reach the rock, a mere forty meters from my squad. My men could observe my moves, but the enemy couldn't see my position, or the fact that I was there. Staff Sergeant Han's squad fired so accurately the enemy was unable to detect my quick moves. The Maker helped us too. The dark clouds in the sky made it more difficult for the enemy to spot us. Now we could be victorious, but only if I threw my grenades accurately.

I was so nervous I was sweating. Then I prayed for strength and courage against the Communists and pulled the safety pins from two grenades. Although I was a young man with considerable nerve, my hands trembled. I felt the burden. I knew that I could hit the machine gun window with my grenades easily if it were not such a pressure-cooked situation. I closed my eyes and prayed for the last time. I had to throw the grenades while lying down, rather than standing, and the steep slope made this even more difficult. The area was filled with surreal noise and smell. It was pure hell, the worst of its kind. A few times U.S. tanks hit the bunker with their guns, but they failed to take it out. There was no way to neutralize the machine guns except to throw the grenades. Somehow the enemy sensed something was about to happen. Their gun barrage became intense, while my platoon's response grew weaker. I had to do it right away. I threw the first grenade into the bunker's window, but it exploded just outside of it. I collected myself and threw the second. In a few seconds I heard a muffled explosion. The assault squad dashed forward with great shouting. I threw the third grenade into the bunker, but I had conquered the bunker with the second grenade. I rushed to the bunker and shouted, "Long live!" as loud as I could. The assault squad reached the bunker and answered my shouting with their "Long live!" It was my world; I was on top of the enemy bunker and on top of the world.

Suddenly, the enemy attacked us with machine gun fire from the left ridge. We rushed into the bunker through feed trenches. We counted eighteen enemy bodies and two machine guns. All but three wounded were dead. I ordered the evacuation of the wounded and discussed the plans to capture the other two bunkers with Sergeants Han and Sul.

"Lieutenant Lee, well done. I am so proud of you. You are a phoenix. Take a rest." Captain Jung embraced me with pride and gratitude.

"We will commence the attack on the second bunker immediately," Captain Jung continued. I reported my plan for taking the bunker to Captain Jung.

"No, no. You need some rest," Captain Jung replied. "You have finished your mission by capturing this bunker." Captain Jung rejected my plan for the Third Platoon to attack and ordered the First Platoon to attack the second bunker.

We watched while the First Platoon attacked. The First had much difficulty advancing, however, and suffered heavy casualties. When it became dark Captain Jung ordered our company to form a defensive perimeter at our current position. The Ninth and Tenth Companies both launched attacks against the second bunker, but they also failed.

On August 21, in the morning, my Third Platoon received orders to attack the second enemy bunker. This bunker had been surrounded by many outposts, and the central peak was protected by an all-direction defense. It was not the place where one-man penetration would be effective. I decided to use the whole platoon instead. I reported my offensive plan to Captain Jung.

"I will divide the platoon into two squads," I said. "I will lead the assault squad and Master Sergeant Han will lead the support squad."

"Good idea," Captain Jung replied. "But this time I want you to trade roles. Master Sergeant Han will lead the assault squad." I understood why the CO ordered the trade. He wanted to protect his platoon leaders.

"Yes Sir. This time I will lead." Han quickly obeyed Captain Jung's order.

The attack on the second bunker was soon under way. Han's assault squad rushed forward with great energy and much shouting. But a terrible surprise met them. It was an anti-personnel minefield. Because of the enemy's overnight preparation, our attack stalled. Exploding mines took feet away from my men. I rushed to save Private Kim, who lost one foot. Although the men tried to stop me, I was able to bring Kim back.

"Lieutenant, I am fine. I am still alive." He was bleeding profusely from the wound.

"Kim Bok Man, don't lose your courage. I will make sure you live." To my delight, Kim began to sing a patriotic song.

"Looking to the future, my heart is full of love for the Motherland."

Walking with only one foot, he continued singing with full volume. Tears were rolling down from my eyes. Captain Jung also shed tears. Probably the whole platoon wept at that moment and thought only of one thing— we had to capture that bunker.

"We have to avenge Private Kim," I shouted to my men. "Let's go. Follow me." I led the assault squad to the bunker fifty meters ahead. Han's support squad provided cover for us. I had returned to the assault squad after Kim's injury. I was not ordered to do that. It just happened that way. When we had gone about thirty meters, I quickly removed the safety pins from my grenades with my teeth. Then I threw the grenades into the machine gun window. Fortunately, one exploded in the bunker.

"Attack, forward! Follow me!" I shouted to the squad. We entered into feed trenches and I threw another grenade into the bunker. We gained total control of the second bunker. In a few minutes Master Sergeant Han and Captain Jung joined us. The bunker was much more spacious than we had expected. Moreover, it had three machine gun windows, not just one as we had believed. They deployed two machine guns in the front and two more in the sides. The bunker had twenty-five Chinese soldiers, including two nurses. We were all revolted by what we found—two soldiers tied to the machine guns by a chain and lock. They were not allowed to run away no matter what. I felt outraged by such inhuman behavior. We quickly evacuated three wounded PLA soldiers to save their lives. We knew they were not responsible for the war. It was their Communist masters who deserved real punishment.

During the attack on the second bunker, I lost two men, Private Kim Young Sik and Private Park Ho Young. They were new recruits but always obeyed my orders to the letter. I buried them in a spot where the sun would shine warmer and longer. Then I led a simple sending-off ceremony for the two brave Christians. During the worship I did not post a single guard. But not a single bullet or shell landed around us.

"Let's get ready for battle!" I cried loudly. We have to capture the remaining bunker. As far as I was concerned we couldn't leave the task to anybody else. While moving to a more desirable staging position for the attack, I ran into Captain Jung, who was on his knees praying. It was such a solemn moment. We waited so we would not disturb him. Finally, I approached him and spoke to him quietly.

"Lieutenant Lee," Captain Jung responded. "I have been praying for our two fallen comrades." We saw tears in his eyes. We all silently wept again. But the war was going on all around us.

"Please allow us to take the third bunker. It would be good revenge for our two fallen comrades." Captain Jung answered my request by shaking his head.

"You are too exhausted. You have done enough by taking the two bunkers." The CO seemed to think our platoon needed a rest. But we did not. Moreover, we thought we couldn't rest until we had avenged the men who had given their lives.

"Captain, we are grateful for your concern for my platoon. But we have been successful both times. We have the best chance to do it again. If we encounter another failure like the one we experienced it could ruin the whole offense. Please let us do it," I begged. Captain Jung, with a rather heavy face, finally gave us permission to take the bunker.

"I wish you and your platoon the best."

The enemy resumed its shower of shells on us. The barrage was so intense I had to order the platoon into the bunker. Fortunately, the shells did not penetrate the concrete bunker, and we were safe.

"Do you know how dangerous it will be to attack the third bunker?" I asked my men. "If you are not sure you can do it, raise your hand and I will assign you somewhere else." After the speech I looked at my men one by one. Nobody wanted to be a coward.

"Will you follow me?" I asked one more time.

"Yes, we will." I was so moved by the platoon's confidence in me.

"Okay. Master Sergeant Han will lead the support squad. Again concentrate your fire at the machine gun windows. The assault squad will follow me and rush the bunker the moment my grenade explodes in it."

When the barrage let up, the platoon moved out of the bunker. Han led his squad to find the best position. Smoke rising from the bombs dropped by U.S. planes formed a thick blanket all over Hill 983, presenting us with an ideal cover. Our sister companies, the Ninth and Tenth, continued to attack even after they had been repeatedly turned back by the enemy. I led the assault squad to a potential launching point and observed the situation for a few minutes.

The machine gun window of the third bunker looked ominous and threatening. I evaluated carefully the best possible route to attack the third bunker. Due to the intense air and artillery strikes, the area was full of debris. While some mines were exposed, there were still others that posed a serious threat to us. There were countless craters all over, both large and small, that I thought improved our chances of a successful attack. I immediately assigned duties to each individual in the squad and crawled into the nearest crater. For some reason, the defenders at the top of the bunker remained silent. I became apprehensive over their total lack of response, and I wondered if they were actually observing my movements. But I had the advantage of using the craters to hide from enemy fire. Suddenly, the enemy opened up with an intense volley, using not one but a number of machine guns. To my great relief, they were aiming at other targets. I made good progress and quickly reached a position about twenty meters from my own target. I signaled my next move to the squad and prayed briefly but earnestly.

I removed the safety pin and threw the first grenade with all the strength I could muster. The second grenade followed quickly. I hit the machine gun window with both grenades. In a few seconds we heard the muffled explosions in the bunker.

"Attack, forward!" I shouted and rushed the bunker. As soon as I reached the feed trench the captain followed me.

"Good work, Lieutenant Lee. Let's go and check the bunker together," Captain Jung said to me with a smile.

The third bunker was the same size as the second. There was one difference; it contained thirty rotting and smelling corpses. It was quite difficult to breathe in the bunker because of the overpowering smell. They had chained two soldiers to each machine gun, just like in the second bunker. The barbarism the enemy perpetrated on its own soldiers was something I never wanted to recall. There were more than ten enemy officers killed in the bunker. We evacuated three wounded enemy soldiers for treatment.

A short time later, the enemy began to fire 82mm mortars on the bunkers. Evidently they realized that we had taken the bunkers. When I assembled my platoon in the bunker, only sixteen men were left. Two were seriously injured during the assault on the third bunker. Others had to be evacuated for less serious injuries. The only target left for us to take was Hill 983, known as Sooribong, which the PLA boasted was impregnable.

"We have paid such a high price to take the bunker," I said. "Let's push one more time and take this last hill." I encouraged my men as the final drive began. Both sides used every weapon they had to win the battle. In spite of the enemy's desperate resistance, by making use of the craters, rocks, and fallen trees, my platoon was able to move up to a point where we could launch an assault on the final target. Then we were told that the Sixth Company of the Second Battalion had captured Hill 940, which was connected to the main peak in the northeast. I was quite encouraged by the development because the Sixth Company could help us by pressuring the enemy from Hill 940. But before we were able to launch the final drive the regiment unexpectedly sent word to us that there had been a change in the regiment's battle plan.

The regiment decided to attack Hill 983 from the rear, while the Ninth and Tenth Companies held the enemy at its current position. The regiment picked our company to go around Hill 940 and attack the final target. It may have made good strategic sense to the regiment, but it was unfair and disappointing to me and the platoon. We had suffered plenty to capture the bunkers, and now we had to climb down and abandon them. But orders were orders.

"I believe you are unhappy," Captain Jung said. "But we did not abandon the bunkers. The Ninth and Tenth companies will effectively prevent any enemy attempt to reoccupy them. They will also remember how we took them. Don't be too upset." After the captain had calmed us down, we enjoyed hot soup, a bowl of rice, and a night's restful sleep.

Early on the morning of August 22, Captain Jung gave the assault order to his platoon leaders. "Our objective is Hill 983," he said. "The enemy will throw everything it has at us to defend the hill. The success of the entire battalion depends on the Third Company." As soon as the order was issued, the enemy showered us with a mortar barrage, almost as if they had been listening to what the captain said to us. We quickly took cover behind rocks and trees. Fortunately, we suffered no casualties.

Before attacking Hill 983, we had to take a nearby hill that would provide us an excellent staging position. I led the Third Platoon forward, advancing cautiously to test the enemy's strength. I had decided that an assault would be too costly for us. After we had gone about one hundred meters the

enemy resumed its mortar barrage. As shells rained down, I hid myself behind rocks. One shell hit my backpack and my rib ever so slightly. Then it hit
the ground right in front of my nose. It was a dud. If it had been live I would
have been blown into a thousand pieces. I believed that God had saved me
for better use later.

"Are you okay, Lieutenant?" Han rushed to me after observing the
whole thing himself. He checked my body quickly and looked closely at
the 82mm dud.

"You must bow to that dud. You are a phoenix for sure. I've never heard
of anything like this."

"He saved me for some other mission I guess," I answered Han simply.
The left side of my fatigue was burnt black. But I was not bleeding and
suffered only light skin burns. My humble fatigue uniform had protected
me quite nicely.

"Sergeant, it is time to take that thing." I tried to collect myself for the
assault. I did not fear death anymore. I had a conviction that I wouldn't be
killed. While the support squad was concentrating its fire on the machine
gun window, the assault squad rushed forward like galloping horses for nearly
one hundred meters. The enemy fire was inaccurate, and we managed to kill
more than twenty in the trenches with grenade attacks. Some ran away to
Hill 983. Capturing this hill cost the platoon three men due to injuries, but
we now had the staging point we needed for our last and greatest challenge—Hill 983. As usual, the captain appeared quickly and issued orders for
the company's next move.

"As you know, the top of Hill 983 consists of highly reinforced bunkers.
We have to assume that their troop deployment is based on their firepower
plan. To evade their grid fire, we have to fool the enemy. We will have to find
out their weakness first. Once the company deploys into a battle formation,
I will order you to attack, but we will not move. Just shout and make all the
noise that you can so that the enemy will think we are coming. This way we
may be able to observe their firepower plan." Of course, all platoon leaders
had no objection whatsoever. Captain Jung was the most capable and respected captain in the regiment.

"Attack, forward!" the captain roared. As usual the men repeated his
order at the top of their lungs while making the customary battle noise. The
enemy responded with vengeance in mind, using automatic weapons and
machine guns.

"First Platoon, attack the left flank!"

"Second Platoon, attack the front!"

"Third Platoon, attack the right with everything you have!" The captain issued orders to each platoon. His voice was loud and clear even amid the intense volleys. He made sure that the enemy heard the order so that they would think the whole company was attacking. Luckily, the fog was very heavy, which gave the enemy limited visual observation. We responded to their volleys and grenade attacks with moans and shouting to give them the impression that they were inflicting heavy casualties on us. We fooled the enemy on a grand scale; the Communists wasted a great deal of ammunition firing on an army that was not coming. Moreover, we were able to read their firepower plan, so we knew their strengths and weaknesses.

Meanwhile, the captain scored direct hits with three 60mm mortar rounds on the enemy trenches about 150 meters away. The hits revealed his keen knowledge of weapon systems. The enemy trenches were too far away for grenades, but too close to use our 82mm mortars. The 60mm mortars were the perfect weapon for the situation. When the captain insisted on securing a large number of 60mm shells prior to the offense, none of us understood his intention correctly. As it turned out, the three 60mm mortars worked overtime. When they became too hot to fire, we cooled them off with the water in our canteens. The enemy responded with their 82mm mortars, but they did not know our exact position. Captain Jung, however, soon figured out the location of their 82mm mortars.

"Lieutenant Lee, take your platoon and capture the mortars on the back slope. Then occupy the enemy command post. We will take the top from both sides. I don't believe they have any machine gun windows on the back side. Your chances are good. I will hold the enemy's main force where they are by using the two platoons I have here. I wish you luck!"

I immediately led my platoon south and then turned right into a valley. When we reached the back slope of the hill, we found it much quieter than the front side. While the forest was quite dense, we were able to advance rapidly because I was sure there were no mines. When we were within fifty meters of their positions, the enemy still had not posted guards. They probably didn't imagine that we could move that far so fast. I signaled the platoon to advance, very carefully. When we were within twenty meters of the enemy, I ordered a grenade attack on their positions. More than ten grenades exploded simultaneously, creating tremendous damage and confusion. The enemy mortar position was totally destroyed. A few survivors ran away. But two enemy officers fled only a few meters because Master Sergeant Han and I opened fire on them. Wasting no time, I ordered the final assault on the hill.

"Let's finish it!"

My men were more than brave soldiers. They were flying phoenixes. We quickly overpowered the enemy positions on the top. Finally we did it!

We shouted loudly with our two hands kicking the sky. The captain came up quickly.

"Captain . . ." I could not say anything.

"Lieutenant Lee . . ." We simply embraced each other.

Everyone had tears in their eyes. No one tried to hide them. They were tears of joy rather than sorrow.

We found more than one hundred enemy corpses on the top of Hill 983. Soon both the Ninth and Tenth Companies made their way to the top. U.S. Navy fighters flew over to the hill but headed south after they had determined the hill was in friendly hands. In a few minutes the regiment's top officers were all over the hill, including the regimental commander himself. To my great surprise, Colonel Hwang bestowed the highest military medal on me right on the spot.

"You are the highest decorated second lieutenant in my regiment. I am so proud of you." I was dumfounded and had little to say to the colonel. I didn't fully comprehend the meaning of the medal at the moment.

Chapter 20

The Chinese Go Underground

In the fall of 1951, both sides began to dig in and the stalemated war of the trenches began. The front lines actually changed very little for the remainder of the war. During this period the CPVF concentrated on strengthening their defensive lines, which they did by constructing an elaborate underground tunnel system. Their trench defense and tunnel system were tested by the sudden onset of the UN Kumhwa offensive in mid-October 1952. The U.S. Seventh and ROK Second Divisions began intensive shelling of the Chinese Fifteenth Army's positions in the Osong Mountain region on October 14, and occupied Hills 597.9 and 537.7, two small hills known as Triangle Hill in the West. By October 16, the UN attack had forced the Chinese troops off the ridge and into their tunnels. Captain Zheng Yanman's company joined the tunnel defense as a reinforcement force on October 18. For more than a month his company and other Chinese troops fought a seesaw action in a pattern. During the day, the UN troops would force the Chinese troops into the tunnels, but at night, the Chinese would counterattack and recover their surface positions, only to lose them again when daylight came. The Triangle Hill battle soon turned into one of the bloodiest battles of the war.

Captain Zheng Yanman

Eighth Company, 134th Regiment, Forty-fifth Division, CPVF Fifteenth Army

WE WERE SHOCKED when we heard that our regiments had lost fourteen out of sixteen positions on Hills 597.9 and 537.7 on October 16, 1952. I couldn't believe that the regiment had 550 casualties in a one-day defense. The next day, my Eighth Company received an order to reinforce the First

Company's defense on Hill 597.9. At the company briefing, I didn't tell my men that the First Company had only twenty men left, including the wounded, out of the company's two hundred men. I didn't want to scare a couple dozen new recruits who had been in our company less than a week.

I told my soldiers at the meeting that they could count on a very strong defense system as a result of all our tunnel work on the hill. I was pretty sure about this. In the past four months, we had been constructing tunnel fortifications along the frontal defense line on a rotation basis. Lacking advanced tools and supplies, we depended largely on our own "carry-on" stuff, such as small shovels and pickaxes. After one week of earthwork, when our tools were worn down and our food had run out, we were replaced by another company that continued digging inside the hill. Then we moved to the rear for supplies and carried tools and food back to the hill for another shift. Usually, each combat soldier carried up to sixty or seventy pounds of supplies. Since the logistical service was not really effective, we felt more secure carrying supplies on our own backs than waiting for others to bring them to us.

We dug inside the hill, taking out rocks and sandy grit while trying to avoid cave-ins. Lacking lamps to light the underground tunnels, we burned pine resin instead. Broken glass and metal plaques were also used at tunnel entrances to reflect sunshine inside during the daytime.

By this time, our regiment had constructed an underground network inside Hill 597.9. I had a map describing three tree-shaped tunnel systems. About twenty to thirty feet below the surface, there were three main tunnels, like tree trunks, about seventy yards long, five feet high, and four feet wide. Each main tunnel connected eight short side tunnels, like tree branches. Each side tunnel had several shelters and storage rooms, like tree leaves. I showed my soldiers the entrances, crossing points, and how the network worked.

I told my company that we could defend the hill as long as we had our tunnels. In fact, I was not sure about this. I had never fought from underground against an enemy on the surface. I said it in order to clear up any doubt in the minds of my soldiers so they would maintain high morale. I had to use the Chinese folk tale of the Monkey King (Sun Wukong) as an analogy.

The Monkey King tale in China is as popular as the Superman story in America. "We will make an assault on the hill and move into the tunnels tomorrow night," I said at the briefing. "We are going to be Sun Wukongs who will make trouble in the belly of the monster, the Princess of the Iron Fan. We can defeat the enemy by getting into its stomach, kicking and punching anytime and anywhere we want to. We can turn the enemy upside down on the hill." It made sense to the soldiers. One could tell by their facial expressions and voices they were not lacking in confidence.

As a captain, however, I knew this was going to be a tough fight. At a commanders' meeting held earlier the same day at regimental headquarters, Colonel Liu Zhanhua asked us to defend the hill to the last man. "Our strong defense at Osong Mountain will bring the Americans back to the negotiating table at Panmunjom," Colonel Liu said. "On October 7, the Americans adjourned the Korean truce negotiations. Now they try the battleground again to get what they couldn't get at the negotiations—more territory for South Korea. We can't lose even one bloody inch of land the Chinese and North Korean soldiers have been fighting for during the past two years. The hill belongs to North Korea as long as we can keep it in our hands. We must stop the Americans right here and send them back to Panmunjom."

During the night of October 18, our company moved up to the hill in the dark. "Seek cover," I told my lieutenants. "No contact with the enemy." I wanted to make sure it was a concealed movement. My mission was to reinforce the First Company in the tunnels and to keep these tunnels in our hands. This would be defensive fighting; there would be no attacks against enemy troops, who had dug in. Quietly, the more than two hundred men in my company crept slowly up the hill.

About halfway to the top, our troops stopped. The vanguard squad reported that they had seen ghosts on the hill. Actually, they were black American soldiers sleeping in the trenches. Our new recruits had never seen black people before. Crawling around the enemy positions, we could even hear American soldiers snoring.

At the top of the hill, the troops stopped again. We had an unexpected problem; we couldn't find the entrances to our underground tunnels. Two days of fierce shelling and heavy fighting had changed almost every landmark on the hill. My map didn't work, and we couldn't communicate with our comrades inside the tunnels. Since it was only about an hour before dawn, we didn't have enough time to move back down the hill and withdraw to safety. My two hundred men would be an easy target for enemy artillery fire if we couldn't move into the tunnels before dawn. "Don't panic," I told my lieutenants. "Disperse and look for the tunnel entrances."

We found the new entrances to the tunnels by accident. One of our soldiers fell into a deep shell hole while he was looking for the entrances. At the bottom of the hole several hands suddenly grabbed him, held his legs,

Chinese soldiers work on their underground tunnels, 1951. (Courtesy
of the Center for Archives and Information, Heilongjiang Provincial
Academy of Social Sciences)

Due to the serious water shortage in the underground tunnels, a Chinese soldier patiently waits for a water drop from the rock. (Courtesy of the Center for Archives and Information, Heilongjiang Provincial Academy of Social Sciences)

covered his eyes, and took away his rifle. "Wait! Don't shoot!" he yelled in Chinese, and the hands on his eyes were immediately removed. He found himself among several Chinese soldiers of the First Company at a new, concealed entrance to the tunnels. I asked the First Company to use flour to mark the way to the entrance. Before dawn, the entire Eighth Company moved into the tunnels without any casualties (except two men missing in action).

It was a big mess inside the tunnels. First, the three tunnels were cut off from each other and there was no connection or communication between the tunnels. Each tunnel had suffered severe damage from the enemy attacks on October 17. Bodies, shells, and garbage were everywhere. There were no supplies, no food, and most important, no water.

Understandably, the morale in the tunnels was low. There was no chain of command, communication between the tunnels and our regimental headquarters was nonexistent, and nobody knew what to do. There were about one hundred soldiers inside the tunnels, remnants from six different companies and ranging in ages from sixteen to fifty-two. About fifty of the men were wounded, and they had received no medicine or medical assistance. They were lying around, some of them dying, and nobody seemed to care. In one of the shelter holes there was a pile of more than twenty corpses.

Neither did anybody care about safety. There were seven accidental rifle discharges and two hand grenade discharges in the tunnels during the first morning after we moved in. I was really mad when I learned that several of my men were wounded by these accidental discharges.

Early the next morning, I held an officers' meeting. Sitting around a candle in a tunnel, the commanding officers all agreed with my proposals. First, we must have a chain of command. I would command the defense of the hill and the tunnels. Though there were several other captains who had survived in the tunnels, they had lost most of their men. For example, the First Company had only sixteen men. I was the only captain who had a radio and could keep in touch with our regimental headquarters.

Next, I sent the badly wounded soldiers down the hill and back to our rear area. I asked those who were not severely wounded to stay on a voluntary basis. During the next two nights, about forty wounded were evacuated. I was told later that a battalion officer and several soldiers who pretended to be wounded attempted to leave the hill that night. The officer faced a PLA court martial in China. The soldiers who deserted were executed on the spot.

I decided to attack the enemy surface positions at night so as to secure our tunnels through the daytime. This decision resulted from my experience as a commander during my first two days on the hill.

About 9:00 A.M. on October 19, the first day of my command on Hill 597.9, the enemy discovered two of our entrances. At 1:00 P.M., they attacked, firing recoilless rifles, machine guns, and grenade launchers into our tunnels. The "S-shaped" tunnels, however, limited their firing power, so they tried to get into our tunnels. To defend our small and narrow tunnels, I could only send three soldiers at a time to the entrances. Each team lasted only eight to ten minutes. By sunset, the attacks stopped. We suffered heavy casualties, forty-nine dead and seventeen wounded. Moreover, some of our tunnels collapsed after the enemy's successive bombardments. Several men were buried alive inside the tunnels.

Our soldiers became frustrated. During the evening of October 19, some of them complained to me. "The Eighth Company never fights this kind of battle," they said. "We are not the super Monkey King here. We feel like a monkey that got stuck in the trap inside the hill. The enemy walks around all over our head. We can't do anything about it. All we can do is to wait for another beating." Others wondered how long we would be able to stay on the hill. Three days, maybe four days? It could not be much longer because every day more men were killed and our tunnels were being taken apart, piece by piece.

Colonel Liu also worried about us and asked me on the radio if I needed reinforcement troops on the hill or to be replaced by another company. "Don't send any more apples," I replied to the colonel. (Apples in our radio code words meant reinforcement troops.) We couldn't take any more troops because our tunnels were getting shorter and smaller. "The Eighth is all right. We can stay." A new replacement company wouldn't do any better as long as it used the same kind of defense and continued to sacrifice more soldiers in order to stay in the tunnels longer. What we really needed was to figure out a better way to protect our tunnels.

In the middle of the night, I sent a couple of squads out of the tunnels to look for water and ammunition. "No engagement," I told the sergeants. But some of them ran into the enemy trenches anyway and shots were fired.

To our surprise, as soon as the firefight was over, the American and ROK soldiers pulled out of their positions and moved down to the bottom of the hill. I was so happy to learn that the enemy troops did not seem to be interested in fighting at night. They didn't have their air support and artillery coverage at night, and probably thought they could retake the hill easily the next morning.

A new defense plan came to my mind on October 20. According to my plan, we would first get out of the tunnels at night and attack the enemy troops. After their withdrawal, we would take over their positions on the hill and try to hold them until the enemy counterattacked the next morning. I calculated it would take them two or three hours to put together an assault. When their attack started, we would retreat back into the tunnels. It would take until sometime in the afternoon for the enemy soldiers to secure their surface positions. Thus, they wouldn't have enough time left to find our tunnel entrances and then organize a major attack on our tunnels before dark. Our tunnels as well as our soldiers would be safe during the day. I reported my new defense plan immediately to the regimental headquarters.

Colonel Liu approved my new plan and added that the regimental mortar company could provide supporting fire to slow down the enemy daytime

The 134th Regiment, Forty-fifth Division, CPVF Fifteenth Army uses the tunnels to defend their positions on Hill 597.9, October 1952. (Courtesy of the Center for Archives and Information, Heilongjiang Provincial Academy of Social Sciences)

counteroffensives. He named my plan an "active defense" plan when he reported it to the Forty-fifth Division Headquarters.

Events soon proved my active defense plan worked well. During the night of October 20, I ordered six squads to attack the enemy positions on the hill. When they opened fire, most of the American soldiers (U.S. Seventh Division) and the ROK soldiers (ROK Second Division) withdrew from their trenches and moved down to the bottom of the hill. With a few casualties, we took over twelve out of sixteen positions on Hill 597.9 by the next morning. I reported our success to the regimental headquarters. Colonel Liu told me later that the division headquarters introduced our successful "active defense" experience to other regiments on October 21. The Forty-fifth Division had lost more than four thousand men in its defense of the two hills during the first seven days. My active defense, by improving the defense of our tunnels, probably saved the lives of a number of Chinese soldiers.

Our combat experience on October 22 further supported my proposals. The enemy wasn't in a big hurry to retake their positions and didn't launch their counteroffensive until 11:30 A.M. We spent most of the morning outside the tunnels, repairing the entrances, storing water, and collecting ammunition on the hill. Our soldiers enjoyed the break and the sun for the first time in four days. Their morale was high, and the commanding officers were excited about my new tactics. "Captain, we can build concealed entrances closer to the positions. It will be easier for us to take over these positions again tonight," one of my lieutenants suggested. "Hey, Captain," another lieutenant said, "let's bury our dead comrades inside the bunkers so their bodies won't be destroyed by the shelling and bombing."

About 11:30 A.M., the enemy shelling began. We all moved into the tunnels. That afternoon, the enemy occupied the surface positions on the hill. By 5:00 P.M. they discovered two of our entrances. Just as I thought, however, they didn't have enough time to put together a major assault on our tunnels. They just threw in a dozen hand grenades before dark and left. We had only two soldiers killed and five wounded in a twenty-four-hour period. It was the first time we didn't have to fight a bloody, passive defense during the daytime.

During the night, our attacks started again. The enemy troops seemed better prepared for their withdrawal this time. They had everything ready and just pulled out of their positions as soon as we opened fire. Next morning, they returned to their positions on the hill a little bit earlier. But, again, they didn't organize any major attack on our tunnels. On the third day, October 24, they repeated the same routine again. We discovered, however, that most of the returning troops were ROK soldiers with only a few American soldiers. I reported this to regimental headquarters. Colonel Liu believed that the ROK Second Division was now the main enemy force on Hill 597.9. To strengthen our defense, he sent me sixty soldiers as reinforcements. It didn't matter which unit the soldiers came from; all the Chinese troops on the hill were under my command.

On October 25, the situation on the hill changed. The enemy troops returned to their positions with nine battle tanks and several searchlights. I thought they might attack our tunnels in the late afternoon or even early evening, so I ordered our troops to be ready for tunnel defense. By 8:00 P.M., however, nothing had happened. Again we became excited about our night combat. The night on the hill belonged to us.

In the middle of the night, I began our attack by sending two demolition squads to destroy the enemy tanks. About fifteen minutes later, one of the squads came back without setting off an explosion. They couldn't see the difference between the enemy tanks and our tanks, since both had a big star. "We don't have any tanks on the hill," their lieutenant told them in an angry voice. "The enemy tanks have a white star, and we have a red star. Go and get them!" Twenty minutes later, explosions took place on the hill one after another. Five of the nine light battle tanks were neutralized.

"Charge the enemy positions," I ordered. Immediately my lieutenants, followed by about one hundred men in seven squads, poured out of the tunnels. They attacked the enemy surface positions as they had every night before.

But this time it was a totally different story. The enemy troops didn't withdraw. Instead of packing and leaving, they turned on their searchlights and fought back. The dark hill was suddenly lit up like a giant soccer field by the enemy lights and flash bombs, and our soldiers were all over the hill without any cover or protection.

The enemy machine guns and the four light tanks opened fire, supported by artillery pieces that shelled the hill for the first time at night. Our attacking troops faced a strong defense in front of each enemy position. After taking over two positions, our troops could advance no further. "Pull back!" My voice disappeared in the deafening noise of the battle.

An hour later, ROK soldiers managed to encircle and inflict heavy casualties on our troops in the two positions. I didn't have enough manpower or firepower to rescue them. By 2:00 A.M. the fighting stopped and quietness returned to the hill. Only seventeen of one hundred soldiers were able to fight their way back to the tunnels. I was angry at myself; my miscalculations had resulted in the loss of more than half of the Eighth Company.

Next morning, ROK troops (Thirty-first Regiment, Second Division) on the hill launched their attacks on our tunnels. About 11:00 A.M., the ROK soldiers discovered one of the entrances to our main tunnels. They threw in a couple of dozen grenades and used flamethrowers to keep us away from the entrance. An hour later, about twenty ROK soldiers managed to slip into the tunnel. The S-shaped, narrow, and dark tunnel limited our shooting range. Our soldiers could not see the enemy until they were very close. As a result, it was hand-to-hand combat in the dark. I could hear shooting, yelling, and screaming everywhere in the tunnels. Thanks to our well-organized tunnel defense, we were able to eliminate the invaders inside the tunnels at a cost of thirty-seven of our soldiers.

Before we could identify and remove our dead and wounded comrades in the tunnels, the ROKs sent more soldiers into the tunnels. It was the bloodiest combat I had ever seen. While we managed to stop the second ROK offensive by 5:30 P.M., the ROKs soon returned and smoked the tunnels with gas bombs. They followed by sealing the entrance to our tunnel with rocks and wire nets. They tried to stop us from coming out at night and attacking their surface positions again. We had to wait until dark to open another entrance and get some fresh air. By the end of the day, October 26, I had only sixteen men left, and only four of them were able to fight. Despite our losses, however, we stayed on the hill.

On the morning of October 27, Colonel Liu reinforced Hill 597.9 with 160 men. I was instructed by the regimental staff on the radio to get my men ready and pull off the hill on October 29. The Eighth Company would be replaced by another company.

"No way!" I yelled on the radio. "I have lost two company political instructors, eight lieutenants, all of my sergeants, and almost two hundred men. I am not finished here yet. The fight is not over; how can I leave the hill? How can I face my dead comrades?"

The regimental staff told me that it was Colonel Liu's order.

"Who cares? Nothing can make me withdraw from the hill. You may pull me out of here after I die in the fight." I was really mad and didn't care who heard me.

In fact, Colonel Liu was standing right there in the regimental headquarters and heard everything I said on the radio. He grasped the microphone and yelled back at me: "Are you out of your mind, Zheng Yanman? This is Colonel Liu Zhanhua. How dare you to disobey my order. Get ready and pull your men out of there tomorrow."

I stopped my complaints. I just wanted him to know that we didn't fail. We did our best to defend the tunnels and stay on the hill for twelve days.

Following Colonel Liu's order, I passed the tunnel defense command to a captain from the 135th Regiment during the night on October 28. "I heard everything, Captain Zheng," he said to me. "We will stay in the tunnel and fight to the end."

During the night of October 29, the Eighth Company pulled out of the tunnels and moved down the hill. There were only six men in the company able to make their way back and walk down the hill with me. When we moved up the hill just twelve days ago, I remembered, two hundred young men were running and jumping, full of energy and heroic dreams. Tonight there were only six of them. Tired and wounded, they moved slowly down the hill. Covered by the dust and blood, their faces and arms were black like charcoals. Their uniforms were ragged, shabby, and torn at the elbows. They looked like ghosts walking in the dark. "Wash your face," I told them in a low voice when we stopped at a small pond. "You look terrible, like defeated soldiers. We are the seeds of a new Eighth Company. We will welcome and impress our new comrades."

I washed my face, but I couldn't wash away those familiar faces of my comrades in my mind. My lieutenants, sergeants, and privates had followed me from China all the way to Korea. They could never go back to their homes and see their families. They were only nineteen or twenty years old, and dropped their last blood on this foreign land. I let my tears drop in the pond.

At the regimental headquarters, I learned that this was one of the most bloody battles we ever fought in the Korean War. The 134th Regiment lost most of its companies. The regiment lost 65 percent of its captains, 89 percent of its lieutenants, and 100 percent of its sergeants. Our division lost 5,200 soldiers on the two hills. The Fifteenth Army had a total of 11,400 casualties from late October to early November, when the Battle of Triangle Hill finally came to an end.

Chapter 21

North and South
A Korean Youth Serves in Both Armies

Lee Young Ho was born in Seoul in 1933. He was a high school junior when the North Koreans attacked and captured the city in 1950. Following the invasion, the entire family remained inside their home to avoid contact with the North Koreans. After a few days, however, Lee Young Ho decided to step outside to catch some fresh air. He was spotted by a North Korean soldier, taken into custody, and forced to join the North Korean People's Army without having the opportunity to say goodbye to his family. After a few months as a soldier in the North Korean People's Army, he managed to escape from the NKPA while it was retreating in October 1950. He later joined the South Korean Marine Corps, participating in battles in the Sachonggang district in 1952. He was discharged in 1957 and has since driven a taxicab in Seoul.

Private Lee Young Ho

Third Battalion, Marine Corps, ROK Army

ONE DAY, WHILE returning home from an errand, I overheard several elderly neighbors repeating some strange rumors. It was June 24, 1950.

"It is said that a war has broken out."

"Who in the world says such a thing?"

"Someone heard that the North's Reds are invading."

"That could be major trouble. But could that be true?"

I rushed home, but my anxiety remained unbearable. Could it be true? But nothing happened that night. In the morning, my entire family was terribly uneasy. We heard that war had indeed broken out. My father was out checking on the rumors, but I couldn't stand the worsening anxiety. So I went to the Donghwa movie theater that was pretty close to my home. Soon a jeep with a large speaker passed by blaring this announcement: "All military personnel on leave, you must return to your unit immediately. We have a war along the 38th Parallel."

All the people around us were in a state of shock and fear. Most began packing essentials and preparing for an evacuation. But not many had any idea where to go. Nevertheless, some left home immediately because there were rampant rumors that the Reds would kill everybody.

On the afternoon of June 26, I could see part of the war myself. Some wounded soldiers passed through the neighborhood, which made the war seem real to me. On the next afternoon, we were even more shocked by the news that the enemy was already in Eijungbu. We could hear the sounds of shell explosions and were in a state of near panic. Everybody talked a lot but knew nothing about what we should do.

"We must evacuate. The Reds will shoot anybody they see."

"They are already in Eijungbu. There is nothing we can do now."

We spent the night with all doors locked. But the shells were falling closer and closer. We were totally afraid of the enemy. We heard the Han River Bridge was destroyed, leaving us no way to cross the river. The next morning, June 28, I very carefully approached the street nearby just to check out the situation. We really had no idea on what was going on. There were just a few pedestrians on the street. But to my surprise, some were wearing a red armband. I guessed that they were Communists.

My neighborhood was poor and small, about seventy families. So we knew many of our neighbors, like the Yoos. We soon found Yoo's entire family wore armbands. Everybody was shaken because Mr. Yoo was well respected in the neighborhood as an intellectual. My family spent the entire day inside with the doors locked. We were just trying to understand the things going on outside.

Soon we heard that an enemy tank force had established its headquarters at Duksoo High School. Grownups lamented that there was no way to escape death. But I was curious about the tanks. I had never seen a real tank. In the alley I found several friends.

"Let's go and see the tanks!"

"It is dangerous. What if they catch us?"

Some objected, but we decided to try. Using alleys we approached the high school.

"Ah . . ."

The sight terrified us. There were rows of tanks guarded by the North

Korean soldiers, who struck me as somewhat small and thin. I thought they would be big and powerful. Of course, they had weapons. But I couldn't understand how they were able to overrun our own forces.

My entire family continued to remain indoors, day after day, but very insecure. To make matters worse, I came down with a bad case of malaria, and there was no medicine available. My father used every home remedy to save my life. Luckily, I recovered fully within a few days. During the illness, I missed the fresh air and being outdoors. On the morning of July 12, I decided to go outside for some fresh air. I didn't intend to go far away but just around the neighborhood.

"Comrade, come here!" someone yelled at me. I was frightened by the order and looked back to see who he was. He was wearing a red armband. He stared at my eyes and signaled me to come closer to him.

"Do you want me?"

"That's right!" He told me to follow him. No reason was given, but I was already frozen and unable to do anything contrary to his command. While following him like a loyal dog, I desperately looked for a familiar face. But there was none. I wept in my heart. I was led to a building behind the Hongik elementary school. Inside I found six young men sitting on a long bench. I figured they were in the same boat as me. A middle-aged man greeted me.

"Comrade, I welcome you. You are to fight for the hero of the people, our great leader, Kim Il Sung."

His talk made me shudder. I was not able to think rationally anymore. He gave me a sheet of paper and ordered me write down my basic personal information. I did what he asked. Then some hours passed. To my great surprise the sister of Mr. Yoo entered the room. She wore the red armband like other Communists. Nevertheless, I was delighted to see her.

I greeted Sukgi's sister warmly. To my desperate greeting she didn't respond at all. She was no longer my friend's sister. But I didn't give up hope. I thought she would do something for me. Meanwhile, they brought in more young men. I found another neighbor who wore the red armband. He was the guy known as the "bird's eye."

"Please tell my family where I am." But his face remained cold. He treated me like a total stranger. Soon there were fifteen men. We were hungry, but they didn't feed us. Instead they tied us together with a rope and led us to some unknown destination. I lamented endlessly. It appeared that I would never be able to see my family again. We arrived at the Jaedong elementary school, where I found a group of about 150 young men. They put thirty men in each classroom. In three days the number of so-called volunteers reached over three hundred men. Very quickly they organized us into military units. That afternoon they gave each of us a bowl of food and ordered the group to move out. Just like that I became a North Korean soldier and was on the way to some unknown place.

"We are going to Pyongyang."

"What?" I heard someone saying.

I was no longer afraid of anything. I just tried to concentrate on remaining alert at all times. Our march continued northward. They placed soldiers and security policemen in the area to prevent any attempt to flee. Although exhausted, I kept thinking about my father. Then I missed my mother, who died when I was a kid. She was from Shinmak, Hwanghae-do Province. We went through Hwanghae-do Province on our way to Pyongyang. We passed Moonsan and the Imjin Bridge, marching all night in the dark. Soon I was dead tired, and I could think of nothing else, not even my family. Excruciating pain ruled every second of my life.

A few miles away from the city of Jangdan, we were allowed to take a badly needed rest. More than anything we needed sleep. In the morning, civilian volunteers brought balls of cooked barley, but it did not come close to satisfying our hunger. In the evening we resumed our march. Within a few hours we entered Gaesung. I realized that I was about to enter the land of the Reds. I didn't have much confidence in my future in this strange territory.

Our forced march continued in the same fashion. A rest during the daylight was followed by long, exhausting night marches. We felt the Reds relaxed quite a bit when we reached Shinnamchon. Perhaps they thought the greater distance would make it impossible for us to return to our homes. When I realized we were in Hwanghae-do Province, I thought about my mother's family again. One of her uncles had even visited us after the liberation in 1945. By the time we reached Shinmak I had suffered so much mental anguish I contemplated the feasibility of an escape. I was so desperate I finally asked my platoon leader for permission to leave. He was terribly rude at first, but when I told him my story he was rather sympathetic.

"Is that so? Your mother's home was in the north? Okay, but don't make any foolish mistakes. The next stop is Suhheung."

Permission granted, I set out to visit my maternal grandmother. I tried to find my uncles, but nobody seemed to know any of them. I was terribly disappointed. At the last moment, however, I met a barber who knew one of my uncles. He advised me to go to my aunt's home instead of my uncle's. I didn't even know if my aunt was still alive, but I took his advice and found her home quite easily. She looked very much like my mother.

"I am Young Ho from Shindangdong, Seoul." I identified myself with faltering words. She stared at me for a while and then exploded with joy:

"What? You are Young Ho?" She embraced me and shed a shower of tears.

"You grew up this big without your mama! What are you doing here in the middle of the war?" I explained to her what had happened to me. Quickly my aunt took me to my grandmother's home.

"Mama, here is Young Ho, a son of my sister in Seoul."

"What are you saying?" My grandmother rushed out of the room to greet me. Of course, warm tears streamed down her face. I washed myself at the family well and put on my uncle's clothes. I felt like a new man. I ate and rested for a little while. But I could not ask them to hide me there. Local Communists had already jailed one of my uncles as a counterrevolutionary. Another uncle was out of town to serve the party elsewhere. In addition, they had to worry about the neighbors, who saw me coming. I had to say goodbye to my grandmother and aunt without finding a place to hide, but seeing those two dear ladies did me a world of good.

"You are back. I worried about you," my platoon leader said when I returned.

Escape was really not feasible for me; wherever I fled, they would certainly catch me. There was not a single soul who could protect me from the Communists. Next morning we resumed the march. We walked a whole day, even after it became dark. Everything was pitch dark because we maintained a complete blackout for fear of U.S. air strikes.

In Jaeryung, our group was divided into three units with about one hundred men in each group. We finally arrived at the slope close to Guwolsan Mountain. There we constructed a makeshift barrack with material we harvested locally. Soon we started the training that reminded me of children's play. We used hand-carved wooden sticks for rifles. After three weeks of such training, ox-carts brought us supplies, including rifles and uniforms. Wearing the NKPA uniform, I fired three rifle shots for the first time. In this way, I became a People's Army soldier, just like the one I saw in Seoul. I was Kim

Il Sung's cannon fodder! I accepted this as my fate. But I still couldn't understand how I became an enemy soldier. I hated the leftists with vigor, but now I was a Communist soldier. I missed my family even more.

"Comrades, you should be ready to sacrifice your body for our great leader. You must become a brave fighter," an officer with a star on his shoulder said to us. I sneered at him and resolved to escape whenever I could. After another series of marches we were delivered to a regular North Korean unit. To my great luck I found that one of my new platoon members was from Seoul. His name was Kim Taesik, and he became a good friend of mine. At that moment I badly needed a close friend.

We moved again. This time each company moved independently. My company was the first to move out of the location, but they didn't tell us where we were heading. I guessed that we were going south. When we arrived at the new location I heard it was Jangsangot. From our position we could see the sea. It appeared we were defending the shore areas. The fact that I was now aiming my rifle to the south tormented me endlessly. I was abducted by the Reds and became a Communist soldier against my will. But who would believe that!

In early September, our immediate task was building bunkers to be used for both sleeping and operational quarters. Each squad was divided into two groups. We worked at night and slept during the day. The night work was not that bad because we could steal a catnap from time to time. So I didn't complain much.

That night the sky was particularly full with billions of bright stars. The wind was fresh and cool. Again I was thinking of my family in Seoul. I was sure that my father was wondering about his first son, who had just disappeared without a trace. He couldn't even be sure I was still alive, not to mention being an enemy soldier. I thought about his frustration and despair. But what could I do! Suddenly I thought I saw some lightning far away to the south. It came from the direction where the city of Inchon might be. I guessed a major storm had hit the area.

Strangely, we could still see the lightning a few nights later. The nightly display of lightning showers seemed to make the company tense and unstable. Soon we were ordered to prepare to move. We were dumbfounded and unhappy with the prospect of another torturous march. Regardless, we were ordered to move out. I gathered from the officers' behavior that the situation was rather urgent. The march was exhausting, like the one we had done before. But some rumors I heard during the march gave me reason to hope again.

The rumor was that the United Nation's forces had landed in Inchon. There could be no news more pleasant than that, if true.

"The UN forces undertook the landing operation in Inchon."

"Could that be true?"

"Yes it is. They have already taken Seoul."

"We are finally saved." I heard things like that during the march. Such remarks made it difficult for me to suppress my surging emotions. My heart was about to burst open with hope and expectations. I finally understood the strange lightning that colored the dark sky a few nights earlier. It was not lightning, but artillery fire from the invading UN forces. Our company was ordered to move to Pyongyang as fast as possible. That meant one thing to me—we were going north! Uneasiness spread among the soldiers quickly. Nonetheless, we headed north. Again, our march was restricted to nighttime to avoid the UN air attacks. The night marches exhausted us.

"Hurry up! Hurry up!" Officers kept pushing us, but we walked slowly and reluctantly. Earlier we had been ordered to rush so we could defend Pyongyang. Now we were ordered to march north, through mountain ranges. The order encouraged us to fight the enemy for the party and the people. That was a tall order because we suffered from hunger and extreme fatigue. Nevertheless, we marched over the rough country roads and paths without a word; we just followed the guy in front of us.

"Enemy fighters!"

"Get dispersed and find a shelter quick!" officers shouted desperately. But there was no place to hide our bodies. While passing through a rice field we became targets of sudden air raids. With no place else to go, I crouched along a tiny elevated path that divided one property from another. It was extreme chaos as everybody scrambled to find a place to hide. Our unit countered the air raid with rockets hidden in the ox-carts. Others fired their rifles and machine guns in desperation. But the enemy fighters clearly maintained an overwhelming dominance. Bombs landed all around me, while machine gun bullets hit just inches away. The last thing I remembered was a big boom. When I regained consciousness, there were no UN fighters, only white clouds in the blue sky. The incessant moaning of the wounded filled the air. The raid hit not only soldiers but also animals, which were pulling carts. It was a hellish scene. We moved the wounded to a safer place and took steps to repair the damage.

"You are alive!" I embraced Kim Taesik. He was the only one I could trust in the company.

"We are going to share the same fate," Taesik said. "We will live or die together." Taesik was two years my senior, but less robust in appearance.

Under the circumstances, getting supplies was unthinkable. Instead we were told to eat raw rice if we had it. Gingerly, we began to move again, in the dark. Once again we came under enemy fire, and this time the UN forces made extensive use of flares to locate our positions. In the confusion of the battle Taesik and I were temporarily separated, but I soon located him.

"Will you do what I tell you? We have to act together," I yelled at Taesik.

"No problem. I will follow you," Taesik replied. We waited for a while under a tiny earthen pathway to evaluate the situation. We found several soldiers talking among themselves in low voices. It sounded like they were planning to escape. When they slowly moved away we followed them quietly. Soon we were away from the battlefield. We could see the battle was still going on with even greater intensity. We kept going, believing we were heading south.

"Hands up! Who are you?" We were terrified by the stern order. But soon we realized that we were held up by the same soldiers we were following. I was greatly relieved and said, "We followed you and left the battlefield just because we didn't want to die there."

"Is that right?" Once they found out who we were they didn't ask many questions. They didn't belong to our platoon, but we were somewhat familiar to each other. They were from North Korea, while we were from South Korea.

"We are on the same boat. So let's be careful," the leader of the four said.

"First of all, we have to become civilians. To do that we must get rid of our uniforms." We all agreed to it. We followed their lead although we had no idea where we were going. In the dawn we found a farmhouse nearby. We approached the house very carefully, but it was empty. We emptied the cabinet but there were no suitable clothes for us. But the North Korean soldiers found some cheap cotton clothes and urged us to change. As they asked us to do, Taesik and I buried our uniforms in the backyard and threw away our rifles and munitions. We no longer belonged to the People's Army; we were civilians. That made us feel much better. We continued to walk and to eat the raw corn we found in empty farmhouses.

"It's safer from here on," the group leader announced. "But it will be better if we separate." I felt as if the end had come. They were our colleagues, who had led us safely to the south. I understood their decision, and we were grateful for their help. But we had no idea how to get to Seoul. Then I remembered Shinmak, where my grandmother lived.

"How far is it to Shinmak?" One of the soldiers gave me the directions, and I felt sure we could find it. After exchanging genuine goodbyes, we departed. We felt alone and abandoned, and we were on our own. I told Taesik what I intended to do. He said he would go with me wherever I went. We set out on our new journey to Shinmak.

While our new clothes gave us a humble appearance, we didn't look like farmers because we had covered our hairless heads with pieces of cloth and wore sneakers issued by the People's Army. So we threw away the sneakers and wore homemade straw sandals we obtained from farmers, which hurt my feet badly. When I couldn't stand the pain anymore, I walked barefoot. After a few miles, my feet were in even worse shape. In addition, we were suffering from incredible hunger. We finally decided to stop at a farmhouse on a slope and take our chances.

"Hands up!" Someone stopped us with a rifle. I was stunned but noticed they were wearing a shoulder piece of Taegukgi, the national flag of South Korea. I realized what that meant. We had reached UN territory.

"You Communist bitch! Kim Il Sung's dog!" They started beating us with rifle butts without even checking our identities. Obviously we looked like soldiers from the People's Army to them. I fell down and almost lost consciousness.

"Where are you from, boys?"

I explained to them what had happened to me. But they didn't believe me. Not only that, they threatened to turn us over to the military police. I resigned and was prepared to accept my fate. It seemed a lot better than dying at the hands of our enemies. I couldn't help but feel that the whole thing was terribly unfair. So I tried one more time. I went down on my knees and explained in detail the fateful journey I was forced to take since my abduction. Finally they were convinced that I was telling the truth. I asked them take me to my grandmother's house, but they refused. Instead they cautioned us to be careful. They informed us that there were many stragglers of Communists and local sympathizers staging wanton killings. We spent the night at the village and resumed walking in the morning.

Our feet were all cut up, which made simple walking pure torture. We even walked with four legs like an animal to relieve the pain on our feet. We often discussed death as a better alternative and wept out of pain and desperation. We could see military vehicles going north. But we were escapees from the People's Army. As a last resort, we removed a piece of cloth from our pants and wrapped our badly cut feet. With sheer determination we continued to walk slowly and painfully. After all, we had to live! At last, we arrived at Grandma's house.

"Aunt!" I couldn't say anything else. Aunt rushed to greet me, and Grandma came out, too.

"Oh, my heaven. You are back alive!" Grandma wept uncontrollably.

I immediately went to sleep. Finally, after many hours of sound sleep, I woke up and ate. After a bath and fresh clothes I felt like a new man. It had been about four months since the Communists had abducted me in Seoul. Grandma believed that heaven helped me to return safely. I was not so sure. I heard that my uncle blamed Grandma for not providing a hideout for me the last time. My uncle was a civilian worker at the makeshift airfield in Shinmak, which was under the control of the South Korean air force.

The war was going well for the Republic of Korea. We heard the ROK forces had liberated Pyongyang and were pushing north to capture the Baekdu Mountain and Aprokgang River, which separated the Korean peninsula from China. It looked like the unification of Korea was only steps away. I was hopeful that soon I would be able to return to my family in Seoul. I was troubled, however, by information that the South had established a new national identification system. Every man was required to carry two identification cards; one for citizenship and another for his military service status. We were told that the authorities would arrest anyone as a Red who didn't produce the proper identification. We worried about the new system. We couldn't go to Seoul without the identification cards, but we couldn't obtain the cards without going to Seoul.

With the loving nourishment of Grandma's family, our wounds healed quickly. But the identification problems troubled Taesik and me. We discussed the problem endlessly but saw no easy solution. One night Taesik informed me of his decision.

"Because of you I am here. So I owe you much. But now I have to face my own fate alone. I will go to Seoul. We will meet in Seoul if heaven allows."

"How can you go alone when things are still dangerous and extremely unstable?" I tried to discourage him in every way I could.

"I must go." Since his decision was resolute, I could only let him go. Warm tears rolled down our faces when we said our goodbyes.

In early November, I had a lucky break. My uncle informed me that his base would send a truck to Seoul to pick up some parts.

"If I arrange to take you to Seoul, I assume you can find your house."

"Yes. Just take me to Seoul." My uncle somehow convinced Sergeant Kim to take me along. I said sad farewells to Grandmother and my uncle's family. They were all happy for me but still wept, a Korean way of saying goodbye. Still, I was happy to be going home. The truck, however, was in such bad shape we could drive only at very slow speeds. We also had to stop numerous times to fix something. I worried about falling into enemy hands. The military situation in the area we were passing through was still unstable even though it was under the control of friendly forces. We drove only during the day, and I remained in the truck cab at all times. There were still many checkpoints where they examined everything. Sergeant Kim did his best to protect me at every checkpoint. Finally, after we had crossed the Imjin River, I realized I was really returning to Seoul.

"Ah, how I missed Seoul!" I felt like going outside and shouting "Long Live." The city was dark except for weak lamp lights here and there. I asked the sergeant to let me off at the Gwanghwamoon area. He kindly offered to drive me to my neighborhood, but I declined. He had already done more for me than I had any right to expect. I expressed my heartfelt gratitude for his help and kindness and set out to find my family. Since I knew most back alleys I extensively used them to avoid identification checks. But I was not able to detour the checkpoint at Chunggyechun. I worried about the potential trouble of not having any identification at all. While I was looking for a safe passage I saw a family carrying some heavy bundles. I volunteered my service to carry one of their bundles. Carrying a large bundle on my back, I was able to pass the checkpoint. In my humble clothes, I looked just like a member of the family. That was the last hurdle I had to overcome to return to my own home.

"Father!"

"Is this Young Ho?" Father almost fainted at my sudden appearance. I wept loudly while embracing my father with both hands.

"You are back. . . ." I found my brothers and my stepmother but not grandmother. Father informed me she had passed away. After my disappearance she went out to the street every day and called my name. She refused to eat and died a short time later. I was so sad and felt guilty that my grandmother had died like this.

I was home but had no freedom to move around, because I dared not leave the house. So we considered every method to obtain the necessary identification cards. After the neighborhood police chief rejected the petition submitted by fifteen adults on my behalf there was not much we could do. I was incarcerated in my own home, but I was totally innocent. The only thing I had done wrong was to allow the Communists to abduct me.

Through friends I did receive news about the war. In late November, I saw a newspaper notice on navy recruitment. When I read it I realized that joining the service was the only solution open to me. Moreover, I had an obligation to serve the nation's armed forces just like any other young man in South Korea. I decided to apply, although I still didn't have identification cards. I prepared the application anyway and submitted it to the naval headquarters. I did my best on all four tests, because becoming a sailor was the immediate solution for my involuntary incarceration. My father was pessimistic because of my incomplete documentation. Luckily I passed the tests. Soon I was on my way to boot camp, but to become a marine, not a sailor. I was admitted to the fifth class of the Marine Corps recruits on December 20, 1950. After fifty days of basic training, I became a marine private on February 10, 1951.

As a machine gun operator I participated in many battles, including the Dosolsan battle, one of the worst battles of the war.[1] It was a price you needed to pay to become a ROK Marine. On Hill 86 on the western front, the enemy shelled us constantly, but we never let fear overcome us.

When the enemy shells were incoming, we usually guessed their landing spots by their sound. If we thought it would land nearby, we scrambled for shelter. We found such games to be exciting. We believed that was the reason the ROK Marines got the nickname "Ghost Catchers."

One day, our Third Battalion was scheduled to trade positions with the First Battalion. We were about to become a reserve unit after spending one bloody month on the MLR. Early in the afternoon the enemy began shelling our positions. The shelling was not heavy, and our artillery responded in the same manner. About dusk, however, the enemy shelling became much more intense. Shells were landing on the MLR and our four forward posts. It was the most intense artillery barrage I had ever experienced.

"Those bitches must have heard of our shifting," I thought. They seemed to know that the shift would take place at ten o'clock at night. I wasn't feeling too good. When the darkness engulfed the area the enemy cut loose on our MLR with machine guns. Flares lit up the MLR as the entire front was filled with heavy gunfire from both sides. I was excited by the immediate prospect of being in the middle of a decisive battle.

Under constant flares I could clearly see unfolding a human wave of Chinese soldiers approaching our lines. "You bitches!" I cursed them unconsciously and pulled my heavy machine gun's trigger. The area was nothing short of pure hell. All sorts of weapons were discharging their deadly bullets and shells at hellish rates.

"Oh, no!" It was an emergency and pure bad luck for me. My heavy machine gun's leg was broken by the enemy shell fragments. I was in great panic. While I was trying to fix it a shell landed close to me. There was a great explosion and I lost consciousness, buried under a pile of debris. A little later, I regained consciousness and realized I was still alive. But I couldn't move at all. Worse, I found breathing to be extremely difficult. Realizing that I was buried in dirt, I pushed my upper body with all the might I was able to muster. Finally, I managed to crawl out of the dirt. I became alive again with a supply of fresh air. Enemy shells, however, were still landing with tremendous din. I was surveying the situation with most of my body still buried.

I heard voices. They were Chinese, and I thought the end was at hand. But I tried to remain alert. I had experienced similar dangers in the north many times, I thought. While I was trying to make up my mind on my next move, friendly forces started their counteroffense with an artillery barrage. Shells exploding in mid-air devastated the Chinese with showers of shell fragments. I was close to a trench, but it was heavily damaged. Nevertheless, I managed to make my way into the trench by using my hands. Nearby, in an undamaged trench, I found grenades. I gathered an armful of grenades and attacked the Chinese soldiers, who were carrying their wounded.

"I will kill all of you!" Yelling at the top of my lungs, I threw grenades at the enemy soldiers. All alone on Hill 33, somehow I survived the night. At dawn a squadron of American fighter planes attacked the hill I was holding. Since the bunkers and trenches on the hill were all heavily damaged, I had no place to hide. The planes attacked the hill anyway.

I could see some movement on the MLR that I assumed were position changes taking place after the night's heavy battle. I thought that they should relieve me too. I needed my replacement so I could return to my unit. Finally, I spotted three guys approaching my position. I was so excited that I waved my hand to them to show them where I was. But they mistook me for the enemy and quickly disappeared. It took some yelling on my part to convince them I was one of them. They had reason to be cautious, because they assumed that I had been killed. When I returned to the platoon they informed me that I had been missing for more than twelve hours.

"Private Lee, you are still alive!" my commanding officer greeted me. I embraced my comrades with joy, and with a deeper appreciation for life.

Part Five

Behind the Front Lines

Chapter 22

The "Lighter" Side of the War

When WWII veterans returned, if they talked about the war at all it was most likely about some of the wild and humorous incidents they had experienced. Korean War veterans, on the other hand, seemed to have less to say about the humorous side of the war. This is not easy to explain. Perhaps GIs found it more exciting to liberate a French or an Italian town than a Korean town. American indifference toward the war may also have played a role. Returning Korean War veterans quickly learned Americans were not particularly interested in stories about a war that ended in a stalemate. Nevertheless, regardless of where they were, whenever large numbers of GIs came together some wild and crazy things usually took place. Even in captivity, POWs in communist prison camps found ways to play jokes on one another and sometimes on their captors. The following stories, the first two by First Lieutenant Pendleton Woods and the third by Staff Sergeant Bernard Case, attempt to tell something of the lighter side of the Korean War.

First Lieutenant Pendleton Woods

Public Information Officer, Headquarters and Headquarters Company, Forty-fifth Infantry Division

WHILE I WAS in Korea during the winter of 1951–1952, only one major Hollywood performer visited our troops. It was still cold but not quite as icy when Betty Hutton and a troupe of entertainers came by the Forty-fifth Infantry Division.

Along with others, as Division Public Information officer I was present with a photographer at the time of her arrival. When she got off of the helicopter, I was concerned about her show appearance. She had a bad case of laryngitis and could hardly utter a sound. Nevertheless, she was determined "to go on with the show."

When the opening of the show came that afternoon, despite her ailment and obvious difficulty, she was able to project her lusty voice and sang beautifully. The show was great!

That evening the division commander and his staff, along with top regimental officers, gave a party for Miss Hutton in the general's mess tent.

One of the cooks in the division headquarters mess hall, who had been the head chef at the Skirvin Hotel in Oklahoma City, had prepared a beautiful cake in her honor. We contacted the cook, asking him to meet us at the tent at a certain hour so we could take a picture of our distinguished guest and the cake for a news release. We asked him to wear his white chef's dress, with the high, traditional-type cook's hat, which we knew he had with him.

When my photographer and I arrived at the tent, we were met by my boss, a colonel well known for his arrogance and overbearing manner. He greeted us heartily with, "Hi Pen, come on in; I don't care what you write about me, just spell my name right, heh . . . heh . . . heh."

"We want to take a picture of Betty Hutton and the cook," I said.

"The cook?" he answered. "To hell with the cook."

I explained that the cook, who had been a chef at the Skirvin Hotel, had made the beautiful cake on the table.

"You can't take this picture," the colonel responded. "He's out of uniform."

By this time Betty Hutton had entered the room and saw what was happening. She immediately put her arms around the cook and pulled him over to the cake. "He's not out of uniform," she said. "He's wearing his whites and he looks beautiful. I want a picture with him and my cake!"

We made the picture in three poses. Then the colonel walked out of the tent without another word.

The next day the colonel called me. He said nothing about the Betty Hutton scene, but bawled me out about something unrelated. I simply smiled because I knew what had actually triggered his call.

As Division Public Information officer, I found it interesting to observe which stories received national attention. Most of the time this depended more on their uniqueness than their importance.

Bill Fields, a warrant officer in the Forty-fifth Division, had political ambitions. Realizing his military service would be over before the coming fall elections, he registered by mail to run for sheriff of Tulsa County in Oklahoma. The primary election was scheduled to take place in the summer, while he was still in Korea.

One day Bill came to my tent and told me about his dilemma, at the same time asking me if I could help him publicize his campaign. I suggested we make a political sign. We would shoot a picture of him nailing the sign into the ground on the top of Old Baldy, a nearby mountain so named because the heavy fighting had destroyed all of its vegetation.

This we did. The sign simply said, "VOTE FOR BILL FIELDS FOR SHERIFF OF TULSA COUNTY." The picture caught on nationwide, and Bill was elected in a landslide. After he won the primary, he came to me and asked what he could do to repay me. My answer, "I want one free release from jail if I should ever be arrested in Tulsa County." Fortunately, he never had to make good on his promise.

Staff Sergeant Bernard E. Case

313th Engineer Utility Detachment, X Corps Headquarters

During my tour of duty in Korea in 1951 and 1952, I never saw any hand-to-hand combat or fired my rifle with the intent to kill anyone. Except for incoming artillery now and then, I really had a pretty safe time over there. I do remember one incident, however, that left me shook-up pretty good.

On the troopship coming over, the *General Black,* I met a master sergeant and we became pretty good buddies, despite the fact I can't remember his name. It was a rough crossing and almost everyone was seasick, but the sergeant and I were not bothered by the rocking and rolling of the ship.

Since he was in ordnance and I was assigned to the engineers, we were separated at Camp Drake. They sent me to Camp Gifu in Japan for a few days of training in CBR (Chemical, Biological, and Radiological) warfare, and I suppose he went right on to Korea.

I arrived in Korea a little later and was assigned to the 313th Engineer Utility Detachment at X Corps Headquarters at Kwand-ri on the Inje River. The general's "Latrine Repairers," we were called.

One day I ran across my old friend, the sergeant from the troopship. We talked for a while, and he told me about his sister who had passed away and another sister who was in poor health. He also told me his outfit was just

Working on a supply road, Punchbowl, early 1953. (Courtesy of Richard Peters)

down the road, where he had a couple of bottles stashed away. He suggested that I pay him a visit sometime and we would see what we could do about the bottles.

A few days later I visited the sergeant, and after he had introduced me to some of his buddies, we started in on the booze. I hadn't had much to drink for some time, so it didn't take long before I needed to lay down and take a nap. Sometime later the sergeant woke me up and told me I'd better get started back to my outfit.

The sergeant offered to drive me back in his jeep, and I accepted. But when we started to drive out the gate the guard held us up. He said the officer of the day had issued orders prohibiting all vehicles from leaving the area that night. The sergeant started arguing with the guard, so I butted in and said, "No problem, I will walk back." But the sergeant just ignored me; he was determined to drive me back. When I continued to insist on walking, he snapped, "Shut up, I'm driving you back."

The sergeant and the guard continued to debate their differences of opinion with increasing volume and impatience, occasionally inserting a few choice words from their rich, army vocabularies. Suddenly, the sergeant asked the guard, "Do you have ammo in the carbine?" After the guard replied "yes," the sergeant said, "Well then, start shooting." Then he told me to lie down in the jeep, and we took off like a bat out of hell. We heard shots, followed by the shattering of our windshield. Obviously, the guard was serious when he told us no vehicles were to leave the area that night.

Since I was crouched down in the jeep I really couldn't see what was going on. When we got to my unit I asked the sergeant if we had hit a tree limb or something and smashed out our windshield. "Hell no," he roared, "the guard shot it out."

Despite a few too many nips on the bottle, at that point my mind began to clear up. That bullet, I reasoned, hit the windshield of the jeep, and if I had been sitting up straight in the seat, it damn well could have hit me. This was not a pleasant thought, especially in my hungover condition. I went to bed that night all shook-up and ended up wetting my bed.

After this I was transferred to another outfit in Eighth Army Headquarters in Taegu, so I didn't see the sergeant again for some time. After a while, however, I found myself back in the X Corps area, but now assigned to the 116th Combat Engineers. One day, when looking for a new generator, I ran into the sergeant again. I asked him if he had survived the jeep deal without any serious problems. He admitted it had cost him a promotion, but it didn't seem to bother him. I told him I wouldn't be riding with him in a jeep anymore because I didn't want to sleep in a wet bunk.

We laughed about the matter and that was that. I never saw the sergeant again.

Chapter 23

A Korean Housewife's Story

Sometimes the saddest and most tragic stories in war are not about the soldiers, but about the civilians, especially the women and children. The Korean War, like WWII, saw thousands of civilian refugees on the roads enduring the hardships of a homeless existence while trying to flee from an invading army. This is a story about one South Korean family, living in Seoul, who fled from the North Korean army in the early days of the war. Told by a Korean housewife and mother, she describes the hardships the family suffered while trying to survive during the brief but oppressive North Korean occupation of South Korea.

Lee Hyun Sook

Housewife in Seoul, Korea
(Translated by her daughter, Lee Hong Im)

AT THE BEGINNING of the Korean War in 1950, I lived in Seoul with my husband, Lee I. Won, and our nearly two-year-old daughter, Lee Hong Im. I was twenty-four years old at the time, and I stayed home to take care of the house and my little girl. My husband had an office job working for the electric department in Seoul.

At the time, we knew there were big problems between South and North Korea. Sometimes we heard about shootings around the 38th Parallel, which divided the two Koreas. We also knew that sometimes those living in North Korea crossed the Han River by boat to get into South Korea. Some even paid money to cross the river.

The North Koreans attacked on June 25, early in the morning. I was home and first heard the news on the radio. At that time most people had very little money or food, because it was near the end of the month, but we knew we still had to leave before the North Koreans arrived in Seoul. Fortunately, every day I had saved a handful of rice, so we had some food to take with us on our journey to the South.

Together with my sister and her family, we crossed the Han River on a boat, with my husband carrying the bag of rice. Unfortunately, my sister was not a very healthy person, and she had several small children, so we could only walk about ten miles a day. We walked for about fifteen days to Hong Song, a city about seventy miles south of Seoul near the West Coast. We chose Hong Song because this is where my husband's family lived. There were many others trying to escape the North Koreans, and some became so weak from lack of food they dropped out along the way and died. We saw many dead people on the way to Hong Song. Because we had some rice, we were okay. We even had some rice left over when we finally arrived in Hong Song.

Everything seemed so peaceful when we entered the city, and we were quite hopeful. We lived with my husband's family, and everything seemed to be okay. Then, after we had been in Hong Song only about two days, the North Koreans arrived, and our lives were changed forever.

Because he loved his country so much, in Hong Song my husband belonged to a local patriotic society. He received no pay, but sometimes gave the local police information on those who supported the North Koreans. The North Koreans, however, regularly arrested and put in jail anyone they suspected of supporting South Korea.

To stay out of jail, my husband and some of his friends hid in the basement of his older brother, Lee Chang Won, who lived in a very big house in Hong Song. He was an important official in the South Korean government, and sometimes he would hide as many as fifty people at one time in his basement.

At this time it was very difficult to know who to trust because there were many people in the South who welcomed the North Koreans, especially in the early part of the war. The North Koreans made Communism sound so wonderful that many thought it must be like heaven. It seemed to have a special appeal for both those with very little education and those with a lot of education. Many college students supported the North Koreans, especially those who studied in Japan.

While my husband's older brother was very helpful to those who were wanted by the North Koreans, and hid many of them in his basement, he had a friend who supported the North Koreans and who became an important head man in the North Korean police. Even so, he didn't interfere with my family as long as we all stayed out of sight and caused no problems.

Unfortunately, one day my husband got tired of his basement hideout and decided to walk around outside. He was seized by the North Korean police, who brutally beat him up. When the friend of my husband's brother learned what happened, he came to our house and took my husband to the police station.

That night my husband never came home. I went to see my husband's brother to see if he knew what happened. Together, we went down to the police station and found my husband so badly beaten he was near death. His clothes were so soaked in blood they stuck to his skin when removed. When the head policeman, the friend of my husband's brother, learned what happened he made sure my husband received medical attention. Then he permitted my husband to go home. Without his help, I'm quite sure my husband would have died.

While my husband continued to suffer terribly from the beatings, it was no longer safe for him to remain in our house. Fortunately, the friend of my husband's brother understood this. So late one night he came to our house and took my husband to another house about five miles away, where he could hide more safely.

My husband stayed in this house for several months, almost like a dead person. During the day he had to be very quiet and could hardly move. At first he still could not walk, but at night he exercised with a rope, and he built up his strength until he could walk again. Eventually, however, even this house became too dangerous for him to stay. So, with some other South Koreans who were wanted by the North Korean police, my husband and the others moved into the mountains, where they all lived in a cave.

Many of those who hid from the North Koreans were the former leaders of South Korea, often professional people with a college education. The North Koreans especially disliked these people and treated them with great cruelty. I know of one occasion when the North Koreans gathered about twenty to thirty of these people in a large building, then closed the door and gave each a good beating. Then they gave shovels to each person and led them into nearby mountains. After they had all dug a hole with their shovels, the North Koreans tied their hands behind their backs and shot them beside the holes. They just toppled over and fell into the holes all by themselves.

My husband and his friends remained hidden in the mountains about two months, until the UN forces drove the Communist forces back into North Korea. When they finally emerged from their cave they were angry toward all of those who had worked for the North Koreans, and they tried to make sure they were arrested and sent to jail.

Gradually, my husband recovered from the beatings by the North Korean police. He spent the rest of the war in the South Korean army, although he was restricted to light duty because of his injuries. My daughter and I continued to live in Hong Song with my husband's family until the war ended and he returned from the army in 1953. Then we all went back to Seoul, to the same house, which somehow had survived all the fighting. My husband went back to his old job in the electric department, but unfortunately he died in 1958. Since my daughter eventually married an American serviceman from Oklahoma, in 1985 I came to Oklahoma. In 1989 my daughter and I went into the laundry business in Edmond, Oklahoma. We called the company "Tammys." Together, my daughter and I owned and operated Tammys until the early part of 2002, when we sold it and started a new business. We still live in Edmond today.

Part Six

POW Camps

North and South

Chapter 24

An American Officer Observes the Koje Island Uprising

In the spring of 1952, prisoner revolts on Koje Island and other POW camps were not only a gargantuan headache for UN Command, they were also a major obstacle to reaching an agreement in the peace negotiations. President Truman was determined no prisoners in UN custody would be forced to return against their will. Unfortunately, this policy led to pandemonium inside the camps. It divided the prisoners, leading to beatings and even murders. The hard-core Communist prisoners, supported by the governments of North Korea and China, were determined that all POWs must return to their homelands. The non-Communist prisoners, however, adamantly refused to go back. Whichever group controlled the compound imposed brutal justice on the other group, often through kangaroo courts set up in the camp. In the following story, First Lieutenant Pendleton Woods describes some of the horrors of the fighting he witnessed on Koje Island.

First Lieutenant Pendleton Woods

Public Information Officer, Headquarters and Headquarters Company, Forty-fifth Infantry Division

IN THE EARLY spring of 1952, the big news from Korea, which I followed in the *Stars and Stripes,* dealt with the American prison camp on Koje Island, located just offshore from Pusan.

This prison had become so overloaded that control was almost impossible. The Communist prisoners had fashioned eating utensils into knives that they could use as weapons within the compound. Behind the chain link and barbed wire fences they were conducting kangaroo courts, and maiming and even killing their fellow prisoners.

Finally, the situation became so bad that the Americans had to move in with tanks to literally retake their own prison compound. In doing so, they removed the weapons that the Communist prisoners had fashioned. This brought the maiming and killing of fellow prisoners to a halt.

Only two days after the Americans had retaken the prison, we moved our newspaper copy to Pusan for typesetting and printing. This time I chose to go myself, because I wanted to visit Koje Island and see what was happening.

I arrived by train, took the copy to the printer, then crossed by boat to Koje Island. There I had arranged to spend the night with a former room-mate in Japan, a Red Cross representative with the army who had been transferred to the island from Hokkaido.

Arriving on Koje shortly before dusk, as soon as possible I went to a hill overlooking the prison compound. Although the killing had stopped after the American "invasion," the demonstrations had not. By the time I arrived on the hill, the prisoners were getting ready for a demonstration.

The action reminded me in some ways of a football pep rally. A "cheer-leader" mounted a box, facing the mass of prisoners. He would yell out a sentence, and the prisoners would repeat it over and over.

I was standing beside a South Korean soldier who spoke both English and Chinese, so I asked him what they were yelling.

The first yell, the soldier said, was "Down with the American Imperial-ists." The next was "Down with Capitalism," followed by "Up with Com-munism." Finally, they yelled, "Hooray for Mao Zedong," the leader of the Chinese Communist government. All the yells were repeated many times and they went on for more than an hour, until almost dark.

After spending the night on Koje Island, I returned to the prison com-pound the next morning, this time with my Red Cross friend. Everything was quiet within the compound, but nearby, outside the prison walls, I saw a platoon of men digging holes. I went over to see what was happening. They allowed me in the area, but not my friend, the Red Cross representative.

I could see that they were digging graves and placing bodies, wrapped in shelter halves, in the holes and covering them with dirt. These were the bodies of the numerous Chinese and North Korean prisoners who had been killed by their fellow prisoners following their convictions by the kangaroo courts. Many of the bodies had partially decayed by the time Americans stormed into the prison compound and retrieved them.

The platoon leader of those digging the holes told me that they would not allow the Red Cross representative to come into the area because hasty burial in shelter-halves was against the Geneva Convention. They had no choice, he pointed out, because the bodies were decaying and there was an immediate threat of an epidemic disease. The smell was unbelievably strong and nauseating.

Then I noticed a large tent nearby and asked what it was for. I was taken there and shown its contents. Packed within the tent were the bodies of literally scores of prisoners, each wrapped in a separate shelter-half.

In combat, an infantry soldier is often exposed to the dead. In seeing one or two, whether allied or enemy, it is easy to relate to the soul that once lay within that body. When seeing large numbers of dead, it is much more difficult. One can relate to this by realizing that when one reads about a few people who are trapped in a mine or well, it is easy to relate to each as an individual. On the other hand, when reading about several hundred killed in a tornado, relating to these unknown individuals is much more difficult. In this case, however, I had no trouble relating to the men who had once occupied those bodies, even though there may have been two or three hundred packed into the tent. I removed my helmet and bowed my head. I thought to myself, "Why did these men die? Did they speak out against Communism? Did they speak up for freedom? Perhaps they refused to participate in a demonstration, like the one I had seen the evening before."

The more I reflected on this event, the more I thought that "These men were heroes. They would have made great Americans." I knew that they never had and never would experience the freedom that we have in America. The Koje Island experience made a great imprint upon my life.

Chapter 25

One Week of War, Three Years of Captivity

This story is about a young American officer, First Lieutenant Wadie Rountree, who saw only about one week of action before his capture in July 1950. During the early weeks of his captivity, he survived the brutality of the "Tiger," a North Korean officer known for his inhumane treatment of prisoners. A prisoner for over three years, mostly in camps near the Yalu River, Lieutenant Rountree experienced the brutal North Korean winters with inadequate clothing, housing, food, and medical care. As a result, he dropped from two hundred pounds to about one hundred pounds during his captivity. Despite the harsh conditions, he and his fellow prisoners revealed amazing creativity in their attempts to relieve their boredom. They organized classes, miraculously made bats and balls for softball, and played jokes on their Chinese captors. One POW stole the antique Chinese dinner bell used to summon the men to assembly, often for indoctrination classes, and dumped it into the latrine. The Chinese found it only after the North Korean laborers had empted the latrine much later. Finally freed on September 6, 1953, Lieutenant Rountree remained in the army and retired as a lieutenant colonel.

First Lieutenant Wadie J. Rountree

*I Company, Twenty-first Infantry Regiment,
Twenty-fourth Infantry Division*

I GREW UP in Twin City, Georgia, and saw service in the Army Air Corps at the end of WWII. Out of the service in 1945, I went back to college and was commissioned a second lieutenant in 1947 through the Army ROTC program. By March 1948, I was back on active duty. Later assigned to the

Twenty-fourth Infantry Division in Japan, I was in just the right place to see action when the North Koreans invaded South Korea on June 25, 1950.

As it turned out, elements of the Twenty-fourth Division were the very first U.S. forces assigned to the task of stopping the North Korean army and defending the Pusan perimeter. Major General William F. Dean, the division commander, ordered his Twenty-first Infantry regimental commander, Colonel Robert (Big Six) Stephens, to form a reinforced battalion for deployment to Korea as soon as possible. The task of commanding this battalion fell to Lieutenant Colonel Charles B. Smith, commander of the First Battalion. Consisting of 440 bewildered soldiers, "Task Force Smith," as they became known, climbed aboard C-54 Skymasters and landed at Pusan airport on the morning of July 1, 1950. They were promptly loaded on trains and transported north, where they first engaged the North Korean army near the town of Osan, about fifty miles south of Seoul. On July 5, 1950, the battalion was overrun by the North Korean forces. In this way the American soldier was introduced to the Korean War.

My unit, the Third Battalion, followed the First Battalion by two days, landing at Pusan on the 4th of July. At the time I served as a platoon leader in I Company. By July 9, my battalion occupied positions south of Chonan, a city between Osan and Taejon. About noon on July 10, the North Korean army completely overran elements of the First Battalion, and we were ordered to counterattack. We managed to recover most of the lost ground and evacuate the dead and wounded, but we also made some shocking discoveries. We found several GIs shot in the head with their hands tied behind their backs. These were the first known North Korean atrocities of the war. There would be many others.

Altogether we lost about a dozen men during the attack, including my platoon sergeant, W.P. Darah, who was hit by machine gun fire and had to be evacuated. He recovered from his wounds in Japan and returned to Korea in the fall but was killed in an attack against the same enemy.

A short time later our company commander, Lieutenant Cliff Barrington, ordered my platoon to secure the base of a hill, and we moved out immediately. When we drew near our destination, all hell broke loose and we found ourselves under heavy fire. Approaching tanks and increasing small arms fire forced us to withdraw and rejoin the main positions of the company. With the assistance of our own tanks and a 2.36-inch rocket launcher we made certain two North Korean tanks had completed their service for the Communist bastards.

No sooner had we stopped the enemy tanks when a sniper bullet ripped through the chest of Lieutenant Barrington and pierced his spinal column. He well knew the seriousness of his wound, and I can still hear him murmuring Hail Mary's. None of us expected to see him alive again, but after the war, I learned with great delight that he survived and became a certified public accountant, although confined to a wheelchair.

Fortunately, Lieutenant Brockman, the company executive officer and an ex-WWII platoon leader, carried on as if nothing had happened. For a while things quieted down, and the men in I Company got a little rest. On our left, however, K Company got hit pretty good and sustained a number of casualties.

At this time the positions we occupied put us at a disadvantage, since the North Koreans were literally breathing down our necks from the surrounding hills. Realizing this, our regimental commander, Colonel Stevens, gave the order to withdraw to the positions we had previously held. We carried out the withdrawal at midnight, but discovered that enemy soldiers had occupied some of our old foxholes. We got them out, but only after some tough fighting.

The next morning, July 11, we were hit hard by the Third Division of the North Korean army in a major attack. The fog was so thick the enemy could approach within fifty yards of our positions before we could see them. By the time the fog began to lift, about 9:00 A.M., my machine gun section had nearly run out of ammunition, and hordes of North Korean soldiers were advancing on our position from practically every direction. One North Korean crawled to within twenty-five feet of our position undetected before the machine gunner, Private First Class Guidry, gave him about a half pound of lead.

Suddenly I realized our supporting artillery was no longer firing. Unknown to us, the enemy had overrun our artillery positions. To determine what had happened, I decided to visit company headquarters, about one hundred yards away. When passing the crest of a hill to get there, however, I heard the rattle of a machine gun burst. One round struck the metal link of my cartridge belt, another hit the stock of my rifle, and a third ripped through my pants leg. I wasted no time in diving into the trenches of our mortar positions a few feet away. Miraculously, I didn't receive a scratch.

With the help of Sergeant Wilson, whom I had never met before, we managed to silence the enemy machine gun. Then, during a lull in the fighting, I heard Lieutenant Brockman shout, "Wadie, we're moving out." By this time enemy tanks and infantry had penetrated and surrounded our positions; we were even receiving fire from our rear.

For the most part my platoon was still intact. Only when we attempted to withdraw did we become separated and disorganized. As we fell back we were bitterly disappointed to see an enemy tank covering a shallow river that we had to cross. We paused for a few moments and watched while the tank cut down about two dozen people trying to cross the river.

Since there seemed to be no firing to the east of our position, we assumed this direction offered our best hope of escaping the enemy trap. We soon found out differently. We had moved only a few yards in this direction when we came under heavy enemy fire. From out of nowhere the enemy swarmed all over us. Outnumbered and surrounded, further resistance would have been futile. Suddenly, we were prisoners of war. The time was 10:30 A.M. on July 11, 1950, the beginning of what can only be described as three years of living hell.

Immediately after we were captured, the enemy tied our hands behind our backs with U.S. Army communications wire and prepared us for the march to the north. They assembled more than three hundred of us on a road that led to Seoul and marched us off in columns. It would be two months before we reached our destination near the Yalu River.

We got a pretty good idea of how the North Koreans intended to treat us on our first day as captives, July 11, an extremely hot day in Korea. Burning with thirst, we halted late that afternoon close to a cool, clear running stream but were not allowed to drink from it. Nor did we did receive any food until about thirty-six hours later, and then only a handful of rice.

Very quickly, however, we learned that our North Korean captors were capable of much worse behavior. Shortly after our capture, I witnessed a North Korean soldier approach one of our men, point a muzzle of a rifle to his head, and pull the trigger. This in turn prompted Lieutenant William Jester, our battalion S–2 officer, to attempt an escape. Assuming he was next, Lieutenant Jester started running like hell, with his hands tied behind his back. It was a futile effort. The North Koreans didn't shoot him, but did club him to the ground with rifle butts. He managed to survive the beating but died in a prison camp during the spring of 1951.

On July 12, we moved into Chonan, and from there north until we reached Seoul. In Seoul I underwent my first real interrogation during my captivity. The interrogator demanded to know about my unit, and when I refused to give him what he wanted, he asked me if I cared to go on living.

I told him they could shoot me, but I still wouldn't answer his questions. He replied that the Korean People's Army did not shoot their prisoners; they had other means. That was a radical departure from what I had observed in the past, I thought. Amazingly, I was not interrogated again until January 1952.

Seoul proved to be only a temporary collecting point for POWs, and we remained there only a few days. It was long enough, however, for the North Koreans to march some of us down the main streets of the city as exhibits, much to the delight of our captors.

During the latter part of July or early August, we were moved to Pyongyang, the capitol of North Korea. This time we were transported by rail, in cattle cars. At Pyongyang we joined approximately three hundred other American prisoners from Task Force Smith, plus those from our sister regiment, the Thirty-fourth Infantry. The total number in our group was 778, a number that decreased rapidly during the next year.

Like Seoul, Pyongyang proved to be only a temporary collecting point for POWs. During the early part of September we were moved to Manpo, a North Korean city located on the Yalu River. We traveled mostly at night, because the U.S. Air Force made movement during the day extremely hazardous for trains. During the daylight hours we stopped and held up in one of the many tunnels along the route. After five full days, on September 11, 1950, we finally arrived at Manpo.

Our new home was a former Japanese prison, located on a high cliff overlooking the Yalu. The place had its share of natural beauty, and from the prison we could see the river meandering through the narrow valleys. In the distance we could see the three railroad bridges that spanned the Yalu and separated Korea from Manchuria.

In October 1950, UN forces were advancing rapidly toward the Yalu, and our captors decided we must move again. To our surprise, we moved south along the Yalu. We stayed in several small towns, and everything was pretty routine until three of our men, Gonzales, Stallings, and one other I can't recall, attempted to escape. They were all recaptured within two or three days, and two of them were shot. Corporal Gonzales, for some reason, was allowed to return to camp.

About this time we witnessed something that for us was nothing less than disastrous—the entry of the Chinese Communists into the war. Early one morning we watched thousands of Chinese soldiers streaming down the main road bordering the Yalu River. It was one of the saddest moments of my life. None of us needed to be told how much this event could affect our lives.

On October 25, we began the march back to Manpo along the same route. When we arrived, however, we were not allowed to return to the old prison barracks. Instead, we were forced to spend six days and nights bivouacked on the banks of the Yalu, where we watched the never ending stream of Chinese soldiers pouring into Korea. It was a depressing sight, and this was without question one of the most miserable periods of my captivity.

By this time the cold had become the major problem for all of us. Most of the men were still wearing the same fatigue uniforms they had on when captured, totally inadequate for Korean winters. A few had received some discarded Korean padded clothing. The temperature had already dropped to below freezing at night, and we were still forced to sleep outside. We tried everything to keep warm, including snuggling together as close as possible and placing empty rice bags on top of us. We didn't keep warm, but we did survive.

On October 31, we received a new group of guards and a new camp commander, a homicidal maniac who became known as the "Tiger." That same afternoon we began marching north, a death march that did not end until November 8. The Tiger informed us that since no transportation was available, we would have to carry our sick and wounded.

If I had to single out the worst day of my captivity, it would be the following day, November 1, 1950. We began our march shortly after daybreak, after we had been divided into fourteen sections, with about forty men in each section. The Tiger set a blistering pace for the march that would have been difficult under normal conditions. We marched for about an hour when the Tiger suddenly halted the column. Through an interpreter, the Tiger informed Major John Dunn and several section leaders, which included myself, that we had allowed people to fall behind in the march. This was true, of course. The sick and wounded could barely walk, even with the help of our most able-bodied men. Next, the Tiger ordered Lieutenant Cordus Thornton to step forward, after which he tied the lieutenant's hands behind his back and placed a blindfold over his eyes. Then the Tiger turned to his guards and asked them if he should shoot Lieutenant Thornton. The guards roared back their approval. Accordingly, the Tiger calmly aimed his pistol at Lieutenant Thornton and shot him through the head. The lieutenant fell forward and crumbled to the ground—dead. Why the Tiger selected Lieutenant Thornton and no one else is still a mystery to me.

This incident seemed to be the catalyst for which the guards had been waiting. Almost immediately they began to commit similar atrocities. Throughout the eight-day march, if anyone fell behind he was shot, although we did not witness all of the shootings. The guards waited until all the other prisoners were out of sight, and then we would hear the dull thud of a rifle firing at close range. We lost approximately one man per mile during this one hundred–mile trek.

By this time the physical condition of all of us had deteriorated. Everyone had lost weight, some as much as fifty percent. Our diet consisted of rice, millet, or cracked corn twice a day, plus an occasional bowl of soup to be shared by several persons. The quantity of this food was totally insufficient to sustain a person undergoing the physical strain we endured during the march. In addition, sanitary conditions were primitive, and the water undrinkable. As a result of these conditions, virtually everyone had diarrhea.

Relative to the others, I was in good physical condition, so I helped those less fortunate. I carried one soldier, Private Ambrou, for about an hour, only to discover he had died. We moved his body to the side of the road and sadly prepared to leave it behind. Then the guard said, "We think he is dead but we want to be sure." He followed by firing a volley of about fifteen rounds into the body of Private Ambrou.

On the following day, we continued our march. This time I carried Lieutenant Books, who had a bad case of diarrhea and needed help. Eventually, I began to fall back toward the end of the column until I got help from another officer, Major Newton Lantrun. That night we huddled together as much as possible to keep warm. During the night Lieutenant Books died. This was the first of many occasions when I woke up and found a dead person beside me. We buried him early the next morning and resumed the march.

About noon on the fourth or fifth day of the march, we were told to assemble those incapable of walking. We gladly brought about twenty prisoners together, thinking they would finally receive some medical attention. It was not to be. As we departed, Hubert Arthur Lord, the commissioner of the British Salvation Army in Korea who served as our interpreter, overheard the Tiger instructing the local civilians to bury these men in unmarked graves.

On the afternoon of November 8, 1950, our march terminated in the town of Chunggang on the Yalu River. Although we had covered about fifteen miles that day, the Tiger appeared and informed us that we must do thirty minutes of calisthenics. Both Major Dunn and Commissioner Lord objected, but their efforts were futile. Following the calisthenics, the Tiger assembled us and made a short speech. "You have made this march to repent for your sins of coming to Korea," he barked. After this, we entered a vacant school building that served as our quarters for the next two weeks.

By this time our men were dying off quite rapidly. Everyone needed medical attention for something, much of it due to overexposure and malnutrition. Frostbite was a common problem, since the North Koreans had removed the shoes from many of the men, forcing them to walk in grass sandals with their feet wrapped in cloth and other makeshift footwear.

Due largely to the untiring efforts of Dr. Boysen, the Communists finally provided us with a separate room for our most seriously ill. Five American soldiers and a French priest, Father Paul Villemont, were placed in the room, which was equipped with a stove. The guard for this room, however, discovered a small hole in the stove pipe that he used as an excuse to douse the fire with water. Unbelievably, he then preceded to open the door and windows to the room. By morning, all six of the men had frozen to death. This included Sergeant Richard Haley, the first sergeant in my unit at the time of our capture.

After about two weeks we moved again, this time to another vacant school near the Yalu, where the monotony, drudgery, and horror continued. Our daily routine began long before daylight, when the guard stomped through our building screaming and herding everyone outside for "fresh air and exercise." The temperature outside was normally around twenty-five to thirty degrees below zero, and most of us still wore the same fatigue uniforms we were wearing at the time of our capture. While we did have stoves in our rooms, they produced more smoke than heat. I don't believe anyone ever became comfortably warm during that first winter.

The schoolroom in which I stayed was approximately eighteen by twenty feet, with four windows and a door. There were no beds; as a matter of fact, I never slept in a bed during my entire thirty-eight months of captivity. To make things worse, there wasn't enough room for everyone to lie down at the same time. This is the way it worked: Some of us placed our heads against the walls while the others placed their heads together in the center. Our feet and legs overlapped each other up to the waist, and we had to lie on our sides, back to breast, to fit into the existing space. If one man turned over, the entire row had to turn over. When our captors gave us a single blanket in mid-January 1951, we gave it to the unfortunate soul sleeping next to the door. At one point we had over one hundred men in our room. Most of us had to relieve ourselves several times during the night. It was a living hell.

Death, hastened by the cold, diet deficiency, and frequent beatings from the guards, became an everyday occurrence for us. It was not unusual to wake up in the morning and find the man on either side of you dead. I had this happen to me on several occasions. It was during this period I lost two of my closest friends, Lieutenants Brockman and Lewis.

In late January we moved again, this time to separate officers and NCOs from the others. According to their Communist logic, we were capitalist reactionaries and as such exerted a bad influence on the other members of the group. This time we moved only a short distance to a Korean mud house, which we found just as cold and miserable as our previous quarters in the school house. There were only about twenty of us to a room, but the room was so small we were just as cramped for space as before.

Fortunately, by late February conditions began to improve. The worst of the winter was behind us, and the reign of the Tiger came to an end. This came about shortly after a visit by a staff major from the North Korean Army Headquarters in Pyongyang. During the visit he talked to Major Dunn, who bravely told the major about the wretched living conditions we were enduring. A few days later the Tiger was relieved. Major Dunn's frankness had paid off, although he took a great risk. None of us had anything but the greatest respect for Major Dunn. After we were released it came as no surprise to learn he was awarded the Legion of Merit for his courage and leadership while in captivity.

In March 1951, for whatever reason, we moved again. By this time I had concluded it was a waste of time to try and figure out the mind of a Communist; they were completely unpredictable and illogical. Again we moved only a short distance, and this time our living conditions actually improved. For the first time since our capture we were allowed to go outside into a compound. I never realized how nice fresh air and sunshine could be, even though the air was biting cold.

With this new freedom and the coming of spring, our morale improved. On occasion we were taken to neighboring hills, where we gathered firewood. It was a welcome escape from the daily monotony.

Unfortunately, it was during this period that I reached my worst physical condition while in captivity. When captured I weighed 200 pounds; by this time I estimated my weight at about 100 pounds. Even so, I was still in better condition than most of the prisoners. By the early summer of 1951, we had lost more than 400 of our original group of 778 men. When liberated at the end of the war only 280 of us remained alive, a little over one-third. Overall, the death rate among American POWs captured in Korea was about 40 percent, most dying during the first year of captivity. Such a high percentage of deaths can only be the result of a diabolical plan prepared and executed by the North Korean and Chinese Communists.

The summer of 1951 brought warmer weather, welcomed by all, and improved living conditions. The new camp commander was a more sane individual than the Tiger, and deserves to be credited with some of the improvement. The indiscriminate shooting of prisoners had for the most part stopped by this time. Our death rate was still high, however, undoubtedly the result of the hardships suffered by the men during the winter months.

Summer passed, autumn came, and we still had no idea how the war was progressing. For all we knew, it could be over. We still had received no mail, and would not until about a year and half after our capture. No new prisoners had joined us since Thanksgiving 1950, almost one year earlier. It had been nearly six months since we had seen friendly aircraft in the area, which had the effect of increasing our anxiety about the war. Most of all, we were beginning to wonder if we would ever be released.

In the early part of October 1951, our guards informed us we were going to move again. At the time we welcomed the news. Anything, we thought, would be better than spending another winter at Camp #7 in Chunggang.

Our trip began on October 8. We walked about thirty miles and then, to our surprise, they put us aboard sampans (river boats) for our voyage south, down the Yalu. The rapids were swift, and at times our small boat seemed to completely submerge as it balanced from rock to rock. Then, much to our relief, the boat emerged undamaged and we continued our voyage.

Finally, we reached the backwaters of the Suiho Reservoir, where we boarded a tugboat in a driving rainstorm for the rest of our journey. Soaking wet, we eventually docked at a small Korean village south of Pyokdong. For about two weeks we stayed at Camp #3, but then moved to Camp #2, a consolidated camp for officers. Sadly, this was the last time we saw the NCOs and enlisted men until we were released. I have never been associated with a better group and leaving them was difficult.

Upon arriving in Pyokdong we had a change in command; the Chinese took over for their Korean comrades. By November 1951, the Chinese had placed all military prisoners under their authority. There was one exception,

Major General William F. Dean, who remained under the control of the North Koreans. On the surface, the Chinese were a little more sensible than the Koreans, but underneath they were just as dirty and filthy rotten as their Korean counterparts.

When we arrived at Camp #2 in Pyokdong in November 1951, little did we realize that we had reached our last POW camp. The camp was located in the little village of Pi-Chong-ni, our "home" until repatriated in September 1953.

Unfortunately, by this time we had not only been separated from the enlisted men but from the civilian prisoners as well. I regretted this very much. Most of the civilians were missionaries, who had spent the greater part of their adult lives devoted to the spiritual and physical well-being of the Korean people. They were a fine group of people, and I became good friends with many of them. I might add, they received no privileges as a result of their civilian status. They made the same marches and endured the same savage treatment as the military prisoners. Some of the civilians in our group were women. I especially remember two wonderful American ladies, Miss Nellie Dyer from North Little Rock, Arkansas, and Miss Helen Rosser from Atlanta, Georgia, both missionaries.

My favorite civilian, however, was Monsignor Thomas Quinlan. A tall, impressive man with a black beard, he had served in China and Korea since 1920. I loved to listen to the soft tones of his beautiful Irish accent, always giving us words of encouragement. "Well, me lads, it won't be long now," he would say, or, when referring to the UN forces, "they're fighting well." Most of us knew that he manufactured about 90 percent of this for our benefit, but we didn't care. We welcomed good news of any kind, and we had faith in the bishop. After the war he returned to Korea and continued his missionary service.

I also have fond memories of the nuns in our group, who performed countless acts of mercy for everyone. Somehow they found the time to launder our soiled clothing and care for the seriously ill. And the nuns received the same treatment as the rest of us. If they fell behind when we marched, they were shot, just like the others. Most of the nuns were elderly, but somehow all but three of the group of about fifteen managed to survive the ordeal.

Our stay at Camp #2 in Pi-Chong-ni, a quiet little village located on the main route connecting Pyokdong and Manpo, lasted twenty-one months, much longer than any of the other camps. At the beginning of our stay, we assumed the nightmare of prison life would continue, but this time conditions did improve. For the first time we received mail from home. We also had the opportunity to speak with prisoners outside our group, who provided us with some of the first news of the world we had received in about a year and a half.

Camp #2 also had better facilities than the other camps. Our room was actually large enough for all of us to lie down at the same time, a real improvement. We had barrels for hot water, and the morning after we arrived we had our first hot bath. The same morning we received a change of clothing and they boiled our old clothing to kill the body lice. Amazingly, we were never bothered with body lice again, and this amounted to a significant improvement in our living conditions. We were also given one blanket per individual, the first since our capture. Our food improved, with increased rations of rice, and flour from which we made bread.

The Chinese even permitted us to attend religious services, something the North Koreans had never allowed. Unfortunately, the saintly Father (Captain) Emil J. Kapaun had died in the spring of 1951, so we had no Catholic clergy. We were allowed, however, to put together a makeshift chapel in a large room that also served as a library. One of our officers made a beautiful crucifix from an oak limb, and another officer, Captain Ralph Nardello, conducted our services. Protestant services were conducted by a British chaplain, Captain Stanley J. Davies.

Receiving mail from home, especially from my wife, was a real morale booster. She actually was on her way to join me in Japan when the war began. Unfortunately, by the time she arrived I had shipped out for Korea. I learned from her letter that she landed in Japan on July 12, 1950, the day following my capture. She spent about six weeks in Japan trying to learn something official about my fate, but eventually gave up and returned to Ft. Smith, Arkansas. She wrote the letter out of sheer hope I might still be alive. Not until the list of prisoners was exchanged in late 1953 did she have any realistic expectation that this might be true.

By the spring of 1952, most of us had recuperated to the point where we could actively engage in athletics, which the Chinese permitted. Our big problem—we had no equipment. We pooled our creative talents and amazed ourselves with the results. Somehow, softballs miraculously emerged from discarded combat boots. Coming up with suitable wood for bats was tough, but we managed. Whenever firewood was delivered to the camp, we rummaged through the pile until we found the right limb with a good grain for a bat. Then we would cut and scrape until we produced a reasonable fac-simile. In the summer of 1952, we were actually provided with equipment for volleyball, soccer, and basketball, which gave us more options. The games were a big help in breaking the monotony of prison life.

Since we were given flour to make bread, Lieutenant Bill Watson de-cided to build an oven, which he did from two fifty-five-gallon oil drums, rock, mud, and an axe. To our great delight, it worked. We still needed bread pans, which we made from some stove pipe stolen from a Chinese guard house. The yeast came from fermented potatoes. Believe it or not, the bread tasted pretty good, or at least we thought it did at the time.

We even held classes at Camp #2, although we had to do this surrepti-tiously, because the Chinese forbade POWs from engaging in any organized activity. Classes were offered in math, science, and languages. There was an amazing range of talent among the POWs, and the instructors knew their stuff. No textbooks were available, of course, but the POWs still came up with some very creative teaching aids. During the latter period of our captivity, we even produced our own plays, some of which were hilariously funny.

Our conditions improved so dramatically at Camp #2, we began to wonder what the motives of our captors were. We really had no way of knowing at the time. We only knew that since July 1951 the two sides had been engaged in peace talks at Panmunjom, and we thought this might have something to do with it. In December 1951, the Chinese and UN represen-tatives even concluded an agreement to exchange lists of prisoners then held in custody. When the war finally did end, surely there would be an exchange of prisoners. Most of us who had been in captivity since the early part of the war had lost as much as half of our weight, and we were literally walking skeletons. The Chinese were well aware of this, and knew that if we were released in this condition they would be at a disadvantage in the propaganda war. Better to give us more rice and fatten us up a bit before our release.

Whatever the motives of our captors, we definitely received more hu-mane treatment. Between November 1951 and September 1953, we re-corded no deaths at Camp #2. The Chinese did kill one British officer, but they claimed he was trying to escape. Perhaps. In any case, we were far better off than during the first year and a half of captivity, when we lost two-thirds of our original group. While the peace negotiations seemed to drag on for-ever, partially because the UN representatives insisted that no prisoners would be forcibly repatriated, these talks were still instrumental in improving our living conditions while in captivity.

One very obvious improvement at Camp #2 came in the form of better medical treatment. Previously, medical care for POWs was almost nonexistent, in part because the Communists would not permit our own excellent doctors to practice their profession. As a result, our wounded were often left unattended, sometimes for days. Now we received much more medical attention than before, but the quality of care was often laughable. When I was suffering from beriberi, diarrhea, and malnutrition, a Chinese doctor told me Americans got sick because we walked on the floor with our shoes on, which was "not sanitary." Then he cleared his throat and spat against the wall. When Lieutenant Bob Howell came down with some mysterious ailment, the Chinese sewed a chicken liver to his intestine. The camp was alive with stories about incompetent Chinese doctors and their weird practices.

Work details were often a part of our daily activity. Frequently, the Chinese marched us to the Yalu River, about two miles away, where we unloaded supplies from incoming barges. On our trips to the Yalu we passed through Pi-Chong-ni, a village that the Chinese used to keep POWs in solitary confinement. They were mostly prisoners who had tried to escape and failed, or, according to Chinese logic, were "plotting against the people." We shouted words of encouragement to them as we passed through, which they generally acknowledged from their manmade caves, basements, cell blocks, and other creative places of confinement.

There was one thing about Camp #2 we all intensely disliked—the systematic program of indoctrination initiated by the Chinese Communists. Widely publicized as brainwashing, this was something quite new to us. While we had been brutalized by the North Koreans in every way, they had never subjected us to a program of organized indoctrination. The Chinese were different.

To launch their campaign, the Chinese put us through a complete course on the "Causes of the Korean War." In their view, of course, the United States was totally responsible for the war. They also hammered us on the use of germ warfare by the United States. The Chinese claimed the tinsel foil dropped by UN planes to jam their radar was laded with germs. A propaganda poster depicted American planes parachuting rats into North Korea to spread disease. To make sure the Americans were identified with capitalism, the eyes of the rats were replaced with dollar signs.

The Chinese also gave us a heavy dose of stuff on the merits of Communism and the wonderful progress the "New China" was making since the "People's Enemies" had been eliminated. We learned all about their new roads, dams, and schools, and the happy life of the peasants. We also sat through lectures on the "Capitalists of WWII." The Soviet Union, we were told, not only won all the important battles in Europe but also played the major role in the defeat of Japan.

The biggest problem presented by all of this indoctrination garbage was boredom. Every day we attended lectures for about an hour and a half each morning and afternoon. Then in the evenings we were supposed to read and have group discussions on Communist literature. The lectures were so distorted and biased it was difficult to take them seriously. Also, we attended the lectures seated on the floor in unheated rooms, which did not help our attitude.

Despite all the time and energy the Chinese put into their indoctrination program, several months passed and they still had nothing to show for their efforts. They apparently understood this, because in the spring of 1952 they discontinued the program, at least in Camp #2. We had witnessed far too many atrocities and suffered too much to be taken in by Communist lies and propaganda. With a very few exceptions, the UN prisoners rejected Communism as an ideology and as a way of life.

Despite our captivity, we somehow managed to find ways and the courage to harass our captors. Sometimes these antics were organized and sometimes they were spontaneous, but either way they provided great entertainment for all the prisoners. We discovered we could easily frustrate the Chinese guards at roll call, which normally took place about 4:30 A.M. One morning everyone in a particular room would go into a delaying pattern and hold up roll call, perhaps as much as thirty minutes. The next morning the same guys would get up early, dress, and wait for the guard to open the door. Then they would burst through the door wildly, yelling as they ran from the building to the parade ground, and fall into ranks with the precision and smartness of West Point cadets. Such erratic behavior totally baffled the Chinese.

One of our best pranks involved the antique dinner bell that the Chinese rang whenever they wished to assemble the prisoners, often for indoctrination lectures. While I was never quite sure who did it, one of the guys managed to steal it and dump it into our latrine, a simple hole in the ground about eight to ten feet deep. Only when the Korean laborers emptied the latrine later, a chore they carried out regularly because they used the human waste for fertilizer, did the Chinese locate their missing bell.

Finally, I must tell the story about Lieutenant John Thornton (USN) and his "motorcycle." Every morning and afternoon he appeared for roll call riding his imaginary motorcycle. With unmistakable sound effects, John would circle the group several times, park his motorcycle, and join the formation. Not surprisingly, the Chinese thought he was a little affected. They called John to their headquarters and informed him that he could no longer keep his motorcycle, because it was against camp "rules and regulations." When John returned and told the story to the men, some of them actually approached the Chinese and demanded they return his motorcycle. The story is almost unbelievable, but it is true. It just reflects the crazy things men will do in captivity to find relief from the boredom.

As the winter of 1952–1953 neared the end, we really began to look forward to spring and summer. While the winter had been milder than the previous winters, and we did have warmer clothing by this time, we still looked forward to milder weather. We continued to receive letters from home regularly, but they took nearly two months to arrive. When they did arrive, we remained just as ignorant about the war as before; letters that contained war news didn't make it through the Chinese censors.

Since Camp #2 was located at the northern end of MiG Alley, we sometimes entertained ourselves by watching the air battles in the sky. These battles were usually fought so far away we couldn't see the identification markings on the planes, but we could still tell the "good guys" from the "bad guys" by the sound of their weapons when they fired.

By the late spring of 1953, we could tell from the mood of our captors that the war was slowly coming to a close. Finally, the last contentious point, the forced repatriation of POWs, was settled. The signing of the armistice took place at Panmunjom at 10:00 A.M. on July 27, 1953, exactly three years, one month, and two days after North Korea invaded South Korea.

In compliance with the armistice agreement, all prisoners were to be informed the hostilities had ended. During the late evening hours of July 27, we were pleasantly surprised to hear American jazz played over the Chinese loudspeakers, something we had never heard before. We all knew the day we had been dreaming about for so long was now at hand.

About mid-afternoon on the following day, the Chinese finally assembled the prisoners and officially gave us the good news. We received the news quietly, without cheers and applause. Apparently the Chinese were expecting a wild melee of jubilation, because they had placed cameras all over the place.

After three years of waiting and abusive treatment, we were more than ready to go home. All of us, except a few—the twenty-one "turncoats." In compliance with the armistice agreements, there would be no forced repatriation, and twenty-one Americans chose to remain in Communist China. I personally knew only one of these men, Private First Class William Cowart, who had been a member of my platoon prior to the war. I remembered him as a kind of perpetual sorehead with a bad attitude. I was not aware, however, of any particular ideological or political beliefs that he possessed prior to his capture. According to reports I have subsequently received, he accepted personal favors from the Chinese and eventually moved into their billets. I really don't think he refused repatriation because he had embraced Communism as a better way of life. In my opinion, he stayed behind because he feared reprisals from other prisoners as well as from the U.S. government. Much the same may be said for the others who remained in China.

Once we realized we would soon be repatriated, the days passed with the speed of a slow turtle. Each day seemed like an eternity. The Chinese told us only that we would be released "soon," but they never gave us a definite date.

Finally, one day in late August, a large convoy of trucks appeared, and we knew this was it. We fell out in formation and, after a period of time, climbed aboard Soviet-built trucks. But the trucks did not move. At last, after more waiting, we heard the order, "Unload, unload."

At first we thought the Chinese were playing one more dirty trick on us before we left, but this time we were wrong. Flash floods the previous week had caused several mud slides, and time was needed to repair the roads.

The next day went much better. The rain let up, the sun came up over the mountains, and once again we climbed aboard the trucks. Even the Chinese seemed to be in a good mood. While we waited for the trucks to start their engines, someone passed a bottle of Chinese whiskey around, which made the time go faster.

Finally, the truck engines roared, and we began one of the happiest days of our lives—the first leg of our journey home. We actually headed north, along the Yalu to Manpo, where we arrived late that same evening. At Manpo, after joining up with other prisoners, we boarded a POW troop train. Once again we were in box cars, but unlike the cattle cars used on our trip north three years earlier, this time we had mattresses and straw on the floors.

The rail portion of our trip lasted two days, slowed by the condition of the bridges and tracks along the way. We traveled virtually the same route south we had taken north after our capture. All along the way we saw the

Stuck in the mud, not an uncommon problem in Korea, especially in the spring. (Courtesy of Forty-fifth Infantry Division Museum)

results of the war—ruined locomotives and vehicles and destroyed bridges. Finally, the train came to a halt, and suddenly I realized we were in Panmunjom.

Operation Big Switch, as it was known, began on August 5, 1953. On average, about three hundred UN prisoners were released each day until the final day of repatriation on September 6. Until our release, we lived in a tent city purposely constructed for the prisoners. Those to be released on a particular day were generally given only a few hours' notice.

I began to grow impatient; it seemed they were never going to call my name. At last, on September 4, when I was about to give up hope and prepare for another long day of waiting, it happened. The Chinese finally called out my name for repatriation, the next to the last name on the list to be called. It was like a dream, and while I went to bed that night, I didn't sleep a wink.

The next morning, those of us to be released were up at dawn, restless and nervous. After breakfast we were assembled, searched, and loaded on the Soviet-built trucks for our journey to the exchange point, located about halfway between Panmunjom and Freedom Village. At the exchange point we were transferred from the trucks to U.S. Army ambulances, where two huge marines assisted us.

"Welcome back," they said smartly. I can think of nothing in the English language they could have said at the time that would have sounded any sweeter than those two little words.

Chapter 26

A First Sergeant's Experience

Not many soldiers wanted to go to Korea, but WWII veterans found it especially hard; after all, they had already served. In the early part of the war, however, their leadership and skills were desperately needed, and many veterans were called up. James Hart, a reservist with mortar experience, was typical of these veterans. Arriving in Korea in January 1951, he was first placed in charge of a 60mm mortar section, then became the company's first sergeant. Unfortunately, during the massive Chinese offensive on April 22, 1951, his company was cut off and surrounded. As a result, Sergeant Hart spent the remainder of the war in captivity. After a hard march, he experienced the same horrors endured by other POWs in the Communist prison camps, including hunger, the terrible cold, unbelievable filth, and brainwashing. Sergeant Hart strongly opposed the "limited" war policy and believed the UN armies should have continued offensive operations until the Communist forces were crushed.

Master Sergeant James Hart

F Company, Second Battalion, Fifth Regimental Combat Team

LIKE SO MANY others, when the Korean War began in June 1950, I entered the war as a WWII retread. I had served in the First Cavalry Division in the Philippines, then spent a year with the occupation forces in Japan. In December 1948, after a year and a half of college, I had started a new job. Since I had stayed in the reserves in order to preserve my rank as staff sergeant, and the army desperately needed experienced personnel, I was just right to be called up.

In September, I received my notice to report for active duty on October 1. I reported to Fort Hood, Texas, which was the same place I had completed my basic training during WWII. I stayed there until I received my orders, sometime in December, which were "pipeline" for Korea. After a few days traveling I arrived at Camp Stoneman, California. A short time later they trucked us to a troopship, and we embarked for Japan. We arrived in Yokohama in early January 1951.

Since I had served in WWII, I was not at all happy about returning to active duty, and especially for duty in Korea. The other reservists felt pretty much the same way. We all very much resented going back into the army when there were so many others who had never served. I will admit we didn't fully understand the army's desperate need for trained personnel with combat experience. Especially in those critical days early in the war, we provided the skills and leadership that were so essential for success on the battlefield.

After disembarking at Yokohama, we spent one day processing at Camp Drake and promptly shipped out for Korea. After about a day on a ferryboat, we arrived at the port of Pusan. Almost immediately the army put us on board an unheated train with straight, wooden seats, and we headed north to a replacement depot somewhere near the front lines. From there we went our separate ways to our assigned units. I was assigned to the Fifth Regimental Combat Team (RCT), which at that time was attached to the Twenty-fourth Division. I arrived at the Fifth RCT Headquarters sometime in the early part of January 1951, and from there on to Fox Company, Second Battalion. Since I had experience in an 81mm mortar section during WWII, they made me a squad leader in charge of a section of 60mm mortars.

In the early part of February, we went into combat. At the time I thought I was in pretty good physical condition, but I found out differently. Korea is just one hill and one mountain after the other, and since we also carried about eighty pounds of equipment, soldiering in Korea was pretty exhausting. Most of us required another six to eight weeks after arriving to get in top condition.

By late February, General Ridgway had ordered a major counterattack along a wide front, known as Operation Killer. It aimed at making a clean sweep across Korea and driving the Chinese and North Korean armies back across the 38th Parallel. To do this, it was very important for us to keep the Chinese and North Korean troops in front of us. We had learned, through bitter experience, that it was a favorite tactic of the Communist forces to break through our lines and set up roadblocks behind us. Then, when we tried to go through a mountain pass, they would cut us to pieces with small arms fire coming from each side of the mountain. In the early days of the war, this tactic had succeeded far too often.

Not long after we hit the front lines, one of the guys I had met coming over on the ship, who had become a good friend of mine, was killed. We were going up a hill when an enemy machine gun opened up, badly wounding him. Even so, he still managed to knock out the machine gun with a grenade before he died. I think he received the Silver Star for this action, but I'm not positive. This was the first casualty I witnessed in the war.

During the early part of April, I became the first sergeant for Fox Company. I also became a master sergeant a little later, but I was already in captivity when I learned about it. I didn't have long to enjoy my promotion anyway. On April 22, 1951, the Chinese army attacked with a quarter million men along a forty-mile front north of Seoul. They just sent masses of humanity at us and suffered the consequences. We had a lot of firepower, so we inflicted heavy casualties, but they just kept on coming. Unfortunately, my company was cut off and surrounded.

At the time, we were fighting just north of the 38th Parallel in the Kumhwa area. When the attack came, I was several miles behind the Fox Company positions at our company command post (CP). We knew as soon as we received news of the Chinese attack that the men would quickly run out of ammunition, so we loaded up a jeep and a trailer with ammo and took off for the front. There was much confusion that night, and it seemed like it took forever to reach the front. Fortunately, there was a full moon, which did help some. While we were in the process of getting the ammo to the men, the Chinese managed to surround the company. I had six or seven men with me, and we fought a fierce rearguard action, repulsing four or five attacks in about a two-hour period. While we managed to get most of the ammo to the company, we had to fight our way out, and in the process we became separated. I managed to elude the Chinese for about eighteen hours before they grabbed me. All the other men with me also became POWs.

After my capture the Chinese put me through one of their interrogations. They told me they were getting ready to surround another American unit, and they wanted me to tell them to surrender. This I refused to do. In hindsight, I probably should have done it. I would have been closer to the front, and the confusion that accompanies heavy fighting would have provided me with a better chance of escaping. Of course, I also would have stood a better chance of getting killed, so maybe things worked out for the best after all.

As a POW the Chinese bounced me around from one group to another. At first I seemed to be the only POW in the area, but soon others were added and we kept getting larger and larger until finally there were about four hundred of us gathered in a place we called Peaceful Valley. It actually was a place near Kumhwa in central Korea, and we stayed there about three weeks. Our food was the bare minimum for survival. They fed us very little because they were getting ready to brainwash us and they wanted to degrade us to an animal existence. The Chinese reasoned that this way we would credit them for the improved conditions we received later. Thus, we would be more likely to accept them as friends, or so they thought.

As the UN forces pushed the Chinese and North Korean forces back to the north, the POWs moved north as well. On May 19, we started marching, and for about thirty days we just kept going. It was a tough march, and we lost about 10 percent of the men along the way. Finally, on June 19, we reached the Yalu River, the border between North Korea and China. This is where the POW camps were located, our "homes" for the remaining part of the war. Unfortunately, our suffering and our losses were just starting. There were about sixteen hundred prisoners in each of the two major POW camps, and I think we lost about 60 percent of them by the time the war was over. Some days we would bury as many as twenty men.

Ironically, in July 1951, not long after I was captured, the peace talks began. The Chinese wanted to talk because they wanted to buy some time; they weren't interested in serious peace talks. They wanted to use the time to dig in and build up their defensive lines, which would make it more difficult for us to push them back. At the time I was not aware of this, but after the war I learned how successful they were in using the time for this purpose. I believe President Truman made a serious mistake when he stopped our offensive operations and allowed the Communist forces the opportunity to dig in; we should have continued to attack while we had them on the run. Then we could have negotiated from a position of strength and made the Chinese get serious about the talks.

The first winter I spent in Korea as a POW, 1951–1952, was the toughest. I spent this time at Changsong, a prison camp near the Yalu River in the northwestern part of North Korea. A whole lot of people died that winter from simple malnutrition and disease. Beriberi and pellagra were very common. Everybody lost weight, some guys getting down to around eighty pounds. Also, we had to go through what the Chinese called reeducation, better known in the United States as brainwashing. They tried to get us to accept Communism as the best form of government possible, and they made this an important part of their agenda. Those who openly opposed the Communist ideas were placed in solitary confinement. The Chinese had what they called "reactionary camps," where they kept the most difficult prisoners. The majority, I think, tried to forestall punishment by avoiding open resistance, but still remained unchanged by the Communist propaganda they threw at us. There were a few individuals, however, who were either so weak or so uneducated they went along with the Communist line of thinking. Fortunately, they represented only a very small minority of the POWs.

One of the worst things about being a prisoner in those early months of captivity was the lack of any opportunity to clean up. Our hair grew down to our shoulders, our beards to our chests, we had lice, and all of us were filthy. In the winter, the cold was a major problem, because the temperature could get down as low as thirty to forty degrees below zero. Since we stayed in simple mud huts with no heat, we had very little protection from the cold. A lot of the guys ended up with frozen fingers, hands, and feet, which they eventually lost, and almost all of us had frostbite in some form. In the summer, in addition to the heat and humidity, flies were a major problem. The walls and ceilings of our huts were literally black with flies.

As time passed, our treatment did improve, but we still didn't know how the war was going or how the peace talks were progressing. The Chinese would tell us the peace talks were going very well and that we would be going home soon. Then, a week or so later, they would say the peace talks had broken down and we would have to remain prisoners indefinitely. Naturally, this kind of thing kept us upset. Eventually we got to the point where we just didn't believe anything they said, and this made things a little easier from a mental point of view. Life was tough enough; we didn't need all that psychological garbage the Chinese were throwing at us to go along with the cold, the hunger, and the lack of anything even remotely approaching decent sanitary conditions.

Most of us who managed to make it through the first winter to the fall of 1951 survived the remaining years of imprisonment and eventually went home. After that first year, for whatever reason, we did receive better treatment, and the death rate dropped considerably.

On July 27, 1953, the war finally came to an end when an armistice was signed at Panmunjom. Ironically, July 27 happens to be my birthday. I figured an armistice was a pretty good birthday present. The exchange of prisoners had actually begun in April with the exchange of the sick and wounded

Silver Star winner Master Sergeant James Hart, Fifth RCT, getting off a plane in Amarillo, Texas, September 18, 1953, following his return from Korea as a POW. (Courtesy of James Hart)

(Operation Little Switch). Then, between August 5 and September 6, the other prisoners were exchanged (Operation Big Switch).

At the time it seemed to us that the prisoners who had given the Chinese a hard time were the last to be repatriated. Usually these people were the NCOs and officers. I came out on September 5, the next to the last day. It was a large group, but I don't remember anybody who was not an NCO or an officer. Furthermore, most of those left behind who came out on the last day were also NCOs or officers. This last group also included a few hardcore guys that had never cooperated with the Chinese in any way.

One thing always bothered me about the war, not only at the time but also after I got out. I believe we should have defeated the Chinese and North Korean armies decisively when we had the opportunity. If we had committed our forces in full strength, I think we could have crushed the Communist forces and ended the war much sooner. I hated the idea of a "limited" war and the restrictions placed on the military that kept us from winning the war. The limited war concept meant that Washington politics determined how we conducted the war, and the shape of the victory, if any. I didn't want to be in Korea, but if I did have to be there, I wanted to fight to win and go home.

I must admit, however, that while I was in Korea I really didn't understand how we ever got involved in that mess. As far as I was concerned, it really didn't mean anything if South Korea did fall to the North Koreans. In retrospect, I do confess I see the war a little differently now. For the first time, we stopped the expansion of Communism, and this has had a great effect on the events which followed. While the Communists may not have given up their expansionist ideas, they were at least stalemated. So I feel our involvement in the forgotten war was not all in vain, and I'm proud to have been a participant. I also feel good when I think of the millions of South Koreans who now live in a free society, something that so far is not even remotely possible in North Korea.

Chapter 27

Organizing the Riots on Koje
Colonel Zhao's Story

By 1952, there were 132,000 Chinese and North Korean Communist prisoners in the UNC camps. About 70,000 of them were held at Koje Island, an isolated, hilly island a few miles across the sea from the shore of Pusan. On May 7, the prisoners in Compound 76 seized UNC Brigadier General Francis T. Dodd as a hostage. On May 9, General James Van Fleet arrived with 15,000 heavily armed UN troops to face the mass of prisoners behind the wire. Though Dodd was released the next day after negotiations, the conflict continued. By July, the rioting had claimed the lives of 115 prisoners. As the secretary general of the "Chinese Communist United Front" at Koje-do, Colonel Zhao Zuorui's reflections provide an untold story about the fighting that took place inside the camps among the Communist and non-Communist prisoners, and the efforts of the Communist prisoners to organize and plan the 1951–1952 riots.

Colonel Zhao Zuorui

Secretary General, "Chinese Communist United Front,"
UNC Koje-do Camp

Former Political Commissar, 538th Regiment,
180th Division, CPVF Sixtieth Army

DURING THE CHINESE People's Volunteer Forces' Fifth Campaign in the spring of 1951, the UN forces managed to surround the 180th Division. The 538th Regiment, my regiment, was assigned the mission of breaking through the enemy lines and leading the division's retreat to the north. When we attempted to carry out our mission during the night of May 24, we failed. I lost contact with regimental headquarters during the night and was captured by the UN forces on May 25. By May 28, most of the division was gone, and nine thousand Chinese soldiers, I learned later, became prisoners of war.

On May 26, I was sent to Suwon. About one thousand Chinese prisoners had already gathered there. Defeated and uncertain about their future, many of them seemed to have lost their courage and spirit. Those who were from my regiment felt a little bit better when they saw me there with them. I told my captors that my name was "Wang Fang," not Zhao Zuorui, and that I was a cook, not a regiment officer. The UN personnel couldn't identify our ranks since we all wore the same uniforms, wore no officer's insignia, and had our heads shaved (including division and regimental commanders). Later, we were shipped by train to Pusan, where we were registered. The Koreans working at the UNC registration tables were prisoners from the North Korean People's Army. Speaking both Chinese and Korean, they were friendly and supportive. While they gave us encouragement, they also indicated we might be shipped to Taiwan.

On June 16, we boarded UNC landing crafts. On my landing ship there were about two hundred Chinese prisoners, and none of us knew where we were going. We did know it could be really bad if we were sent to Taiwan. The Chinese Nationalist Army could easily identify the Chinese Communist Army officers, and they would execute all the commanders. I had to do something before it was too late. After the ship left the port of Pusan, I sat around with a couple of regimental and battalion commanders on board, and we discussed the possibility of killing the guards and taking over the ship when it got close to the Shanghai coast, about halfway to Taiwan. About two hours later, however, before we could come up with a plan, the ship stopped at an island not far from Pusan. It was Koje Island.

We got off the ship and walked into a camp, numbered 72. A UN officer asked us, "Who are the battalion officers?" No answer. "Any company commanders?" Again, no answer. Two days later, however, on June 18, all the Chinese officers in Compound 72 were identified by the UN interrogators. Somebody in our division had betrayed the CPVF. These scums apparently told everything to the enemy.

The UN guards transferred seven of us, the regimental and battalion officers, from Compound 72 to a "POW Officer Compound." There I met other Chinese and North Korean officers, including a North Korean governor. They told me that there were about one hundred thousand North Korean prisoners and more than twenty thousand Chinese prisoners detained on Koje-do Island. Most of the Chinese prisoners were in Compounds 71, 72, and 86. Many North Korean compounds had been organized by leaders of the Communist Party, who were preparing for a general riot in September. The North Korean officers hoped that the Chinese compounds could be organized and join in their struggle. Having learned a lot in the "Officer Camp," I became confident. I knew what I could do and how to do it. I was ready to carry on my duty in the POW camp and continue to fight the Korean War on Koje Island. It was the second front of the Korean War.

A month later, in late July, we were sent back to Compound 72. The situation, however, had totally changed there. The Chinese prisoners, including my own men, didn't want to talk to either me or the other officers. They wouldn't even look at me. I could feel a heavy pressure and a terrible fear over the entire compound. The UN camp officers had changed their policy. They now allowed those Chinese prisoners who had turned traitors and cooperated with the enemy to run the camps.

After the Chinese prisoners had been interrogated and sent to their camps, like Koje-do, they became both useless and a burden for the UNC. Many of the guards treated the prisoners like animals. The UN officers and men believed that we, the Chinese and North Koreans, were not people like themselves, but near animals, who could be controlled by the use of the same brutality we were accustomed to employ against each other. They selected the traitors and defectors from the prisoners and used them to watch us. These Chinese turncoats, I have to say, were worse than the American and South Korean guards in dealing with the problems in the camp.

The Chinese traitors, supported by the UN guards, controlled Compound 72 by terror. They organized the compound into a brigade, which included six prisoner teams, and took charge of both the brigade and the teams. Then the leaders and their deputies installed rules that forbade the prisoners from talking to each other, holding meetings, and passing notes. They also hand-picked individuals from their own people and organized them into "prisoner guards" that they armed with knives, steel pickets, spiked clubs, barbed wire flails, and blackjacks to enforce their regulations. If you violated their rules, the "PGs" would take you to an isolated room and beat you up. Some of our comrades were beaten to death.

In early 1952, the brigade leader, Li Da-an, wanted to tattoo every prisoner in Compound 72 with an anti-Communist slogan. Some prisoners objected because a permanent and visible tattoo like "*fangong kanger*" (fight against the Communists and the Soviets) on their bodies would cause problems when they returned to China.

One morning, Li called a general assembly in the compound exercise field. He ordered the prisoner guards (PGs) to beat those who refused the tattoo in front of the five thousand prisoners. Some of those who couldn't stand the beatings gave up and agreed to the tattoo.

One prisoner, however, Lin Xuepu, continued to refuse the tattoo. Li Da-an finally dragged Lin up to the stage and in a loud voice asked Lin: "Do you want it or not?" Bleeding and barely able to stand up, Lin, a nineteen-year-old college freshman, replied with a loud "No!" Li Da-an responded by cutting off one of Lin's arms with his big dagger. Lin screamed but still shook his head when Li repeated the question. Humiliated and angry, Li followed by stabbing Lin with his dagger. After Lin finally collapsed, Li opened Lin's chest and pulled out his heart. Holding the bleeding but still beating heart, Li yelled to all the prisoners in the field: "Whoever dares to refuse the tattoo will be like him!"

I cried quietly that morning. It was not because of Lin's death—I had seen many young comrades fall on the battleground. Nor was it because of the traitors' atrocities—this happened all the time in the camp, and I was prepared for the worst. I cried because I felt so useless and powerless when Lin was brutally murdered. Later, I used these savage acts to mobilize prisoners and organize our resistance movement. More and more prisoners became angry about these outrageous acts of violence by their own countrymen. More and more prisoners realized that there was a life-and-death struggle in the camp between the Chinese prisoners and the Chinese traitors.

Why were there so many turncoats among the Chinese prisoners? Why did so many turn after they became prisoners of the UNC? Unfortunately, the Chinese army had its own problems.

First of all, there were some bad elements in the CPVF carried over from its past. When WWII ended in 1945, the Chinese Communist Army with about 3 million troops engaged the Chinese Nationalist Army with more than 7 million troops in the Chinese Civil War. In 1948, the Chinese Communist Army was reorganized into the Chinese People's Liberation Army. In October 1950, the Chinese Communist Party's Central Committee made its decision to send the Chinese troops, the PLA troops, to Korea. In order to avoid a risk of being in a direct state of war with the United States and other nations that had joined the UN forces in Korea, the CCP

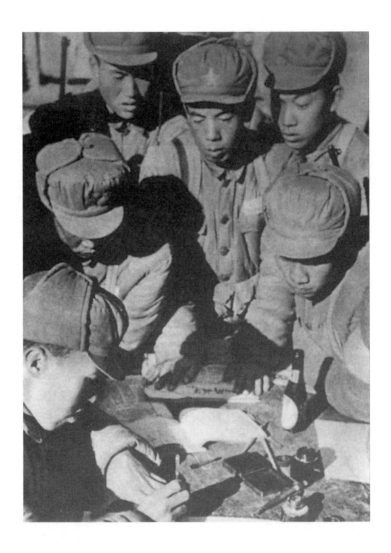

Chinese soldiers sign up to go to the Korean War, October 1950.
(Courtesy of Zhao Zuorui)

Central Committee established the CPVF by using the name "volunteers." In fact, the CPVF soldiers were not volunteers; they were exactly the same Chinese Communist troops, the PLA troops. They were the Chinese troops assigned to the Korean War. The CPVF command was actually the PLA's front command in Korea. The Chinese leaders expected to convince the world that the CPV Forces were organized by Chinese volunteers, not the Chinese government.

Although the PLA won the Chinese Civil War in 1949, it also lost most of its WWII veterans and seasoned Communist soldiers. The civil war proved to be one of the bloodiest wars in Chinese history, and total military casualties on both sides were about 10 million in three years.

During the Chinese Civil War the PLA completely exhausted itself. It desperately needed new recruits as replacements to enable it to continue the fight against the Chinese Nationalists. In order to meet the PLA's large demand for new recruits, some recruiting officers ignored the army's criteria and practiced an "open door" policy, accepting almost all the applicants. Now the "bad elements" were able to join the PLA.

Some of the new recruits came from wealthy families, such as landlords, business owners, bankers, and other bourgeois and capitalist classes accustomed to exploiting the less fortunate members of society. Others had lost their land or business during our land reform. In some cases their parents were jailed or sentenced to death, and they joined the PLA to escape the revolutionary movement or class struggle. They hated the PLA and the Chinese Communist Party.

Obviously, the PLA contained some anti-Communist elements. During the civil war, the PLA began to look for new recruits who could fill their technical and engineering positions. The PLA began to consider a person's training and career more important than his political background. Unfortunately, there were many "bad elements" among these new recruits. When they were sent into the Korean War, many of them defected to the enemy. As prisoners, they now had the opportunity to take revenge against the Communist prisoners in the camps, like those at Koje-do Island. For instance, Li Da-an, the brigade head of Compound 72 at Koje-do, had been a police officer in the Nationalist government in Northeast China. He hated the Communists. When the Nationalist army was defeated and fled south in 1948, Li didn't have a chance to go with them during the civil war. In 1949, he was recruited by the Communist local government and joined the PLA as a truck driver because he knew how to drive.

Li Da-an came to Korea with his truck transportation regiment in 1951. During a supply mission to the CPVF frontline troops, Li drove his truck across the MLR and went over to the enemy. The UNC sent Li and other Chinese defectors to the POW camps and let them deal with the Chinese prisoners. As we know, Li became a diehard traitor and a nightmare to the CPVF, but a "model collaborator" to the UNC at Koje-do.

One day, Li and a dozen traitors followed me into my tent and began to beat me with big sticks and bricks.

"Why, what for?" I tried to defend myself, but my moves attracted more attacks.

"Why? You know why." One traitor answered by shouting at me: "Because you Communists beat me in China. Now I can beat you back here!"

Another shouted, "You Communists took my land and killed my father. I want to even up this bloody debt with you today."

While I was beaten to near death, Li watched and laughed at me. Differences over the class struggle and hatred became one of the important sources of conflict in the camp.

Another source of camp problems was the conflict between the Chinese Communist soldiers and the former Chinese Nationalist soldiers. During the Chinese Civil War, the PLA enlisted a large number of the so-called "liberated" soldiers. These were former Chinese Nationalist soldiers who accepted the Nationalist army's defeat and were willing to cooperate with the Communists and join the PLA. For example, the PLA took over Beijing in January 1949. There were about 200,000 Nationalist troops who surrendered to the PLA during the Peking campaign. From February to April, more than 150,000 former Nationalist troops were inducted into the PLA. This included commanding officers at the regiment, division, and army levels of command.

Some of these former Nationalist soldiers and officers had no choice, but they concealed their unwillingness to join and waited for the right opportunity to defect. Wei Sixi, the brigade deputy for Compound 72 and a former Nationalist captain, is a good example. His entire regiment was inducted into the PLA after the Nationalist army lost Beijing. He kept his Nationalist Party membership card and sewed his Nationalist army ID inside his uniform. After his regiment entered Korea, he went over to the enemy, using his Nationalist Party card for identification.

The conflict between the Chinese Communist prisoners and Nationalist traitors became more serious after July 1951, when the peace negotiations began in Korea. The POW issue became one of the most important and difficult issues in the peace talks. It took two more years of bloody fighting before the POW problems were settled. The fighting took place both on the battleground and in the POW camps.

While the Chinese–North Korean delegation demanded a total repatriation of "all the current prisoners in the Korean War," the UN delegation insisted on a "voluntary" or a "self-motivated" repatriation. That meant the released prisoners could go wherever they were "willing" to go. Thus, the Chinese prisoners had their choices. They could either go back to Communist China where they came from, or join the Chinese Nationalists on Taiwan. The compound brigade leaders, or the traitors, tried to persuade Chinese prisoners to go to Taiwan. We had to stop their efforts and bring all our men back to China.

First, we established Communist organizations in the camp. We developed the underground CCP groups in the fall of 1951. We recruited the party members from those who had belonged to the same CPVF unit and knew each other. Each party group had six to ten party members. The group leaders called secret meetings, exchanged information, and made plans to fight against the PGs. There were about two thousand CCP members among the Chinese prisoners, and at least half of the party members were organized into the underground party groups. Meanwhile, Chinese Communist Youth League (CCYL) groups were also organized among the CCYL members.

Next, CCP and CCYL branches were established. Each branch included four to seven party groups and had about fifty party members. The branch had a secretary and a committee with five to seven committee members as the leaders. Most of the party branch secretaries and committee members were CPVF officers. There were about one thousand officers among the Chinese prisoners at Koje-do, and they played a very important role in our struggle. They met secretly on a regular basis, gave assignments to their groups, and coordinated the plans for the fight. For example, the CCP branches organized a campwide hunger strike on October 1, 1951, China's National Day, to protest the brutal treatment of the prisoners by the UNC guards. The organized CCP party members and CCYL members played a very important role in the hunger strike, and made the campwide collective effort possible and successful.

We also established the CCP-sponsored mass leadership in the camp. The CCP party members made up only 20 percent of the Chinese prisoners. And the CCP groups and branches operated secretly. The party leaders were usually active behind the scene. Our goal was to unite the Chinese prisoners, including those who were neither CCP nor CCYL members, and involve all of them in our struggle. We needed elected leaders who could speak for all the Chinese prisoners, organize public meetings, and negotiate with the UNC camp officers on the table.

Finally, in April 1952, after careful preparations and many discussions, the "Communist United Front" (CUF) was founded and I was elected secretary general. I had three deputy secretaries and a standing committee of eleven members. Most of them were CPVF regimental or battalion commanding officers. The CUF organized several subcommittees, which included public relations, propaganda, communication, information, security, and counterintelligence. The CUF also established a branch committee in each brigade.

On April 8, the UNC began the screening of the so-called voluntary repatriates in Compound 72. In order to persuade more prisoners to return to China, the CUF called an emergency committee meeting. We decided at the meeting to demand the following from the UNC: (1) the CPVF-NKPA statement must be read to all the prisoners; (2) all prisoner guards must be removed from the compound so the prisoners could make their own decisions without any pressure or fear; and (3) the UNC camp officers must agree to meet the CUF representatives and discuss the improvement of camp life.[1] It came as no surprise that the UNC refused our proposals. The UNC thus supported the atrocious tortures of the prisoner guards against those who wanted to go back to China.

One by one, the UNC and the PGs screened the prisoners to determine who wished to be repatriated to China. They tried to create a picture of mass defections on the part of the Chinese prisoners, hoping this would persuade the Chinese–North Korean delegation to agree to the proposals favored by the UN delegation. In order to force the prisoners to say "no" to repatriation, the UNC reduced our rations, cut off our medical service, and stopped our water supply. Also, the PGs became even more violent. Whenever the prisoners told the UN screening authorities they did not want to go to Taiwan but wished to be repatriated to China, the PGs tortured and sometimes murdered them. There were ten prisoners fatally beaten by the PGs. On April 10, fighting between the guards and prisoners during the screening led to the deaths of seventy-five Chinese prisoners and the murder of an American guard.

To counter the UNC's suppressive measures and the prisoner guards' atrocities, the Communist United Front encouraged the prisoners to go to the "Returning Home Compound," or Compound 602. The new camp was established by the UNC in April for those who had been confirmed for repatriation. But prisoners who wished to move into Compound 602 took a big risk of first being beaten or even killed.

When my turn came for the repatriation screening, I told a half dozen PGs that I wished to go to Compound 602 and return to China. Several PGs came up and hit me really hard. After I passed out, they said I couldn't make any decision and took me back to my room. A couple of days later, they did the same thing. I kept telling them, "I don't want to go to Taiwan. I want to go back to China." Finally, they gave up and let me go to Compound 602. About six thousand out of twenty thousand Chinese prisoners moved to Compound 602 and waited for their repatriation. I wish we could have convinced more Chinese prisoners to move to Compound 602.

In the new compound, we continued our fight and tried to persuade more prisoners to join us in 602. We exposed the UNC and PG crimes, and held the funeral services for the murdered prisoners. To protest the UNC plots, we organized hunger strikes, mass allies, and parades. We also communicated with other compounds and supported the North Korean prisoners' struggle for their repatriation. We used the camp clinic as our message exchange point.

On May 1, our compound liaison person came back from the clinic and brought us an important message from the North Korean Communist leadership. The underground North Korean Workers' Party committee in the camp had decided to capture Brigadier General Francis T. Dodd, the American commander at Koje-do and a staff member of the U.S. Eighth Army. The Koreans planned to capture Dodd at one of the Korean compounds and then use the event and world attention to expose the UNC prisoner abuses to the world. The Korean party leaders asked us to assist them by organizing the Chinese prisoners and starting a mass protest rally and hunger strike.

I called a CUF standing committee meeting and discussed the situation. All the committee members were excited and wanted to kidnap Dodd at one of the Chinese compounds. But our Korean comrades insisted on carrying out this action themselves. They also asked us to carry out two more assignments. First, during our protests, we needed to demand face-to-face negotiations with Dodd. Second, when Dodd appeared, we must stop all protesting activities so Dodd would believe that he was the only person who could deal with the camp problems, thus making his personal appearance very important.

Our committee made a detailed plan and gave assignments to the Chinese party branches in each compound. On May 2, the CUF presented a public letter to Dodd, demanding direct negotiations between himself and the Chinese prisoner representatives. On May 3, we organized a general protest rally in all the Chinese compounds.

On May 4, our general hunger strike began. At Compound 602, the prisoners hung up their dinner plates, rice bowls, and spoons on the wires. At Compound 72, the grain and vegetables were moved out of the kitchens and storage rooms and thrown outside the compound gates. Meanwhile, we informed the camp headquarters that our hunger strike would continue until we met with Dodd.

During the afternoon of May 4, we were told that Dodd would meet the Chinese prisoner representatives in his headquarters. We refused the invitation in his office and insisted on a meeting inside Compound 602. We said that our representatives' safety could not be guaranteed in his headquarters.

On the morning of May 6, Dodd arrived at Compound 602 with his aide and a platoon of armed guards. We asked him to come inside the compound. His aide declined our request by using the same security excuse. Following this exchange, an unusual meeting took place at the compound gate between Dodd and the Chinese prisoner representatives. The compound gates at Koje-do were see-through gates made of wood logs and wire net.

The three Chinese representatives, standing inside the gate, were Sun Zhenguan, Zhang Zeshi, and myself. General Dodd got out of his jeep, walked toward us, and stopped outside the gate, about two or three yards from us. The gate remained closed, but both sides were close enough to hear and talk to each other through the wire net gate. It was my first time to meet Dodd. Well built and well dressed, Dodd looked fit and sharp. His uniform and golden badges were shining, and his eyeglasses gave him an intellectual look. "Welcome, General Dodd," Sun greeted him in Chinese. "We appreciate your visit since you have a very busy schedule." After Zhang's translation into English, Dodd nodded and said: "I always respect the Chinese people. Please tell me what you need."

"We'd like to have your personal inspection on the serious problems of our poor nutrition and lack of medication in our compound," I said. "We hope the Chinese prisoners will be given humanitarian treatment, which is clearly stated in the *Geneva Joint Pledge on POW's Rights.* Your country was one of the signatories."

"We always follow the *Geneva Pledge,*" Dodd argued. "With a minimum staff and limited transportation sources, we have tried our best to follow the Geneva Convention Agreement." Dodd became impatient and asked his aide to read some related articles in the *Geneva Pledge*.

"Obviously, the current treatment we have here is way below the standard set up by the *Geneva Pledge*," Sun declared in a loud voice as soon as the Chinese translator finished. "Two bowls of rice per day is not enough for one prisoner. No meat and very little vegetables. If your country has difficulties fixing the problems in the camp, please inform our country. We believe China will help you improve the starving situation here immediately."

When the English translator finished, Dodd became upset. "If you are starving, I don't think it necessary at all for you to organize this hunger strike. Your action certainly puts more pain and miseries on your fellow countrymen." Then he added, "Well, I will consider your unusual appetite and the Chinese diet habits. And I will think about how to improve the medical care in the camp."

"If Your Respectable General can seriously consider our requests and solve our problems," I replied, "we will end our hunger strike and resume our regular meal schedule."

"I am fully responsible for my own words," Dodd said. He seemed serious.

The three of us nodded to each other with a smile of understanding. Then, Sun said to Dodd: "We are willing to believe Your Respectable General's sincerity. We appreciate it that you came to this meeting in person. Thank you very much."

Dodd seemed satisfied and glad it was over. He nodded to us through the gate, went back to his jeep, and left with his aide and guards.

We were also happy, because we had accomplished our goal of luring Dodd to the compounds. By setting up a gate-side meeting format, we made possible the successful kidnaping of Dodd by the North Korean prisoners a short time later.

As planned, the actual kidnaping of Dodd took place in one of the North Korean prisoner compounds, Compound 76. I learned about it only after it happened.

After a three-day protest, at 1:30 P.M. on May 7, Dodd finally arrived at Compound 76. With Dodd were Lieutenant Colonel Wilbur Ravin and a platoon of armed guards in armored vehicles. The meeting was held at the compound gate much the same as before. After discussing some differences and reading the *Geneva Pledge*, Dodd became impatient and asked Ravin to negotiate with the North Korean representatives. At the same time Dodd began to cut his fingernails with a nail scissor. His guards were also relaxed, talking to each other and looking around. They were about ten yards behind Dodd, Ravin, and their aide.

At that moment, a prisoner janitor group approached the gate from the compound kitchen. They were doing their daily routine of taking the garbage outside and dumping it into the sea. The wire gate opened, and Dodd and Ravin stepped aside to let the janitors walk through the gate. When the janitors walked out of the gate and lined up between Dodd and his guards, several of the North Korean representatives suddenly jumped outside the gate and grasped Dodd and Ravin. Tall and young, Major Ravin managed to avoid capture by hanging on to the gate post until he received help from the guards. Dodd, however, was captured and carried by four Korean prisoners inside the compound before he realized what was going on. The gate was closed immediately and locked by the prisoners.

"Save me! Save me!" Dodd shouted to his guards from inside the compound. The guards rushed to the gate, but it was too late. Dodd struggled with his North Korean captors but soon disappeared in the tents.

Dodd became a prisoner of his prisoners. The news shocked the entire world. The event is known as the "Dodd Incident" or the "Koje-do Riot."

That afternoon, UNC forces armed with tanks, heavy machine guns, and offshore gunboats placed Compound 76 under siege. Two helicopters also patrolled the area. About 3:00 P.M., the North Koreans hung up a big sign in English at the compound's gate: "WE CAPTURE DODD AS LONG AS OUR DEMAND WILL BE SOLVED HIS SAFETY IS SECURED. IF THERE HAPPEN BRUTAL ACT SUCH AS SHOOTING, HIS LIFE IS IN DANGER." At 3:30 P.M., a note from Dodd was handed over to the UNC officers outside the compound. Dodd asked the UNC officers to set up a telephone line for him from the outside to his tent in the compound, to send him some personal items for his daily needs, to reduce the number of the surrounding troops, and to invite prisoner representatives from other compounds to Compound 76 for talks.

As the secretary general of the Chinese Communist United Front, I attended the meetings in Compound 76 with the other three Chinese representatives.

During the late evening of May 7, before the negotiations with Dodd, about thirty Chinese and North Korean prisoner representatives met in Compound 76. It was the first time for such a joint meeting. We were representing seventy thousand prisoners on Koje Island. The Korean leaders at

Compound 76 chaired the meeting. We discussed three topics: first, the agenda for the negotiations; second, when and under what conditions Dodd should be released; and third, what our next step should be in the event the negotiations broke down.

Regarding the negotiations with Dodd, our Korean comrades made three proposals: (1) stop the abuse and murder of the prisoners; (2) stop the "voluntary repatriation" preparations; and (3) agree to the organization of a "Chinese–North Korean Prisoner Delegation" to coordinate the camp activities. I agreed with their proposals but suggested the termination of repatriation screening should be added as a separate item. Some comrades said that the "termination of the voluntary repatriation efforts" item had included my suggestion, but I continued to insist the item must be added. I said, "We should emphasize the illegality of the screening in order to stop the brutal and forceful repatriation screening immediately." Finally, they agreed to add this item to the negotiation agenda.

Regarding Dodd, some representatives wanted to execute him for his crimes and to avenge our dead comrades on Koje Island. Others wanted to keep him a hostage as long as possible to protect the prisoners. In case of a UNC rescue attempt, he would be eliminated before the UN troops could free him. I disagreed by arguing that "An alive and a freed Dodd out there could do much more for our cause than a dead or a detained Dodd in here." I explained that a hostage situation might give the UNC an excuse to murder more prisoners and put more pressure on the Chinese–North Korean delegation at the truce negotiations. The situation might get out of control and turn into a real riot, as the UNC had already declared in its anti-Communist propaganda. It would not help us in our efforts to improve camp life or to achieve a total repatriation of the prisoners and a cease-fire in the war. I suggested we protect Dodd during the negotiations and release him as soon as he accepted our four demands in writing. After our discussions, the other representatives agreed with my views.

During the meeting, we elected a Chinese–North Korean Prisoner Delegation. I was elected one of the deputy chiefs of the delegation. We chose General Lee Jong-jun, a division commander in the North Korean People's Army, as the chief of the delegation.

On the morning of May 8, we met with Dodd in a new tent. The setting inside the tent looked like a courtroom. The head table had five seats for the delegation chief and deputies. A small table with one chair, facing the head table and in the middle of the tent, was reserved for Dodd, the defendant.

The forty-three representatives from the seventeen Chinese and North Korean prison compounds sat on both sides as jurors. I sat at the head table next to our delegation chief and negotiation chairman.

Dodd was called in. He slowly walked to his table and sat down. His red eyes and tired-looking appearance revealed he had spent a sleepless night in the compound. He also wore a dirty uniform with missing buttons, indicating his desperate struggle during the capture. Our chair addressed the purpose of the meeting and read our four demands to him. Dodd refused to accept our proposal. He didn't believe the murders and brutal screening in the compounds took place under his command. We invited badly beaten and wounded prisoners, who testified to the brutality of the prisoner guards during their screening. The clinic nurses brought their medical records to show Dodd and provided additional eyewitness testimony. The warehouse bookkeepers explained how the camp supplies were sold by ROK soldiers to the black market. Two female prisoners told their stories about frequent rapes and gang rapes by both guards and prisoners. Dodd became nervous and sometimes seemed touched by the stories. He just said, "I can't believe it. I can't believe it."

The negotiations continued the next day. On May 9, we learned by listening to Dodd's telephone calls that the UNC had appointed Brigadier General Charles Colson as the new commandant of the Koje-do POW Camp. Our delegation discussed the changing situation and decided to deal with Dodd inside and Colson outside the compound at the same time. By listening to their telephone conversations, we knew that Dodd and Colson were classmates at the West Point Military Academy, and that Dodd's wife called Colson day and night asking him to save her husband's life. Furthermore, she was coming to Koje-do from Tokyo, Japan. We took the opportunity and applied even more pressure on Dodd. We added individual meetings to the general meetings. General Lee met Dodd after dinner on May 9. Then I talked to Dodd. Thereafter, two more meetings were held in Dodd's tent that evening. Meanwhile, we translated and made copies of the minutes of the meetings for Colson.

Finally, Dodd gave up. On the morning of May 10, after another round of prisoners' testimony, Dodd stood up from his chair and said in a low voice: "I am responsible for what happened here. And I am guilty." After Korean and Chinese translations, General Lee stood up and read our requests again. Dodd agreed to sign it. Lee also asked him to sign the minutes of the meetings. He agreed.

By noon, two documents were ready for Dodd to sign. One document,

UNC guards bring the Chinese POWs back to their compound after the Koje riots, May 1952. (Courtesy of the Center for Archives and Information, Heilongjiang Provincial Academy of Social Sciences)

entitled "Korean–Chinese Prisoners' Grievances to the World," contained the testimonies of the witnesses of the meeting. The other document, entitled "UNC POW Camp Affidavit," contained our four demands. At the same time, copies of the two documents were sent to Colson for his signature. Dodd inside the compound and Colson outside the compound both signed the two documents, thus accepting the charge that the UNC had forced the prisoners to refuse their repatriation, and promising to improve the camp conditions. These documents embarrassed the UNC by acknowledging the measure of justice in the Communist prisoners' case. We had scored a propaganda triumph for the Chinese and North Korean prisoners at the Koje-do Camp. The documents revealed to the entire world the UN forces as the brutal persecutors and murderers of their prisoners. In Compound 76, about seven thousand Korean prisoners who had been waiting outside the negotiating tent for the signature ceremony learned the good news and cheered the victory. We released Dodd unharmed on the night of May 10.

Colson, however, didn't keep his promise. Instead of improving the living conditions in the camp, he brought excessive violence and brutal suppression to Koje-do. On May 11, he refused to return the Chinese and Korean representatives to their own compounds. I was stuck in Compound 76 and lost contact with the Chinese Communist United Front in the Chinese compounds. In late May, Colson divided the compounds, which had an average of several thousand prisoners in each, into much smaller camps of about several hundred prisoners each. His new policy made any organized resistance very difficult, if not impossible. In early June, Colson transferred all the Chinese prisoners in Compound 602 to another island, Cheju-do. At the Cheju-do Camp, six thousand Chinese prisoners were divided into ten small compounds.

The North Korean prisoners in Compound 76 opposed the division and refused to leave their compound for relocation. On June 10, Colson personally commanded an attack against Compound 76. The North Korean prisoners used bricks and wooden sticks against tanks, machine guns, gas bombs, and over one thousand UN troops. After a bloody two-day fight, more than five hundred Korean prisoners were killed or wounded. Most of the tents were burned down to the ground. All of the Korean and Chinese representatives and delegates were sent to the "War Criminal Camp" at Koje-do.

I was jailed there with eighteen other Chinese representatives until the fall of 1953. The Korean Armistice was signed in July 1953. On September 5, we were told that we had visitors. When I saw the Chinese government delegation waiting for us in the visiting room, I cried. The delegates told us that we would be released the next day and returned to China soon. By the end of September, 7,094 Chinese prisoners had been repatriated to China. Meanwhile, more than 14,000 Chinese prisoners refused to return to China. They went to Taiwan.

Perspectives on the War

IN JUNE 1950, the invading North Korean army, trained and advised by the Soviets, armed with Soviet weapons, and indoctrinated with the Communist rhetoric of its leader, Kim Il Sung, quickly forced the ROK Army into a hasty retreat. Labeling themselves as "liberators" who invaded to free the enslaved South Koreans from the tyranny of Syngman Rhee and the capitalist-imperialist Americans, many South Koreans initially saw the invasion as a means of achieving a unified Korea and welcomed the invaders. The North Korean army's brutal persecution and needless killings, however, quickly turned the South Koreans against the invaders.

When American troops began arriving in Korea in July, they found the retreating ROK Army in disarray. American soldiers in Korea were often critical of the performance of the ROKA, especially in the early part of the war. It is true there were serious problems in the ROKA of 1950. It lacked effective leadership in the higher commands, its communications were poor, and many soldiers were anything but enthusiastic about their president, Syngman Rhee. The ROKs also lacked the air force, tanks, and heavy artillery necessary for a successful defense against the larger and more mechanized North Korean army. While the Soviets had generously provided these weapons to North Korea, the Americans refused to do the same for the ROKA, primarily because they feared President Rhee would use them to invade North Korea. Given these factors, plus the element of surprise, the retreat of the South Korean forces during the first days of the war was virtually inevitable. Although many GIs considered the ROK units to be unreliable and inclined to "bug out," later experience revealed that when ROK soldiers were well trained and well led, they could fight with great tenacity and courage.

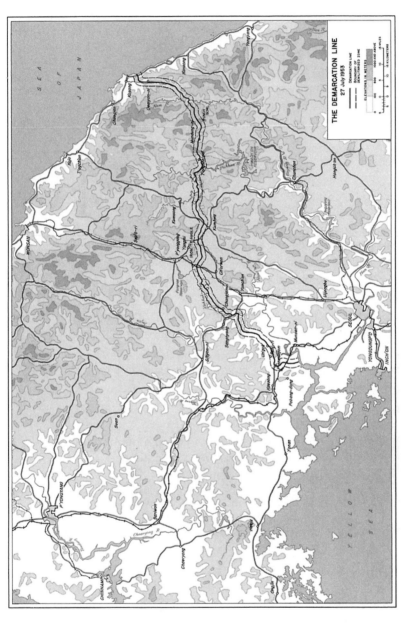

The Demarcation Line, July 27, 1953. Source: Department of the Army, *United States Army in the Korean War: Truce Tent and Fighting Front* (Washington, D.C.: U.S. Government Printing Office, 1988), Map IX.

If the South Korean army had problems in 1950, so did the American army that came to its rescue. Starved for funds during the military cutbacks of the immediate postwar period, the battalions were short on both manpower and equipment. In part this may be explained by the belief of American military planners that the dark shadow of Soviet Communism was most likely to fall on western Europe, an area still torn by the war and economic distress. Hence, first priority in men and weapons went to American troops in Europe, not Asia. Furthermore, the first GIs to land in Korea were troops from Japan. They had been steeped in occupation duty, not rigorous combat training. It may also be said that much of the American army underestimated the strength of the North Korean army. Combined, these factors undermined the effectiveness of the first U.S. troops to reach Korea, and the North Korean People's Army continued to advance south. This came as a great shock to most Americans, who expected that the presence of a single American division would be sufficient to roll back the army of a backward and underdeveloped nation such as North Korea.

As the North Korean army drew closer to Pusan, American reinforcements began to pour into Korea. Green American troops quickly gained battlefield experience, helped immensely by a nucleus of career officers and noncoms who had served in WWII. Increased American firepower, much of it from the air force and navy, was just enough to prevent the fall of Pusan. The much celebrated Inchon landings followed in September, which placed the North Korean forces in great danger of being trapped and cut off. MacArthur's admirers believe these landings stand out as one of the masterful military strokes in history; his detractors consider them largely the result of good fortune. Whatever the truth, it is a fact the Inchon landings went smoothly, and they so enhanced MacArthur's reputation as a military genius that his opinions took on godlike dimensions in the days ahead, not to be questioned by anyone. Urged on by MacArthur, the American army and UN forces crossed the 38th Parallel and advanced toward the Yalu River.

As the U.S. and UN forces moved northward, the North Korean People's Army began to fall apart. Part of the NKPA fled to the hills and conducted guerrilla warfare operations, for which they had been thoroughly trained. Other North Korean soldiers were reorganized into small, lightly armed units and employed hit-and-run tactics. By this time the American and UN forces had overwhelming firepower superiority, both on the ground and in the air, and they met only light resistance as they pushed on toward the Yalu. Both troop morale and support for the war back in the States had never been higher. The war, it appeared, would be short, and President Truman could take pride in his risky decision to commit American troops to this distant peninsula.

Suddenly, the Chinese entered the war, and the American army found itself engaged in a different kind of war against a different kind of enemy. The Chinese People's Volunteer Forces consisted largely of conscripted peasants, most of whom were illiterate. The CPVF's command structure was chaotic, and often favored personal relationships and political orthodoxy at the expense of ability and performance. While the Chinese were rich in manpower, their lack of an industrial base preordained weakness in armor and technical expertise.

The Chinese reliance upon manpower rather than armor reflected both the social-economic reality of China and the philosophy of their leader, Mao Zedong. Mao believed that although weapons were important in war, "It is people, not things, that are decisive." Not only did Mao believe that a highly spirited warrior could vanquish a stronger opponent in battle, this belief was deeply rooted in Chinese culture. In part, as least, this explains why the Chinese repeatedly sent masses of whistle-blowing soldiers against overwhelming American firepower, knowing the cost in casualties would be enormous.

In contrast, the Americans utilized armor, artillery, and air power at every possible opportunity. This allowed them to both minimize casualties and draw on the vast industrial capacity of the United States. Morale and fighting spirit were important assets in war, but they could not be expected to replace artillery and air power.

The logistics of supplying the two armies also reveal striking differences. American air power forced the Chinese to take to the hills, and Chinese soldiers carried a large portion of their supplies on foot. Since the average Chinese soldier (as well as the Korean) had tremendous physical endurance and could live on far less food than American soldiers, this primitive supply system worked reasonably well, except when attempting to supply large-scale offensive operations. Amazingly, the Chinese even found ways of moving artillery to their frontline positions high in the mountains of Korea. In contrast, the American army relied much more on motor transport to move supplies to the front. Supply roads carved out of the mountains by huge bulldozers went right up to the MLR.

After entering the war in the fall of 1950, the Chinese employed their hit-and-run guerrilla tactics against the Americans. Initially these tactics worked well, especially in the Chosin Reservoir fighting. The Chinese flanked the American troops and attacked from the surrounding hills, forcing them to withdraw to the south. The heroic and much publicized retreat of the First Marine Division, now so much a part of marine legend, was part of a general UNF withdrawal. Frequently, the Chinese established roadblocks that not only obstructed the retreat but at some points threatened to cut it off altogether. The combination of hard fighting and intense cold at the Chosin Reservoir made this engagement one of the worst of the entire war, for all participants. Dressed in their light canvas shoes and cotton-quilt uniforms, the Chinese suffered from the cold even more than the Americans.

The Chinese entry into the war collapsed American morale overnight. In Korea, American soldiers knew there would be no quick victory and prepared for a long war. Back in the States, most Americans assumed the Soviet Union had orchestrated the Chinese entry and feared the Korean conflict would lead to World War III. There was also fear of a third world war in other countries, especially in Europe.

The Chinese offensive, however, soon exhausted itself. By early 1951, the American and UN forces carried out their own offensive operations and began moving north. In part, this amazing turnaround may be attributed to the new Eighth Army commander, General Matthew G. Ridgway. When the Chinese army attacked and their troops were exposed, Ridgway hit them with everything in the Eighth Army arsenal, plus whatever the navy and the air force could deliver. Although the Chinese usually advanced at the outset of the attack, they did so at the cost of horrendous casualties. When the attack faltered, as it inevitably did when the Chinese had exhausted their supplies, the Eighth Army attacked. After each advance a new defensive line would be established, and the troops would hold their positions until the next offensive. In this way the U.S.-UN forces again worked their way up the peninsula to the 38th Parallel.

By the late fall of 1951, the war had become a stalemated war of the trenches. Despite the overwhelming firepower possessed by the U.S.-UN forces, the UNC was unwilling to pay the price essential for a total victory, especially in casualties. No doubt this reflected the opposition to the war that had developed in many UN countries, including the United States, where the war had become very unpopular. It had become a "limited" political war, which Americans neither understood nor supported. As news of the war moved from the front pages to the back pages, most Americans viewed it with either complacency or hostility. They did not understand a war where political decisions made in Washington constrained the decisions of the generals on the battlefield. The ceaseless arguing over trivial matters in the truce negotiations only added to their frustration over the war.

In the meantime, the war continued and the casualty figures mounted on both sides. Many young American men still received their "Greetings" from the local draft board and ended up in Korea as replacements, where most were more interested in acquiring the thirty-six points necessary for rotation home than in winning the war. Worldwide, public opinion clearly favored bringing the war to a close. The exceptions were Syngman Rhee and his supporters, who wanted to continue the war until Korean unification had been achieved. Mercifully, agreement was finally reached on the terms for a truce, and on July 27, 1953, the guns fell silent.

Although the human costs of the war were much higher than anyone expected at the outset, the Korean War succeeded in achieving its original goal—the expulsion of the North Korean Communist forces from South Korea back to the 38th Parallel. Yet, Americans have tended to ignore this achievement about the war. Most remember it as an unpopular war of the trenches, the war the United States failed to win. Thus, Korean veterans returned home to a silent welcome, uncertain about their standing with their "big brothers," the heroes of World War II, and the American public in general.

Notes

1. Background and Origins of the War

1. Stanley Sandler, *The Korean War: No Victors, No Vanquished* (Lexington: Univ. Press of Kentucky, 1999), 2–3.

2. Bruce Cumings, *Korea's Place in the Sun: A Modern History* (New York: Norton, 1997), 140 (hereafter cited as *Korea's Place*).

3. For the Japanese occupation of Korea, see ibid., chapter 3; Walter B. Jung, *Nation Building: The Geopolitical History of Korea* (Lanham, Md.: Univ. Press of America, 1998), chapter 8; and Geoff Simons, *Korea: The Search for Sovereignty* (New York: St. Martin's Press, 1995), chapter 4.

4. Jung, 238; Michael Hickey, *The Korean War: The West Confronts Communism* (Woodstock, N.Y.: The Overlook Press, 1999), 6.

5. Jung, 238–39; Bruce Cumings, *The Origins of the Korean War: Liberation and the Emergence of Separate Regimes, 1945–1947,* vol. 1 (Princeton, N.J.: Princeton Univ. Press, 1981), 395–403 (hereafter cited as *Origins,* vol. 1); Sergei N. Goncharov, John W. Lewis, and Xue Litai, *Uncertain Partners: Stalin, Mao, and the Korean War* (Stanford, Calif.: Stanford Univ. Press, 1993), 131–32.

6. For the full text of the communique, see *Foreign Relations of the United States: Diplomatic Papers. The Conferences of Cairo and Tehran, 1943* (Washington, D.C.: U.S. Government Printing Office, 1961), 448–49.

7. Young Whan Kihl, *Politics and Policies in Divided Korea: Regimes in Contest* (Boulder and London: Westview Press, 1984), 29.

8. Cumings, *Korea's Place,* 187–88. For a much fuller discussion of U.S. and Allied planning for Korea during World War II, see Cumings, *Origins,* vol. 1, 120–21.

9. Young Whan Kihl, 28–32; Cumings, *Origins,* vol. 1, 120–21.

10. Simons, 159–60.

11. Cumings, *Korea's Place,* 189; Hickey, 10.

12. Simons, 162–65; Hickey, 11.

13. Burton I. Kaufman, *The Korean Conflict* (Westport, Conn.: Greenwood Press, 1999), 5; Cumings, *Korea's Place,* 189–90.

14. Kaufman, 5; Cumings, *Korea's Place,* 190–91.

15. Sandler, 26.

16. Cumings, *Korea's Place,* 192.

17. Ibid., 195; Hickey, 18.

18. Cumings, *Korea's Place,* 193–95.

19. Jung, 240–41; Sandler, 25–27.

20. Jung, 241–42; Hickey, 18–19.

21. Jung, 242; Cumings, *Korea's Place,* 211–12.

22. Cumings, *Korea's Place,* 212–14.

23. Jung, 242–43.

24. Cumings, *Korea's Place,* 224–28.

25. Ibid., 238–43; Chen Jian, *China's Road to the Korean War: The Making of the Sino-American Confrontation* (New York: Columbia Univ. Press, 1994), 109.

26. Ibid., 243–47; Sandler, 37–39; Goncharov, Lewis, and Xue Litai, 135–36.

27. Hickey, 25.

28. Kaufman, 6–7; Bruce Cumings, *The Origins of the Korean War: The Roaring of the Cataract, 1947–1950,* vol. 2 (Princeton, N.J.: Princeton Univ. Press, 1990), 158 (hereafter cited as *Origins,* vol. 2).

29. Simons, 161–62.

30. Cumings, *Origins,* vol. 2, 379–82; Patrick C. Roe, *The Dragon Strikes: China and the Korean War: June–December 1950* (Novato, Calif.: Presidio Press, 2000), 10–11.

31. Cumings, *Korea's Place,* 247–51; Sandler, 40–41.

32. Dean Acheson, *Present at the Creation: My Years in the State Department* (New York: Norton, 1969), 355–57.

33. Ibid., 357.

34. Goncharov, Lewis, and Xue Litai, 142. For a discussion of the Acheson speech, see Cumings, *Origins,* vol. 2, chapter 13.

35. Intelligence reports just prior to the outbreak of war are often in conflict. General MacArthur's intelligence section did predict in March 1950 that an invasion was possible, but exhibited no sense of urgency. Reports on the ability of the ROK Army to stop an invasion are also confusing. KMAG officers were well aware of the serious deficiencies in the ROK Army in weapons, equipment, and training of officers. Yet, General Roberts, the KMAG chief, described the ROK Army in an article published in *Time* magazine on June 5, 1950, as the "best doggone shooting army outside the United States" (quoted in Roe, 12). See also Sandler, 42–45, and Hickey, 21, 28.

36. Goncharov, Lewis, and Xue Litai, 136–37, note.

37. Zhihua Shen, "China Sends Troops to Korea: Beijing's Policy-Making Process," chapter 2 in *China and the United States: A New Cold War History,* ed. Xiaobing Li and Hongshan Li (Lanham, Md.: Univ. Press of America, 1998), 15–18; Kaufman, 37–38.

38. Quoted in Goncharov, Lewis, and Xue Litai, 145.

39. Ibid., 151–52.

40. Formally, the Treaty of Friendship, Alliance, and Mutual Assistance, signed February 14, 1950. See ibid., chapter 4.

41. Zhihua Shen, 16–21; Goncharov, Lewis, and Xue Litai, 145–48.

42. Goncharov, Lewis, and Xue Litai, 147.

43. Cumings, *Korea's Place,* 262–64.

2. The Opening Phase

1. Max Hastings, *The Korean War* (New York: Simon and Schuster, 1987), 58; Matthew B. Ridgway, *The Korean War* (Garden City, N.Y.: Doubleday, 1967, 15–16; John Edward Wiltz, "The Korean War and American Society," chapter 4 in *The Korean War: A 25-Year Perspective,* ed. Francis H. Heller (Lawrence, Kans.: The Regents Press of Kansas, 1977), 116–17.

2. Bevin Alexander, *Korea: The First War We Lost,* rev. ed. (New York: Hippocrene Books, 1998), 46–47.

3. Ibid., 17; Wiltz, 114.

4. Alexander, 32–45; Harry S. Truman, *Memoirs,* vol. 2, *Years of Trial and Hope* (Garden City, N.Y.: Doubleday, 1956), 335–40.

5. Hastings, 15–22.

6. Sandler, 196.

7. Ibid., 194–95.

8. Quoted in ibid., 196.

9. Ibid., 171–74.

10. For the decision on the Inchon invasion, see James F. Schnabel, *Policy and Direction: The First Year, U.S. Army in the Korean War* (Washington, D.C.: Office of the Chief of Military History, U.S. Government Printing Office, 1972), 146–54; James L. Stokesbury, *A Short History of the Korean War* (New York: William Morrow, 1988), chapter 4; and Alexander, chapter 22. General Bradley received his fifth star in September 1950.

11. Roy E. Appleman, *South to the Naktong, North to the Yalu (June–November 1950), U.S. Army in the Korean War* (Washington, D.C.: Office of the Chief of Military History, U.S. Government Printing Office, 1961), 587, 600–604.

12. Joseph C. Goulden, *Korea: The Untold Story of the War* (New York: Times Books, 1982), 241.

13. Ibid., 242–43; Alexander, 228–29.

14. Omar N. Bradley and Clay Blair, *A General's Life: An Autobiography* (New York: Simon and Schuster, 1983), 570.

15. Schnabel, 186–87. The key part of the UN resolution may be found in James F. Schnabel and Robert J. Watson, *The History of the Joint Chiefs of Staff, The Joint Chiefs of Staff and National Policy,* vol. 3, *The Korean War,* part 1 (Wilmington, Del.: Produced by the Historical Division, Joint Secretariat, Joint Chiefs of Staff, published by Michael Glazier, 1979), 244–45. See also Acheson, 454–55.

16. Quoted in Schnabel and Watson, vol. 3, part 1, 247. According to one military historian, MacArthur's conduct in driving to the Yalu "reflected a contempt for intelligence, for the cardinal principles of military prudence, seldom matched in twentieth-century warfare." Hastings, 130.

3. China Enters the War

1. Quoted in Appleman, *South to the Naktong,* 608.
2. William Stueck, *The Korean War:An International History* (Princeton, N.J.: Princeton Univ. Press, 1995), 94.
3. Goncharov, Lewis, and Xue Litai, 173–75.
4. Zhihua Shen, 27–28.
5. For the full text of this interesting telegram, see Goncharov, Lewis, and Xue Litai, 177–78. Mao actually discusses the possibility of a stalemated war.
6. Zhihua Shen, 28–29; Goncharov, Lewis, and Xue Litai, 180.
7. Mao considered the liberation of Taiwan a part of the Chinese Civil War, and planning for an attack on Taiwan began in the early spring of 1950. The outbreak of the Korean War, however, changed everything. When President Truman ordered the U.S. Seventh Fleet to patrol the Taiwan Straits on June 27, 1950, he realistically ended Mao's plans to attack Taiwan anytime in the near future. If Mao did attack, he would risk war with the United States, with its vastly superior air and naval power. See Xiaobing Li, "Making of Mao's Cold War: The Taiwan Straits Crises Revised," in *China and the United States: A New Cold War History,* ed. Xiaobing Li and Hongshan Li (Lanham, Md.: Univ. Press of America, 1998), 51.
8. Zhihua Shen, 36–39; Goncharov, Lewis, and Xue Litai, 181–84; 194.
9. Zhihua Shen, 28–29; Goncharov, Lewis, and Xue Litai, 180.
10. Goncharov, Lewis, and Xue Litai, 198–200.
11. Shu Guang Zhang, *Mao's Military Romanticism: China and the Korean War, 1950–1953* (Lawrence, Kans.: Univ. of Kansas Press, 1995), 10–13.
12. Mao Zedong, "Problems of War and Strategy," November 6, 1938, in *Selected Works of Mao Tse-tung,* vol. 2, 4th ed. (Peking: Foreign Languages Press, 1977), 224.
13. Mao Zedong, *Quotations from Chairman Mao Tse-tung* (New York: Bantam Books, 1967), 85 and 93.
14. Mao Zedong, "On Protracted War," May 26, 1938, in *Selected Works of Mao Tse-tung,* vol. 2, 4th ed. (Peking: Foreign Languages Press, 1977), 143.
15. Zhang, 18.
16. Quoted in Roe, 78–79.
17. Mao Zedong, "Problems of Strategy in Guerrilla War Against Japan," May 1938, in *Selected Works of Mao Tse-tung,* vol. 2, 4th ed. (Peking: Foreign Languages, Press, 1977), 81.
18. Mao Zedong, *Quotations from Chairman Mao Tse-tung,* 52.
19. Zhang, chapter 2.
20. Sandler, 115; Hickey, 119, 163.
21. Brian Catchpole, *The Korean War, 1950–1953* (New York: Carroll and Graf, 2000), 75.

4. The Chosin Reservoir and Advance to the North

1. Alexander, chapter 36, "Disaster at Unsan," 269–77.

2. Clay Blair, *The Forgotten War: America in Korea, 1950–1953* (New York: Times Books, 1987), 376–77; Alexander, 285–86; Appleman, *South to the Naktong,* 763–65.

3. Stanley Weintraub, *MacArthur's War: Korea and the Undoing of an American Hero* (New York: The Free Press, 2000), 202–4; Stokesbury, 85–86.

4. Appleman, *South to the Naktong,* 772; Hastings, 147–48.

5. Appleman, *South to the Naktong,* 736; Blair, 418.

6. For a comparison of the two jet fighters, see Conrad C. Crane, *American Airpower Strategy in Korea, 1950–1953* (Lawrence, Kans.: Univ. Press of Kansas, 2000), 52–53.

7. Robert Frank Futrell, *The United States Air Force in Korea, 1950–1953* (New York: Duell, Sloan and Pearce, 1961), 278; Sandler, 180–82.

8. Catchpole, 194.

9. While U.S. authorities were aware of the Soviet involvement, it was kept secret for fear the political far-right would demand tougher measures that could lead to a wider war. Sandler, 184–86.

10. Quoted in Crane, 50.

11. Weintraub, 222–23.

12. Quoted in ibid., 231.

13. General Smith's actual words were: "There can be no retreat when there's no rear. You can't retreat, or even withdraw, when you're surrounded. The only thing you can do is break out, and in order to do that you have to attack, and that is what we're about to do." Quoted in Martin Russ, *Breakout: The Chosin Reservoir Campaign, Korea, 1950* (New York: Penguin Books, 1999), 355.

14. Alexander, chapter 47, "The Breakout," 353–67.

15. Truman, vol. 2, 395–96.

16. Acheson, 478–85; Blair, 533–34.

17. Quotations in Appleman, *South to the Naktong,* 720.

18. J. Lawton Collins, *War in Peacetime: The History and Lessons of Korea* (Boston, Mass.: Houghton Mifflin, 1969), 232–33. See also Truman, vol. 2, 410.

19. Quoted in Ridgway, 83. See also Bill C. Mossman, *Ebb and Flow: November 1950–July 1951, U.S. Army in the Korean War* (Washington, D.C.: Center of Military History, U.S. Army, U.S. Government Printing Office, 1990), 177–78.

20. Ridgway, 84–88. Ridgway soon relieved (officially "rotated") four of the six division commanders. Blair, 581.

21. Ridgway, 93–94.

22. Stokesbury, 118–19.

23. Ibid., 117–23.

24. Mossman, 299–300.

25. Ridgway, 116.

26. For the entire statement, see Bradley and Blair, 626.

27. For the entire communique, see Douglas MacArthur, *Reminiscences: General of the Army* (New York: McGraw-Hill, 1964), 387–88.

28. Truman, vol. 2, 441–42. Secretary of State Acheson, equally incensed, described

MacArthur's statement as "defiance of the Chiefs of Staff . . . and insubordination of the grossest sort to his commander in chief." Acheson, 519.

29. MacArthur, 386.

30. For the reaction to MacArthur's return, see Weintraub, 349–56, and Dennis D. Wainstock, *Truman, MacArthur, and the Korean War* (Westport, Conn.: Greenwood Press, 1999), 129–35.

31. Blair, 822–55; Alexander, 419–22.

32. Blair, 901; Stokesbury, 137–38; Alexander, 423–25.

33. Alexander, 425.

5. Truce Talks and Prison Riots

1. Ridgway, 150–51. Ridgway estimated the cost in casualties for such a drive at one hundred thousand.

2. Hastings, 228–30.

3. Ibid., 230; Acheson, 523–33.

4. Acheson, 534–35.

5. Stokesbury, 144–46; Hastings, 231–32.

6. Ridgway, 202–3; Acheson, 535–36.

7. Hastings, 232–33; Blair, 955–61.

8. Stokesbury, 150.

9. Walter G. Hermes, *Truce Tent and Fighting Front, U.S. Army in the Korean War* (Washington, D.C.: Office of the Chief of Military History, U.S. Government Printing Office, 1966; reprinted in 1988), 141; Blair, 961–64.

10. Truman, vol. 2, 460–61.

11. Hastings, 305–6; Acheson, 652–54. Admiral Joy, a strong critic of voluntary repatriation, wrote later that it "cost us over a year of war, and cost our United Nations Command prisoners in Communist camps a year of captivity." Admiral C. Turner Joy, *How Communists Negotiate* (New York: Macmillan, 1955), 152.

12. Catchpole, 207.

13. Sandler, 215; Catchpole, 209.

14. Sandler, 212–13.

15. Catchpole, 208–10; Sandler, 214–15.

6. Trench Warfare and Peace

1. Hastings, 329.

2. Wiltz, 147–48. See also Stokesbury, chapter 15, "The Home Front," 227–37.

3. Catchpole, 155.

4. Ibid., 153.

5. Ibid., 190; Harry G. Summers Jr., *Korean War Almanac* (New York, Oxford, and Sydney: Facts on File, 1990), 135–37.

6. During World War II, 28 percent of wounded Americans died as compared to 22 percent in Korea, and the mortality rate for hospitalized soldiers dropped from 4.5 percent to 2.5 percent. Summers, 182–83.

7. Sandler, 222.

8. Hastings, 280–81.

9. Stokesbury, 212–13; T.R. Fehrenback, *This Kind of War: A Study in Unpreparedness* (New York: Macmillan, 1963), 558; Hermes, 349–51.

10. Based on S.L.A. Marshall's *Pork Chop Hill: The American Fighting Man in Action, Korea, Spring 1953* (New York: Morrow, 1956).

11. Hastings, 324. For a table showing the dramatic increase in casualties and the number of artillery rounds fired between April and July 1953, see Hermes, 477. The figures on Outpost Harry were prepared by James W. Evans, at the time the commanding officer of Company A, Fifth Regimental Combat Team, on Outpost Harry, and published in the *Newsletter of the 5th RCT in Korea*, October 1993, 8.

12. Dwight D. Eisenhower, *Mandate for Change, 1953–1956, The White House Years* (Garden City, N.Y.: Doubleday, 1963), 180–81. Leading Democrats and prominent newspapers in Great Britain and India expressed concern that such steps could lead to an extension of the war. See Hermes, 408–9.

13. Blair, 971; Hermes, 412.

14. Kaufman, 65.

15. Ibid.; Blair, 971–72.

16. Hermes, 412–13.

17. Ibid., 417–19.

18. Ibid., 431–32; Kaufman, 66–67.

19. Hermes, 450–51; Stokesbury, 247–48.

20. Hermes, 489–90; Goulden, 644–46. For the text of the armistice see Hermes, Appendix C.

21. For a complete list of the prisoners exchanged see Hermes, Appendix B, 514–15.

22. The treatment of American POWs upon their return is one of the saddest chapters of the Korean War. They were regarded by many as soft, undisciplined, lacking strength of character, and deficient in their knowledge of American history and democratic values (thus making them vulnerable to Communist brainwashing techniques). Also, unlike their heroic World War II brothers, they had failed to escape from the prison camps. Fortunately, a very excellent and recently published book on Korean War prisoners has set the record straight. See Lewis H. Carlson, *Remembered Prisoners of a Forgotten War: An Oral History of the Korean War* (New York: St. Martin's Press, 2002).

23. Hastings, 327.

24. Spencer C. Tucker, ed., *Encyclopedia of the Korean War: A Political, Social, and Military History*, vol. 1 (Santa Barbara, Calif.: ABC-CLIO, 2000), 98–101. Some estimates of Korean War deaths run even higher. See Jon Halliday and Bruce Cumings, *Korea: The Unknown War* (New York: Pantheon, 1988), 200.

8. *A Mortar Man's Story*

1. "Bedcheck Charlie" is a nickname for the slow-flying Soviet-built aircraft the Communists used to fly over UN positions, usually on dark nights. Capable of carrying

only one or two small bombs, they actually did very little damage. They were a source of irritation to UN troops, however, and their harassment value was high. See Summers, 61.

19. A ROK Lieutenant Survives the Bloody Ridges

1. The expression "commodity lieutenant," widely used in the wartime South Korean army, has no equivalent in English. In practice, it referred to the new second lieutenants who were killed in large numbers as soon as they assumed command of a platoon in combat. Unlike American officers, who received proper training after an established selection process, wartime South Korean officers were usually appointed by their commanders on the battlefield. Any training they received as officers was brief, no more than a few weeks. In spite of their meager training, they were eager to prove their ability and courage to their men by leading their platoon in front, often paying the ultimate price.

21. North and South

1. The battle for Dosolsan Mountain referred to by Private Lee is one of many battles fought over hills or mountains and is not commonly mentioned in Korean War histories published in English. The battle took place near Yanggoo (west of Injui) in the Taebeck Mountain range. The Fifth Regiment of the First U.S. Marine Division participated in the early part of the fighting, but on June 4, 1951, they were replaced by the ROK Marines. Intense fighting followed between ROK Marines and the North Korean forces defending the mountain. For more on the subject, see Lynn Montross, Hubard D. Kuokka, and Norman W. Hicks, *The East-Central Front,* vol. 4, *U.S. Marine Operations in Korea, 1950–1953* (Washington, D.C.: Historical Branch, G-3, Headquarters, U.S. Marine Corps, 1962), 138–48.

27. Organizing the Riots on Koje

1. On March 27, 1952, the Chinese–North Korean delegation at Panmunjom issued the following statement on releasing and repatriating the prisoners: "Both sides should release and repatriate all the non-Korean and Korean prisoners who did not live in the areas under the detaining side's control before the war. The Korean prisoners who had lived in the areas under the detaining side's control before the war could return to their homes themselves and resume their peaceful lives according to their own will and without formal repatriation." Chai Chengwen, *Panmunjom Tanpan* (Panmunjom Negotiations) (Beijing, China: The PLA Press, 1992), 227–28.

Selected Bibliography

Acheson, Dean. *Present at the Creation: My Years in the State Department.* New York: Norton, 1969.

Alexander, Bevin. *Korea: The First War We Lost,* rev. ed. New York: Hippocrene Books, 1998.

Appleman, Roy E. *Disaster in Korea: The Chinese Confront MacArthur.* College Station, Tex.: Texas A&M Univ. Press, 1989.

———. *South to the Naktong, North to the Yalu (June–November 1950), U.S. Army in the Korean War.* Washington, D.C.: Office of the Chief of Military History, U.S. Government Printing Office, 1961.

Avakian, Bob. *Mao Tsetung's Immortal Contributions.* Chicago: RCP Publications, 1979.

Barnett, A. Doak. *China and the Major Powers in East Asia.* Washington, D.C.: Brookings Institution, 1977.

Blair, Clay. *The Forgotten War: America in Korea, 1950–1953.* New York: Times Books, 1987.

Bradley, Omar N., and Clay Blair. *A General's Life: An Autobiography.* New York: Simon and Schuster, 1983.

Carlson, Lewis H. *Remembered Prisoners of a Forgotten War: An Oral History of the Korean War.* New York: St. Martin's Press, 2002.

Catchpole, Brian. *The Korean War, 1950–53.* New York: Carroll and Graf, 2000.

Chai Chengwen. *Panmunjom Tanpan* (Panmunjom Negotiations). Beijing, China: The PLA Press, 1992.

Chang, Gordon H. *Friends and Enemies: The United States, China, and the Soviet Union, 1948–1972.* Stanford, Calif.: Stanford Univ. Press, 1990.

Chen Jian. "China's Changing Aims during the Korean War." *Journal of American–East Asian Relations* 1 (spring 1992).

———. *China's Road to the Korean War: The Making of the Sino-American Confrontation.* New York: Columbia Univ. Press, 1994.

———. "The Sino-Soviet Alliance and China's Entry into the Korean War." Working

Paper No. 1. *The Cold War International History Project*. Washington, D.C.: Woodrow Wilson Center, 1992.

"Chinese Generals Recall the Korean War." Trans. and ed. Xiaobing Li and Donald Duffy. *Chinese Historians* 13–14 (1994).

Christensen, Thomas. "Threats, Assurances, and the Last Chance for Peace: The Lessons of Mao's Korean War Telegrams." *International Security* 17 (summer 1992).

Cohen, Warren I. *America's Response to China: An Interpretive History of Sino-American Relations.* 3d ed. New York: Columbia Univ. Press, 1990.

———. "Conversations with Chinese Friends: Zhou Enlai's Associates Reflect on Chinese-American Relations in the 1940s and the Korean War." *Diplomatic History* 11, no. 2 (1987).

Collins, J. Lawton. *War in Peacetime: The History and Lessons of Korea.* Boston, Mass.: Houghton Mifflin, 1969.

Crane, Conrad C. *American Airpower Strategy in Korea, 1950–1953.* Lawrence, Kans.: Univ. Press of Kansas, 2000.

Cumings, Bruce. *Korea's Place in the Sun: A Modern History.* New York: Norton, 1997.

———. *The Origins of the Korean War.* 2 vols. Princeton, N.J.: Princeton Univ. Press, 1981 and 1990.

Documents and Commentaries on the Cease-Fire and Armistice Negotiations in Korea. 2 vols. Beijing, China: Foreign Languages Press, 1953.

Domes, Jurgen. *Peng Te-huai: The Man and the Image.* Stanford, Calif.: Stanford Univ. Press, 1985.

Eight Years of the Chinese People's Volunteer Forces' Resistance to American Aggression and Aiding Korea. Beijing, China: Foreign Languages Press, 1958.

Eisenhower, Dwight D. *Mandate for Change, 1953–1956, The White House Years.* Garden City, N.Y.: Doubleday, 1963.

Farrar-Hockley, Anthony. "A Reminiscence of the Chinese People's Volunteers in the Korean War." *China Quarterly* 98 (June 1984).

Fehrenback, T.R. *This Kind of War: A Study in Unpreparedness.* New York: Macmillan, 1963.

Foot, Rosemary. "Make the Unknown War Known: Policy Analysis of the Korean Conflict in the Last Decade." *Diplomatic History* 15, no. 3 (1991).

———. *A Substitute for Victory: The Politics of Peacemaking at the Korean Armistice Talks.* Ithaca, N.Y.: Cornell Univ. Press, 1990.

Foreign Relations of the United States: Diplomatic Papers. The Conferences of Cairo and Tehran, 1943. Washington, D.C.: U.S. Government Printing Office, 1961.

Futrell, Robert Frank. *The United States Air Force in Korea, 1950–1953.* New York: Duell, Sloan and Pearce, 1961.

George, Alexander L. *The Chinese Communist Army in Action: The Korean War and Its Aftermath.* New York: Columbia Univ. Press, 1967.

Gittings, John. *The Role of the Chinese Army.* New York: Oxford Univ. Press, 1967.

Godwin, Paul. *The Chinese Communist Armed Forces.* Maxwell, Ala.: Air Force Univ. Press, 1988.

Goldstein, Steven M., and He Di. "New Chinese Sources on the History of the Cold War." *The Cold War International History Bulletin,* Woodrow Wilson International Center (spring 1992).

Goncharov, Sergei N., John W. Lewis, and Xue Litai. *Uncertain Partners: Stalin, Mao, and the Korean War.* Stanford, Calif.: Stanford Univ. Press, 1993.

Goulden, Joseph C. *Korea: The Untold Story of the War.* New York: Times Books, 1982.

Halliday, Jon, and Bruce Cumings. *Korea: The Unknown War.* New York: Pantheon Books, 1988.

Hanrahan, Gene Z., and Edward L. Katzenback Jr. "The Revolutionary Strategy of Mao Tse-tung." In *Modern Guerrilla Warfare,* ed. Franklin Mark Osanka. New York: Free Press of Glencoe, 1969.

Hao Yufan and Zhai Zhihai. "China's Decision to Enter the Korean War: History Revisited." *China Quarterly* 121 (March 1990).

Harding, Harry, and Yuan Ming, eds. *Sino-American Relations, 1945–1955: A Joint Reassessment of a Critical Decade.* Wilmington, Del.: Scholarly Resources, 1989.

Hastings, Max. *The Korean War.* New York: Simon and Schuster, 1987.

Hermes, Walter G. *Truce Tent and Fighting Front, U.S. Army in the Korean War.* Washington, D.C.: Office of the Chief of Military History, U.S. Government Printing Office, 1966; reprinted in 1988.

Hickey, Michael. *The Korean War: The West Confronts Communism.* Woodstock, N.Y.: The Overlook Press, 1999.

Holliday, Jon. "Air Operations in Korea: The Soviet Side of the Story." In *A Revolutionary War: Korea and the Transformation of the Postwar World,* ed. William J. Williams. Chicago: Imprint, 1993.

Hoyt, Edwin P. *The Day the Chinese Attacked Korea, 1950.* New York: McGraw-Hill, 1990.

Hunt, Michael H. "Beijing and the Korean Crisis, June 1950–June 1951." *Political Science Quarterly* 107, no. 3 (1992).

Hunt, Michael H., and Odd Arne Westad. "The Chinese Communist Party and International Affairs: A Field Report on New Historical Sources and Old Research Problems." *China Quarterly* 122 (1990).

Joffe, Ellis. *Party and Army: Professionalism and Political Control in the Chinese Officer Corps, 1948–1964.* Cambridge, Mass.: Harvard Univ. Press, 1967.

Joy, Admiral C. Turner. *How Communists Negotiate.* New York: Macmillan, 1955.

Jung, Walter B. *Nation Building: The Geopolitical History of Korea.* Lanham, Md.: Univ. Press of America, 1998.

Kalicki, J.H. *The Pattern of Sino-American Crises: Political-Military Interactions in the 1950s.* New York: Cambridge Univ. Press, 1975.

Kau, Michael Y.M., and John K. Leung, eds. *The Writings of Mao Zedong, 1946–1976.* Vol. 1, *September 1949–October 1955.* Armonk, New York: M.E. Sharpe, 1986.

Kaufman, Burton I. *The Korean Conflict.* Westport, Conn.: Greenwood Press, 1999.

Khrushchev, Nikita S. "Truth About the Korean War." *Far Eastern Affairs* [Moscow] 1 (1990).

Kihl, Young Whan. *Politics and Policies in Divided Korea: Regimes in Contest.* Boulder, Colo., and London: Westview Press, 1984.

Kim, Chullbaum, ed. *The Truth About the Korean War: Testimony 40 Years Later.* Seoul, South Korea: Eulyoo Publishing, 1991.

Kim, Chum-kon. *The Korean War, 1950–1953.* Seoul, South Korea: Kwangmyong Publishing, 1980.

Lewis, John Wilson, and Xue Litai. *China Builds the Bomb.* Stanford, Calif.: Stanford Univ. Press, 1988.

Li Haiwen. "How and When Did China Decide to Enter the Korean War?" Trans. Chen Jian. *Korea and World Affairs* 18, no. 1 (spring 1994).

Li, Xiaobing. "Making of Mao's Cold War: The Taiwan Straits Crises Revised." In *China and the United States: A New Cold War History,* ed. Xiaobing Li and Hongshan Li. Lanham, Md.: Univ. Press of America, 1998.

Li, Xiaobing, Allan Millett, and Bing Yu. *Mao's Generals Remember Korea.* Lawrence, Kans.: Univ. of Kansas Press, 2001.

Li, Xiaobing, and Hongshan Li. *China and the United States: A New Cold War History.* Lanham, Md.: Univ. Press of America, 1998.

MacArthur, Douglas. *Reminiscences: General of the Army.* New York: McGraw-Hill, 1964.

MacFarquhar, Roderick, ed. *Sino-American Relations, 1949–1971.* New York: Praeger, 1972.

"Mao's Dispatch of Chinese Troops to Korea: Forty-Six Telegrams, July–October 1950." Trans. and ed. Xiaobing Li, Wang Xi, and Chen Jian. *Chinese Historians* 5, no. 1 (spring 1992).

"Mao's Forty-Nine Telegrams during the Korean War, October–December 1950." Trans. and ed. Xiaobing Li and Glenn Tracy. *Chinese Historians* 5, no. 2 (fall 1992): 65–85.

Mao Zedong. "On Protracted War." May 26, 1938. In *Selected Works of Mao Tse-tung.* Vol. 2. 4th ed. Peking (Beijing), China: Foreign Languages Press, 1977.

——. "Problems of War and Strategy." November 6, 1938. In *Selected Works of Mao Tse-tung.* Vol. 2. 4th ed. Peking (Beijing), China: Foreign Languages Press, 1977.

——. *Quotations from Chairman Mao Tse-tung.* New York: Bantam Books, 1967.

——. "Problems of Strategy in Guerrilla War Against Japan." May 1938. In *Selected Works of Mao Tse-tung.* Vol. 2. 4th ed. Peking (Beijing), China: Foreign Languages Press, 1977.

"Mao Zedong Informs Stalin of China's Decision to Enter the Korean War, 1950." Trans. Xiaobing Li and Chen Jian. In *Major Problems in American Foreign Relations.* Vol. 2, *Since 1914,* ed. Dennis Merrill and Thomas Paterson. New York: Houghton Mifflin, 2000.

Marshall, S.L.A. *Pork Chop Hill: The American Fighting Man in Action, Korea, Spring 1953.* New York: Morrow, 1956.

Millett, Allan R. "Understanding Is Better Than Remembering: The Korean War, 1945–1954." In *The 7th Eisenhower Lecture in Military History.* Manhattan, Kans.: Kansas State Univ. Press, 1997.

Montross, Lynn, Hubard D. Kuokka, and Norman W. Hicks. *U.S. Marine Operations in*

Korea, 1950–1953. Vol. 4, *The East-Central Front.* Washington, D.C.: Historical Branch, G-3, Headquarters, U.S. Marine Corps, 1962.

Mossman, Bill C. *Ebb and Flow: November 1950–July 1951, U.S. Army in the Korean War.* Washington, D.C.: Center of Military History, U.S. Government Printing Office, 1990.

Peng Dehuai. *Memoirs of a Chinese Marshal: The Autobiographical Notes of Peng Dehuai, 1898–1974.* Trans. Zheng Longpu. Beijing, China: Foreign Languages Press, 1984.

Pollack, Jonathan D. "The Korean War and Sino-American Relations." In *Sino-American Relations, 1945–1955: A Joint Reassessment of a Critical Decade,* ed. Harry Harding and Yuan Ming. Wilmington, Del.: Scholarly Resources, 1989.

Ridgway, Matthew B. *The Korean War.* Garden City, N.Y.: Doubleday, 1967.

Roe, Patrick C. *The Dragon Strikes: China and the Korean War: June–December 1950.* Novato, Calif.: Presidio Press, 2000.

Russ, Martin. *Breakout: The Chosin Reservoir Campaign, Korea, 1950.* New York: Penguin Books, 1999.

Ryan, Mark A. *Chinese Attitude toward Nuclear Weapons: China and the United States during the Korean War.* Armonk, N.Y.: M.E. Sharpe, 1989.

Sandler, Stanley. *The Korean War: No Victors, No Vanquished.* Lexington, Ky.: Univ. Press of Kentucky, 1999.

Schnabel, James F. *Policy and Direction: The First Year, U.S. Army in the Korean War.* Washington, D.C.: Office of the Chief of Military History, U.S. Government Printing Office, 1972.

Schnabel, James F., and Robert J. Watson. *The History of the Joint Chiefs of Staff, The Joint Chiefs of Staff and National Policy.* Vol. 3, *The Korean War, Part I.* Wilmington, Del.: Produced by the Historical Division, Joint Secretariat, Joint Chiefs of Staff, published by Michael Glazier, 1979.

Schram, Stuart. *The Thought of Mao Tse-tung.* New York: Cambridge Univ. Press, 1989.

Scobell, Andrew. "Soldiers, Statesmen, Strategic Culture and China's 1950 Intervention in Korea." *Journal of Contemporary China* 22, no. 8 (1999).

Segal, Gerald. *Defending China.* New York: Oxford Univ. Press, 1955.

Shambaugh, David. "China's Military in Transition: Politics, Professionalism, Procurement, and Power Projection." *China Quarterly* 146 (June 1996).

Shen, Zhihua. "China Sends Troops to Korea: Beijing's Policy-Making Process." In *China and the United States: A New Cold War History,* ed. Xiaobing Li and Hongshan Li. Lanham, Md.: Univ. Press of America, 1998.

Sheng, Michael M. "Beijing's Decision to Enter the Korean War: A Reappraisal and New Documentation." *Korea and World Affairs* 19, no. 2 (summer 1995).

Shipping Advice Files [*Captured CPVF documents*], no. 2018, box 2,115, Washington National Records Center, Suitland, Maryland.

Simmon, Robert R. *The Strained Alliance: Peking, Pyongyang, and the Politics of the Korean Civil War.* New York: Free Press, 1975.

Simons, Geoff. *Korea: The Search for Sovereignty.* New York: St. Martin's Press, 1995.

Spurr, Russell. *Enter the Dragon: China's Undeclared War against the U.S. in Korea*. New York: New Market Press, 1988.

Stokesbury, James L. *A Short History of the Korean War*. New York: William Morrow, 1988.

Stueck, William. *The Korean War: An International History*. Princeton, N.J.: Princeton Univ. Press, 1995.

Summers, Harry G., Jr. *Korean War Almanac*. New York, Oxford, and Sydney: Facts on File, 1990.

Teiwes, Frederick C. "Peng Dehuai and Mao Zedong." *The Australian Journal of Chinese Affairs* 16 (July 1986).

Truman, Harry S. *Memoirs*. Vol. 2, *Years of Trial and Hope*. Garden City, N.Y.: Doubleday, 1956.

Tuchman, Barbara. "If Mao Had Come to Washington: An Essay in Alternatives." *Foreign Affairs* 51, no. 1 (1971).

Tucker, Nancy Bernkopf. *Patterns in the Dust: Chinese-American Relations and the Recognition Controversy, 1949–1950*. New York: Columbia Univ. Press, 1983.

Tucker, Spencer C. *Encyclopedia of the Korean War: A Political, Social, and Military History*. 3 vols. Santa Barbara, Calif.: ABC-CLIO, 2000.

Usov, Victor. "Who Sent the Chinese Volunteers?" *Far Eastern Affairs* [Moscow] 1 (1991).

Wainstock, Dennis D. *Truman, MacArthur, and the Korean War*. Westport, Conn.: Greenwood Press, 1999.

War Memorial Service–Korea. *The Historical Re-Illumination of the Korean War*. Seoul, South Korea: Korean War Research Conference Committee, 1990.

Weathersby, Kathryn. "Soviet Aim in Korea and the Origins of the Korean War, 1949–1950: New Evidence from Russian Archives." Working Paper No. 8. *The Cold War International History Project*. Washington, D.C.: Woodrow Wilson International Center, 1993.

Weintraub, Stanley. *MacArthur's War: Korea and the Undoing of an American Hero*. New York: The Free Press, 2000.

Weiss, Lawrence S. "Storm around the Cradle: The Korean War and the Early Years of the People's Republic of China, 1949–1953." Ph.D. diss., Columbia University, 1981.

West, Philip. "Confronting the West: China as David and Goliath in the Korean War." *Journal of American–East Asian Relations* 2 (spring 1993).

Whiting, Allen S. *China Crosses the Yalu: The Decision to Enter the Korean War*. New York: Macmillan, 1960.

———. *The Chinese Calculus of Deterrence*. Ann Arbor, Mich.: Univ. of Michigan Press, 1975.

———. "The Sino-Soviet Split." In *The Cambridge History of China*. Vol. 14, "The Emergence of Revolutionary China, 1949–1965," ed. R. MacFarquhar and J.K. Fairbank. Cambridge: Cambridge Univ. Press, 1987.

Whitson, William W. *The Chinese High Command: A History of Communist Military Politics, 1927–1971*. New York: Praeger, 1973.

Wiltz, John Edward. "The Korean War and American Society." In *The Korean War: A 25-*

Year Perspective, ed. Francis H. Heller. Lawrence, Kans.: The Regents Press of Kansas, 1977.

Xu Yan. "Chinese Forces and Their Casualties in the Korean War: Facts and Statistics." Trans. Xiaobing Li. *Chinese Historians* 2 (fall 1993).

Yu, Bin. "Sino-American and Sino-Soviet Relations." In *The Modernization of China's Diplomacy,* ed. Jianwei Wang and Zhinmin Lin. Armonk, New York: M.E. Sharpe, 1997.

———. "What China Learned from Its 'Forgotten War' in Korea." *Strategic Review* (summer 1998).

Zaloga, Steven J. "The Russians in MiG Alley." *Air Force Magazine* 74 (February 1991).

Zelman, Walter A. *Chinese Intervention in the Korean War: A Bilateral Failure of Deterrence.* Los Angeles, Calif.: Univ. of California Press, 1967.

Zhang, Shuguang. *Deterrence and Strategic Culture: Chinese-American Confrontations, 1949–1958.* Ithaca, N.Y.: Cornell Univ. Press, 1992.

———. *Mao's Military Romanticism: China and the Korean War, 1950–1953.* Lawrence, Kans.: Univ. Press of Kansas, 1995.

———. "Preparedness Eliminates Mishap: The CCP's Security Concerns in 1949–1950 and the Origins of Sino-American Confrontation." *The Journal of American–East Asian Relations* 1, no. 1 (1992).

Zhang, Shuguang, and Chen Jian, eds. *Chinese Communist Foreign Policy and the Cold War in Asia: New Documentary Evidence, 1944–1950.* Chicago: Imprint, 1996.

Zhang Xi. "Peng Dehuai and China's Entry into the Korean War." Trans. Chen Jian. *Chinese Historians* 6, no. 1 (1993).

Zhu, Fang. *Gun Barrel Politics: Party-Army Relations in Mao's China.* Boulder, Colo.: Westview Press, 1998.

Index